THE PHILOLOGY OF LIFE

IDIOM INVENTING WRITING THEORY
Jacques Lezra and Paul North, series editors

THE PHILOLOGY OF LIFE

WALTER BENJAMIN'S CRITICAL PROGRAM

KEVIN McLAUGHLIN

Fordham University Press   *New York 2023*

Fordham University Press gratefully acknowledges financial assistance and support provided for the publication of this book by Brown University.

Copyright © 2023 Fordham University Press

All rights reserved. No part of this publication may be reproduced, stored in a retrieval system, or transmitted in any form or by any means—electronic, mechanical, photocopy, recording, or any other—except for brief quotations in printed reviews, without the prior permission of the publisher.

Fordham University Press has no responsibility for the persistence or accuracy of URLs for external or third-party Internet websites referred to in this publication and does not guarantee that any content on such websites is, or will remain, accurate or appropriate.

Fordham University Press also publishes its books in a variety of electronic formats. Some content that appears in print may not be available in electronic books.

Visit us online at www.fordhampress.com.

Library of Congress Cataloging-in-Publication Data available online at https://catalog.loc.gov.

Printed in the United States of America

25 24 23   5 4 3 2 1

First edition

*for Ourida, in memory of our time together
during the plague years*

CONTENTS

	Note on Abbreviations	ix
	Introduction: The Philology of Life	1
1.	"Two Poems by Friedrich Hölderlin"	15
2.	*The Concept of Criticism in German Romanticism*	42
3.	"Goethe's Elective Affinities"	68
	Coda: The Afterlife of Philology	109
	Acknowledgments	127
	Appendix: Sources for Benjamin's "Goethe's Elective Affinities" (1924–25)	129
	Notes	131
	Bibliography	179
	Index	189

NOTE ON ABBREVIATIONS

All citations of the works of Walter Benjamin are to *Gesammelte Schriften*, 7 vols. (Frankfurt am Main: Suhrkamp, 1972–91). Unless otherwise noted, available English translations are from *Selected Writings*, 4 vols., ed. Michael W. Jennings et al. (Cambridge, Mass.: Harvard University Press, 1996–2003). References will be given parenthetically in the text with the German original followed by the English translation in the following form: (*GS*; *SW*). The published translations have occasionally been modified when necessary.

THE PHILOLOGY OF LIFE

INTRODUCTION: THE PHILOLOGY OF LIFE

The outlines of the following study started to appear to me as I was completing my book *Poetic Force* in 2014.[1] That project had taken its initial cues from a pair of essays by Walter Benjamin: "Two Poems by Friedrich Hölderlin" and "Toward the Critique of Violence." Looking back on my work I could see that the theory of force emerging in Benjamin's essays was part of a single literary critical program, the significance and impact of which, it seemed to me, deserved more focused attention: from the commentary on Hölderlin that he began to compose in 1914 to the study of Goethe that he completed in 1922, one year after the publication of the essay on violence. During this time Benjamin elaborated a theory of literature and a method for criticism on the basis of an intensive engagement with three nearly simultaneous developments in German letters around 1800: the poetry of Hölderlin, the literary theory of the romantics, and Goethe's novel *Elective Affinities*. Benjamin approached this nexus as a dynamic field of force in which these three phenomena enter into relation with one another without becoming subject to influence in the conventional sense. In the period immediately following this interval in his work—in the late 1920s—Benjamin adopted the word "entanglement" (*Verschränkung*) from contemporary physics to describe this singular kind of relationship.[2] The implications of the theory and the method that arise out of this critical project are not limited to literary criticism in Benjamin's work: they extend broadly to historical experience as such—specifically, to what he calls "life" in his early writings. In this sense, the critical program undertaken by Benjamin from 1914 through 1922 not only offers a highly innovative and illuminating interpretation of a revolutionary moment in modern literature, it also forms the basis of his remarkable and now widely influential critical project as a whole.

The work presented in the following chapters happens to have been carried out precisely one hundred years after the period on which it focuses in Benjamin's work. To be sure, the political, professional, and personal conditions under which Benjamin realized his project were very different from those under which the present study was completed. For example, although he barely mentions it, Benjamin studied and wrote during these years in the shadow of world war. The commentary on Hölderlin bears traces of this: it was dedicated to his friend the poet Friedrich Heinle, whose suicide was understood as a pacifist protest against the war in 1914, and it was addressed to the Hölderlin editor Norbert von Hellingrath, who died at the Battle of Verdun in 1916 (*GS* 2.3: 921).[3] On a professional level, this period was marked by Benjamin's failure to establish himself in the university.[4] In 1914, he was twenty-two years old, having returned to Berlin after a semester as a student in Freiburg. For the next eight years he pursued his studies in Berlin as well as in Munich (1916) and Bern (1917–19)—where he submitted his dissertation one day before the signing of the Treaty of Versailles (on June 27, 1919)—and at that point returned to his native city where he completed his essay on Goethe in 1922 at the age of thirty.[5] The present study, on the other hand, was undertaken from 2014 through 2022 while its author served as an academic dean at a prominent North American university. To be sure, the political environment in the United States during those eight years was far from peaceful, and the world pandemic that punctuated the end of this period was profoundly destabilizing. However, it would certainly be an exaggeration to compare these circumstances to the extreme carnage and destruction of the war in Europe a century earlier. The world historical conditions under which this book was written were clearly very different from those under which Benjamin worked during the years in question.

Yet the period during which this book was composed came to share a certain time with the one on which it is focused. This time arose out of what I take to be a defining feature of the philological method that is the subject of this book.[6] As I have noted, Benjamin approaches the works of Hölderlin, the romantics, and Goethe not as self-contained literary or historical objects but as phenomena that emerge out of a dynamic field of force. The most developed version of this critical approach is provided by the study of Goethe, the third case to be considered in the chapters that follow. At one point in the analysis—one that I will analyze in greater detail below—Benjamin interprets a remark Goethe is reported to have made about his poetry as revealing the truth content of his novel *Elective Affinities*.[7] In a conversation that took place on September 17, 1823, Goethe is said to have observed that all of his work amounted to "occasional poems" (*Gelegenheitsgedichte*).[8] According to Benjamin, the true meaning of this phrase is revealed by interpreting it first by way of *Elective Affinities* according to the romantic theory of the work as an "immanent structure" and then in the context of Hölderlin's use of a form of the same word (*gelegen*) in his poem "Timidity" (*GS* 1.1: 71; *SW* 1: 155). In the space conjured by Benjamin in which Hölderlin, the romantics, and Goethe are held together—according to a method of "mirroring" juxtaposition that Goethe himself identified as his poetic principle—the word *Gelegenheit*, which can be translated as "occasion" or "opportunity," is thus transformed from referring to a ceremonial occasion to evoking a missed opportunity, as it must be understood through the prism of the novel, and then to characterizing the "sobering" condition of modern life that is "opportune" (*gelegen*) for the poet of "Timidity."⁹ The dense layering of contexts and allusions in this passage bears further scrutiny. But it is important to recognize in advance that for the reader at this point Benjamin's text itself becomes a highly dynamic site for the transmission of what he calls "life." In his essay Benjamin insists on attributing this life to Goethe. But it is crucial to the critical procedure underway in this project that the life in question is not identical with and not reducible to that of the historical person who was living (and dying) around 1800. The life at issue, rather, includes the third thing in the tripartite structure of "human life" to which Benjamin alludes near the end of his essay on violence: there is "earthly life, death, and living on" (*Fortleben*), he says (*GS* 2.1: 201; *SW* 1: 251).¹⁰ This third part of life, which is not a synthesis or sublation of the first two, is also not reducible to the lives of individual living and dying beings—what Benjamin calls "earthly life" and "death." Nevertheless, these senses of life are related to one another: the lives of living and dying beings are interpenetrated by that part of life that lives on. Life encompasses the time of "earthly life" and "death" as well as that of "living on." Even if they are not identical—even if they are not the *same* time—the one can provide the occasion for the other. And this is precisely what happened to the time that my critical effort appeared to share with that of Benjamin over the past eight years: it became the occasion for an encounter with life *tout court*.

The possibility of such an encounter derives from the deep connection between experience and language that is central to all of Benjamin's work. This connection is framed by Benjamin as the relation between history and reading in a note he composed in the late 1930s just before his death: "The historical method is a philological method based on the book of life. 'Read what was never written,' runs a line by Hofmannsthal. The reader one should think of here is the true historian" (*GS* 1.3: 1238; *SW* 4: 405). I will have more to say about this statement at the end of this study. I cite it now as revealing the persistence of the linkage between life and philology that emerged in Benjamin's earliest writings, as we will see. The phrase *philology of life* that I have allowed myself to adopt as the title of this study appears nowhere explicitly in Benjamin's writing. It came to me as the translation of a word that, to my knowledge, has never been written (much less read) in German, namely, *Lebensphilologie*. *Philology of life* succinctly names the relation that lies at the very crux of Benjamin's critical project from his student writings through his late studies of Charles Baudelaire and his reflections on the concept of history. In the context of current critical discussion it is important to begin by pointing out that the life of this philology is certainly not the one that is exclusively subject to what Michel Foucault calls "biopolitics": "numerous and diverse techniques for achieving the subjugation of bodies and the control of populations."[11] It is also not to be confused with the "form-of-life" that Giorgio Agamben has described as "always retaining the character of a possibility" and as "emancipating" the human being from the sovereignty of biopower.[12] Benjamin's statement about life and philology involves a more ambiguous possibility. It recasts the traditional distinction encompassed by the single word life (*Leben*)—between what Agamben characterizes as bare life (*zoé*) and qualified or made life (*bíos*)—in terms of a text (a "book of life") and an interpretation of a text (a "philological method"). Life and philology, Benjamin implies, are connected by a complex and ultimately ambiguous logic of an underlying ground and what is made of it. In view of this fundamental ambiguity, the philological method does not liberate the reader of life from the division within it. Instead, the dual signification in the word "life" (construed by Agamben as *zoé* and *bíos*) corresponds to the irreducible tension between a text and its interpretation that opens the dimension in which the philology that concerns Benjamin operates—one in which it is ultimately impossible to distinguish rigorously between a given text and what is made of it. The paradoxical possibility of the life in Benjamin's philology is inseparable from the ways in which it is repeatedly qualified and limited. The philological method in question exposes the densely layered texture of what Benjamin calls "the book of life."[13]

The specific linkage between this philological method and history is illuminated by a remark made by Thomas Schestag on a phrase that occurs in a letter Benjamin wrote to Gershom Scholem on February 14, 1921—toward the end of the period that concerns us in what follows. Here is the text of Benjamin's letter followed by what Schestag makes of it (the key German words are included because they are indispensable to what Benjamin and Schestag are saying):

BENJAMIN:
I define philology not as a science or history of language [*Geschichte der Sprache*] but rather in its deepest layer as a *history of terminology* [*in ihrer tiefsten Schicht als "Geschichte der Terminologie"*], whereby one has to do then certainly with a highly enigmatic concept of time and very enigmatic phenomenon.[14]

SCHESTAG:
Philology is not *Geschichte* but rather—in its deepest layer [*in ihrer tiefsten Schicht*]—"*Geschichte*." Benjamin places the repetition of the word "*Geschichte*" in italics [*kursiv*], as if to hint at an imperceptible slippage between *Geschichte* and "*Geschichte*." For the *deepest layer* ["*tiefste Schicht*"] that is inserted (or excavated) between history *Geschichte* and "*Geschichte*" separates "*Geschichte*" from the word *-layer-* ["*-schicht-*"] that is in it, letting "*die*" *Geschichte* (history) pass over into "*das*" *Geschichte* (layering) without making the transition.[15]

The "true historian" invoked by Benjamin's late statement on "philological method" and "the book of life" is immersed in the layering that is implied by Benjamin's text and that is made more explicit in Schestag's interpretation of it. Significantly this layering describes both the texture of history and the method by which it is approached. History as layering involves what Schestag goes on to delineate as "overlaying and excavating" (*Überlagerung und Freilegung*), which is precisely the philological method that his text shares with Benjamin's letter. Thus, Benjamin excavates the "layer" (*Schicht*) in the word history ("*Geschichte*") by overlaying it with italics (underlining it in the manuscript)[16]; and Schestag in turn excavates this operation and overlays it with the German word *kursiv* to convey the passing or running over of history into layering—*Geschichte* into "*Geschichte*."

Before going on to explore further the implications of these overlapping philological operations, let us look more closely at the German word—or more precisely, the German *words*—*Geschichte* surfacing in Benjamin's letter and in Schestag's interpretation of it. According to Grimm's dictionary, *(das) Geschichte* signifies: "(1) layering as activity *(das Schichten als Thätigkeit)* and (2) the layered *(das Geschichtete)*; collectively, the totality of layers *(collectiv, die Gesamtheit der Schichten)*." In the second sense, *das Geschichte* is connected in Benjamin's writing to *das Gedichtete* (the poetized): a linkage stressed by his gloss on Goethe's use of the word "the poetized" with regard to his *Elective Affinities* that is cited in Benjamin's essay on that novel (written at the same time as his letter to Scholem).[17] "The poetized," Benjamin notes, is the "mythic material layer *(Stoffschicht)* of the work" (GS 1.1: 146; SW 1: 314). We will return to this point below. Philology is defined above all by the movement from *Geschichte* to "*Geschichte*" in the sentence from the letter to Scholem. It starts with *Geschichte* as "history" in the phrase "history of language" early in the sentence. *Geschichte* in this case, according to Grimm, is derived from the root verb *geschehen*, meaning "to happen." In this sense *Geschichte* is related to the rich semantic field surrounding *schicken*, in which temporal happening or occurrence is connected with something having been ordained or sent. Heidegger delineates this field in his discussion of the historicity *(die Geschichtlichkeit)* or the destiny *(das Geschick)* of Being. But, as manipulated by Benjamin in his letter to Scholem, *Geschichte* becomes more multifaceted. The phrase "*in ihrer tiefsten Schicht*" (in its deepest layer) that introduces the second occurrence of the word "*Geschichte*" in the sentence opens the spatial dimension (depth) of what is translated as "layer." On this level, "*Geschichte*" is embedded, Grimm observes, in the root verb *schihten*, signifying "classification and arrangement" *(Eintheilung und Anordnung)*. The modern German verb form *schichten* is related to the Latin "to divide, to arrange, to order" (*dividere, disponere, ordinare*). The main meaning of *schichten* today, the dictionary states, is "to put one thing on top of another in an ordered layout or series" (*etwas in geordneten Lagen oder Reihen über einander legen*). *Schicht* in this sense is connected to the English word "layer": "someone or something that lays" or "something which is laid," according to the Oxford English Dictionary. *Das "Geschichte"* is formed from the collective prefix in German *Ge-* and *Schicht* in the sense of layer; Grimm states "collectively, the totality of the layers" (*collectiv, die Gesamtheit der Schichten*). Based on this analysis, the phrase in Benjamin's letter might be translated as follows: "I define philology not as science or history of language but rather in its deepest layer as *layering of terminology* (*in ihrer tiefsten Schicht als 'Geschichte der Terminologie'*)." There is yet another signification attributed by Grimm to *Schicht*, namely, "assigned worktime" (*geordnete Arbeitszeit*). *Schicht* in this sense is cognate with the English "shift." From this perspective, the collective form "*Geschichte*" might be understood to refer to a set of arranged or assigned times: a collection of "shifts." It seems awkward to translate the phrase "*in ihrer tiefsten Schicht*" as "in its deepest shift." Nevertheless, the temporal figure of shifts might be understood to point to what Benjamin describes in the second half of his sentence as "a highly enigmatic concept of time." The main point, however, is that as it moves from (*die*) *Geschichte* (history) to (*das*) "*Geschichte*" (layering) the definition of philology is neither exclusively temporal or spatial: it is instead characterized at its deepest level by the oscillation between the temporality of history and the spatiality of layering, which also contains a hint of the temporality of shifts.

Schestag for his part excavates the italicization of history as layering and overlays it with the addition of the definite articles—*die* and *das*—that mark the transition from history to layering (from "*die*" *Geschichte* to "*das*" *Geschichte*) but that Benjamin leaves implicit or indefinite in his definition of philology. Yet the slippage made explicit by Schestag's introduction of the definite articles is in a sense already written into Benjamin's letter as the phrase "in its deepest layer" provides a bridge or transition to the interpretation of history as layering. The word "layer" (*Schicht*), moreover, that separates (and connects) history and layering is excavated in the very texture of the German language. The word *Geschichte* (which is indeed not one word) thus provides an example of the irreducible layering between ground and what is made of it, text and interpretation, that philology shares with the interweaving of *zoé* and *bíos* in life. Schestag also decides to place the word *philology* in italics in his philological commentary on Benjamin's letter where it is not italicized and thus emphasizes its deviation—in the text and in the interpretation—from a "science or history of language" toward what I am calling a *philology of life*. This is the sense in which "the true historian" of which Benjamin writes in "On the Concept of History" is a *philologist of life*. *Philology* as such from this perspective has no conventional concept: no conceptual ground on which to base a science or history of language. At its deepest layer *philology* in this complex sense is to be understood not as a *history* of language but as what Benjamin calls a *layering* of terminology: als "*Geschichte der Terminologie.*" The excavation and overlaying of philology present us with what he describes as "a highly enigmatic concept of time and very enigmatic phenomenon" since neither *philological* time nor the *philological* phenomenon adheres to the concept of chronological time with its logic of an underlying ground and what is progressively made of it. Under the influence of this layering, the words are no longer the means to a predetermined semantic end. Instead the "terminology" becomes fundamentally "enigmatic" with regard to its end and its means—as in the case of the term "history" (*Geschichte*) when the excavation of the "layer" (*Schicht*) redefines it as "layering" ("*Geschichte*"). The time disclosed by this operation might be described as interlinear rather than linear, except that it is not so much a matter of something that is between the lines but rather of a space or a turn that intervenes in a chronological time line. *Philology* in this sense outlines a time emerging from turning points where and when the fundamental ground of language is determined not as a fixed meaning but in ways that imply and make possible further modifications. The "enigmatic" time of the philological "phenomenon" emerges from the interpenetration of the word and what is made of it in a manner that corresponds to the interpolation of *zoé* and *bíos* in what Benjamin calls "the book of life."[18]

Benjamin works out this *philology of life* in relation to the neo-Kantian critique of the philosophy of life (*Lebensphilosophie*)—the diverse range of "fashionable currents" in philosophy that had acquired this name in early twentieth-century German intellectual circles.[19] The philosophy of life can be traced back to Nietzsche, in particular to his reflections on philology and history.[20] If for Nietzsche life is the dynamic force that is abused by the philistine concept of history condemned in his early work, philology designates the love of or friendship with language that is the source of what he regards as a genuine historical experience of antiquity.[21] In this sense, reading and a certain literary criticism become the historical method for Nietzsche's revolutionary "philology of the future."[22] A time inextricably bound to language and diverging from a concept of time as progressive or successive is of deep importance to this philology. Thus, Nietzsche's one enduring contribution to the academic field of classical philology was made with respect to the temporality specific to the Ancient Greek language as expressed in its peculiar rhythm—the purely quantitative and divisible temporality of Greek verse that was rendered inaccessible by the modern theory of Ancient Greek metrics based on the concept of stress (the *ictus*).[23] The untimely time that Benjamin's theory of reading shares with Nietzsche's philology is that of an elusive present made possible by literary texts.[24] If for Nietzsche's philologist "the *present* should now be understood *from the perspective of antiquity*," for Benjamin's critic the time in which literary works are read should be understood from the perspective of "the time in which they arose." This is the time that comes to pass as the layering of history in Benjamin's letter to Scholem and in Schestag's interpretation of it.[25] Thus, like the texts of classical antiquity from the standpoint for which Nietzsche advocates in his philological writings, literary works for Benjamin become what he describes as "an organon of history" (*GS* 3: 290 *SW* 2: 464).

In what follows I propose to retrace the outlines of the philological project developed by Benjamin in his literary critical essays on Hölderlin, the romantics, and Goethe from 1914 through 1922. This philological program provides a key to Benjamin's theoretical and methodological project as a whole. It also touches on three major fields in German studies, each of which has also had considerable significance in literary studies broadly. Yet, with some notable exceptions, Benjamin's work has had relatively little impact on these fields. A comprehensive reassessment of them on the basis of the philological project undertaken by Benjamin in his earlier literary criticism is, however, beyond the scope of this study. Instead, I will call attention to the way that the landscape laid out by Benjamin's work provides a new and illuminating context within which to view some specific contributions to these scholarly areas that have been made over the past century—on versification in Hölderlin, romantic philology, and onomastic technique in Goethe, to cite three examples. But my principal focus in what follows is on retracing the steps in Benjamin's literary critical project through a series of detailed commentaries on the following three documents.

1. "Two Poems by Friedrich Hölderlin": This essay was composed in Berlin from 1914 to 1915, immediately after the outbreak of World War I, and was not published in Benjamin's lifetime. The essay existed as a typescript, a copy of which was kept in the Benjamin archive. It was first published in 1955 in the two-volume edition of Benjamin's *Schriften* prepared by Theodor W. Adorno and Gretel Adorno (Frankfurt am Main: Suhrkamp, 1955) and it was republished in the second volume of the *Gesammelte Schriften* in 1977 (*GS* 2.1: 105–26; *SW* 1: 18–36). The German editors of the *Gesammelte Schriften* note: "Nothing is known about efforts to publish the work; it is not to be excluded that Benjamin did not consider this given its esoteric character. On the

other hand, it was not written to be left locked up in his writing desk; Benjamin had before his eyes selected addressees, who were worthy to receive the work under certain conditions." (*GS* 2.3: 921).

2. *The Concept of Criticism in German Romanticism*: This doctoral dissertation was submitted by Benjamin on June 27, 1919, at the University of Bern. Work on the thesis started in 1917 after Benjamin moved to Switzerland. The dissertation was first published in 1920 (Bern: Verlag von A. Francke, 1920) in a series edited by his dissertation director, Richard Herbertz. It was republished in the second volume of the *Schriften* in 1955 and in the first volume of the *Gesammelte Schriften* in 1974 (*GS* 1.1: 7–122; *SW* 1: 116–200).[26]

3. "Goethe's Elective Affinities": This essay was written from summer 1919 to summer 1922, mainly in Berlin. It was first published in Hugo von Hofmannsthal's series *Neue Deutsche Beiträge* in two installments in April 1924 and January 1925. It appeared in its entirety for the first time in the *Schriften* in 1955 and again in the *Gesammelte Schriften* in 1974 (*GS* 1.1: 123–201; *SW* 1: 297–360).

This literary critical trilogy focuses on what Benjamin calls "perhaps the greatest epoch in the Western philosophy of art" (*GS* 1.1: 103; *SW* 1: 175). The aesthetic development under consideration may be described as *epochal* in the literal sense that it presents in works of literature a temporal layer that *suspends* the "unidirectional" progressive movement of conventional history and "inclines in the end toward the cyclical," as Benjamin writes in a note on "methodical modes of history" composed during the second half of 1918 (*GS* 6: 94).[27] The mode of historiography corresponding to the turn toward cyclical time is what Benjamin calls philology. By concentrating on a cyclically inclined "layer of history" (*Schicht der Historischen*) in the literary work, this philology redefines the term *history* (*Geschichte*) and at the same time undergoes redefinition itself "as a *layering of terminology*" (*Geschichte der Terminologie*). These redefinitions of philology—the redefinition of history by philology and the redefinition of philology itself—are connected to another key term that is transformed in the course of Benjamin's project, namely, *life*. With this term, Benjamin observes two decades later in the context of his study of Baudelaire, philosophy in the late nineteenth century tried to grasp a genuine mode of experience that is opposed to the "standardized, denatured existence of the civilized masses."[28] This "philosophy of life" of the later nineteenth century took as its point of departure "lived experience" (*Erlebnis*), especially, for example, as presented in literary works. The title of Wilhelm Dilthey's famous study—cited by Benjamin in the relevant passage from his essay on Baudelaire—succinctly expresses this life-philosophical methodology: *Das Erlebnis und die Dichtung*. Benjamin's philological project reverses the sequence and proceeds not from the life to the work but from the work to the life. What emerges from this process, however, is the presentation not of "lived experience" but of life—specifically, of the life that is the true content of the work. In this way Benjamin proposes to redefine the false philology of "the philosophy of life" as the true philology of life.

This redefinition of philology entails the central thesis of Benjamin's early literary criticism, namely, that—taken together—the writings of Hölderlin, the romantics, and Goethe constitute a genuinely historical, epochal turn in the Western philosophy of art. This thesis begins with Hölderlin's proposition on the "sobriety" of ancient Greek art that confronts the modern poet as expressed in what became the poem "Timidity." It continues with the development of the German romantic theory of the modern work of art as a "medium of reflection" that derives from the irreducibly interpolated texts of Greek antiquity discovered by the philological investigations of Wolf at the end of the eighteenth century. And it concludes with the figure of Ottilie in *Elective Affinities* as Goethe's concession to a modern aesthetic theory based on a kind of beauty that adheres exclusively to what passes away. But the key to this argument lies in a philological method involving the interweaving and interpolation of textual elements among the three components in this nexus. This is the crucial critical dimension of the philological method that combines with the analytical operation of commentary, according to the simile introduced at the beginning of the essay on Goethe. The combining of the textual elements that reveals the meaning or the "truth content" of the given literary work corresponds to what Benjamin characterizes as the alchemy of critique, which is the indispensable counterpart to the chemistry of commentary. The fundamental importance of this methodological development in Benjamin's work seems not to have been recognized by his contemporary readers, including even Theodor Adorno who considered it simply to be lacking in dialectical rigor—a reaction on which Benjamin turned his philological method in a famous exchange of letters in the late 1930s concerning the late study of Baudelaire, as we will see in the final chapter of this book. It was also not appreciated in the initial reception of the two-volume edition of Benjamin's writings, *Schriften*, in 1955 and in the collections edited by Hannah Arendt and Peter Demetz in the 1960s and 1970s under the titles *Illuminations* and *Reflections*. But the editorial labor led by Rolf Tiedemann, Adorno's student and later assistant, along with that of teams of scholars and translators working in several languages, have made it possible in the intervening decades to retrace the outlines of a distinctive philological project that starts to develop in Benjamin's early literary criticism and that extends into the late studies of Baudelaire and Paris. By bringing this innovative method to light, the chapters that follow propose the philology of life as the key to the critical program of one of the most influential intellectual figures of the past few decades in literary studies and across the humanities.

1
"TWO POEMS BY FRIEDRICH HÖLDERLIN"

The life that is the object of Benjamin's philology can be traced to his earliest writings. A case in point is "The Life of Students."[1] This essay, published in 1915, begins with the distinction between the two perspectives on history that informs the concept of philology developed by Benjamin during his student years: the unidirectional character of conventional or "pragmatic" history, on the one hand, and the cyclical inclination of philological history, on the other. Benjamin's definition of philology, which becomes explicit in the historiographical notes from 1918 and the letter to Scholem in 1921 cited in the preface, is shaped by a conversation with Scholem in August 1916 that focused on the question of the direction of time and specifically on the determination of the "course" (*Ablauf*) of a given series of years.[2] This conversation concerns in particular the mathematical expression of a version of history and of historical time that is not understood to progress infinitely along a straight line—a topic about which Scholem (as a student of mathematics), unlike Benjamin, was expert.[3] At issue, in other words, is the mathematical expression of the "enigmatic" time of philological history to which Benjamin alludes in his 1921 letter to Scholem. Although the mathematical inflection given to the concept of what Benjamin considers genuinely historical time remains legible in the 1918 notes on historiography, neither the conversation with Scholem nor the discourse of mathematics more generally constitutes the starting point of the philological theory developed by Benjamin during the course of these years. Peter Fenves has argued, for example, that the mathematical discussion with Scholem may have been "prompted" by Benjamin's handling of the nonmathematical term "course" or "sequence" (*Ablauf*) in his essay on Hölderlin composed in 1914–15.[4] A similar case could be made with respect to Benjamin's use of the mathematical term "focal point" (*Brennpunkt*) at the beginning of "The Life of Students," which was also written in 1914–15. That is to say, Benjamin's definition of philology during his student years seems to have involved an intertwining of the terminologies of mathematics and the philosophy of history that was underway prior to the 1916 conversation with Scholem. Thus, Benjamin approaches student life philologically a year earlier as a "focal point" (*Brennpunkt*)—a point at which various curves can be constructed: "The following observations . . . delineate a particular condition in which history gathers in a single focal point" (*GS* 2.1: 75; *SW* 1: 37). Student life for Benjamin poses the paradigmatic question of a genuine experience of historical time that suspends the conventional view of history as progression along a straight line.[5] Benjamin's life as a student (what in German would be called his *Lebenslauf*) also poses for the present study of the philology of life a parallel question to the extent that the course of his student years is to be grasped not as a time of the progressive development of a theory of philology but rather as a building up or a transformation of overlapping discursive or, to use his word, "terminological" layers. This life, like the life that is the object of philology, also unfolds as what Benjamin calls "a history of terminology."[6]

The term "life" that "The Life of Students" takes as its point of departure derives to a significant degree from Nietzsche and Bergson. Benjamin read the former in preparation for the speeches to the Berlin Independent Students' Association in 1914 on which the essay builds, and he studied the latter in a seminar offered by Heinrich Rickert in Freiburg during the summer semester of 1913.[7] Like Nietzsche in the inaugural lectures, "On the Future of Our Educational Institutions," Benjamin denounces from the perspective of life the social customs and institutions as well as the academic disciplines and instructional methods of the German university of his day. But "The Life of Students" is, he insists from the start, not a "manifesto" or a "call" for social, institutional, pedagogical, or disciplinary reform (*GS* 2.1: 75; *SW* 1: 37). The specific "condition" of student life on which Benjamin focuses is a "metaphysical structure"—"like the idea of the French Revolution" (rather than its unfolding as a series of political events as these are conventionally understood). In this metaphysical sense, "the idea of the French Revolution" is in turn like the "messianic realm" in that it lies in a sphere that is beyond the reach of what is usually viewed as human affairs and political states. Thus, the specific "condition" of student life that concerns Benjamin "is to be grasped in its metaphysical structure" rather than in its existing social structure or even in any possible alternative socio-institutional manifestation. To invoke a term taken from the discourse of the contemporary phenomenology, with which Benjamin was also engaged during this period, we might say that the specific metaphysical condition at issue in "The Life of Students" *switches off* the existing social, institutional, pedagogical, and disciplinary conditions of student life in the university.[8] It is at this point that Benjamin's essay turns to the question of time as it is taken up in Bergson's transformation of the dynamic understanding of life in Nietzsche's writings into the theory of true time as what is defined as "duration" (*la durée*). This turn becomes explicit near the end of "The Life of Students" in Benjamin's analysis of the transposition of the concept of infinitely progressive history with which we began into the context of the German university of his day. The result, Benjamin concludes, is the conceptualization of the course of the student years as an empty "waiting period" on the path to profession and marriage:

> This entirely irrational period of waiting for marriage and a profession had to be given some kind of content, and it had to be a playful, pseudo-romantic one that would help pass the time.... But because students have sold their souls to the bourgeoisie, along with marriage and profession, they insist on those few years of bourgeois freedom. This exchange is effected in the name of youth. Openly or secretly—in a bar or amid deafening speeches at student meetings—a dearly purchased state of intoxication (*Rausch*) is created, the right to which is not to be denied. (*GS* 2.1: 85; *SW* 1: 45)

To this conception of youth and student years as a "dearly purchased state of intoxication," Benjamin offers a contrasting image—namely, that of a deeply sobering experience of student life as a time of "aging": "For students are not the younger generation; they are the aging generation. For those who have wasted their early years in German schools it is a heroic decision to recognize aging, when their university years appeared to offer them at long last the prospect of a youth full of life, only to postpone it year after year" (*GS* 2.1: 85–86; *SW* 1: 45). Aging in this passage is adopted from Bergson's terminology where it is understood as a trope of genuine time—one of duration and thus of life. "Living consists in aging," Bergson writes in his 1903 essay "Introduction to Metaphysics."[9] In this way the turn to aging allows duration to enter "The Life of Students" and indeed suggests the aging of Nietzsche's understanding of life itself in Bergson's theory of time and in Benjamin's image of student life. It also reveals the influence of what had become known as "the philosophy of life" in Benjamin's early work and raises the question of how the former is transformed by the latter.

This transformation of the life of "the philosophy of life" underway in Benjamin's writings during his student years can be understood as a deviation from the neo-Kantian reception of this philosophical movement in the German university at this time.[10] Especially prominent in this context was Rickert, who published his book *The Philosophy of Life: Presentation and Critique of the Fashionable Philosophical Currents of our Time* in 1920. This study took shape during the years when Benjamin (along with Martin Heidegger) was a student in Rickert's seminar on Bergson's concept of time.[11] The "philosophy of life" is presented in Rickert's book as primarily the legacy of Nietzsche, although its origins are traced to *Sturm und Drang*, in particular as this movement becomes philosophically significant, as Rickert notes, in the work of Goethe. The key contemporary representatives of these "fashionable philosophical currents" are identified as Bergson, Dilthey, and Simmel (interestingly, Husserl is also included in the group in passing).[12] The main thrust of Rickert's work is a philosophical critique of the life, more precisely of what he calls the *"mere* life" (*"bloßen" Leben*; his emphasis), of this "philosophy of life":

> I believe that the philosophical efforts of our day that are the most widespread and that are to be taken most seriously may be best placed under the concept of a philosophy of life. I am attempting to take a critical position toward them. I want thereby at the same time to point to a philosophy of life as a necessary task, the accomplishment of which, however, must result in more than a philosophy of *mere* life (*"bloßen" Lebens*). The main purpose of this book consists in showing that when one philosophizes about life, one is not dealing with life alone.[13]

In other words, to adapt Kant's famous starting point in the introduction to the *Critique of Pure Reason*: although all philosophy begins with life, it does not follow that all philosophy arises from life. The true "philosophy of life" therefore must go beyond *mere* life and become the life of philosophy. Overcoming the *mere* life of "the philosophy of life," Rickert proclaims, serves the life of philosophy: "I believe myself therefore to be serving the life of philosophy when I resist this 'philosophy of life.'"[14] For this reason, presumably, Rickert takes as the title of his book the phrase "the philosophy of life" (*die Philosophie des Lebens*)—and specifically not "life-philosophy" (*Lebensphilosophie*), which is more ambiguous. The philosophy of life, according to Rickert, only makes sense when life remains the object of philosophy (as an objective genitive) and resists becoming its subject or agent (as a subjective genitive). For Rickert there is no genuine philosophy of life in the latter sense. The phrase "the philosophy of life" acquires its true meaning only when life is possessed exclusively by philosophy. This occurs, according to Rickert's system, when life is progressively qualified by values. From the philological perspective being developed by Benjamin, such progressive qualification is the enemy of life. Thus, the student life of Benjamin's essay may be understood to enact the possibility of a philosophy of life in which life is the agent or expression of philosophy instead of its object. In this way, student life can take on what Benjamin calls the genuinely "philosophical form" of a community rooted in "life," rather than the reverse. This alternative understanding of the philosophy of life corresponds to Kantian aesthetics and in particular to Kant's description of the way the poets see the world in the *Critique of the Power of Judgment*, that is to say, "merely" (*bloß*). "*Mere* life," like student life, is understood from this point of view not as simply unqualified by values but as complexly shaped by a paradoxical purposiveness—a purposiveness without purpose. For the students, "life" in the phrase "the philosophy of life" hovers between an objective and a subjective genitive: it is an objective genitive without an object in the sense of something that could be opposed to a subject. In the juridical terms of the critique of violence worked out by Benjamin in the essay that appeared immediately after Rickert's book, the philosophy of life may be said to pose the question of the right not of values to convert "mere life" into "the life of philosophy" but of "mere life" or "bare life" (*bloßes Leben*) to become what Fenves has characterized as the "nucleus" of an alternative *Lebensphilosophie*. Benjamin, Fenves notes, "makes 'bare life' into the nucleus of a 'philosophy of life' that is decidedly neutral with regard to value.

The critical character of this philosophy consists in the identification of 'the law' (*das Recht*) as the value-creating and therefore life-destroying force; the end of the law thus becomes the paradoxical 'purpose' of life."[15] Instead of raw material for conversion into value, "bare life" (*bloßes Leben*) for Benjamin presents an ambiguous matter—at once indivisible and divisible—that is impossible to distinguish rigorously from what philosophy makes of it (it is neither simply *zoé* and *bíos*, to invoke once again Agamben's distinction). Life becomes in short a site of transformation as in the case of Bergson's interpretation of life as duration (or as aging). The law that makes life worth living from the perspective of value-philosophy becomes the destroyer of this dynamic, endlessly transforming life rather than its savior. The hint of a philological inflection in this alternative *Lebensphilosophie* is indeed given in Rickert's own comments on the word "life" in Nietzsche's writing:

> In Nietzsche we find deep insights into the originality of the being alive [*Ursprünglichkeit des Lebendigen*] in relation to merely thought life [*gedachten Leben*]. Above all, he expressed the feeling again with incomparable linguistic force [*unvergleichlicher Sprachgewalt*] that must come over every thinking person as the powerlessness to grasp the fullness of the living world, and precisely the *extra-scientific* linguistic force [*die "außerwissenschaftliche" Sprachgewalt*] is decisive. The ungraspable that one today names "life" enters indeed into no theoretical or scientific linguistic meaning [*keine theoretische oder wissenschaftliche Wortbedeutung*], and its signification as life would thus be just as insufficient as every other name given to it [*Namengebung*], if Nietzsche had not been able to lend to the word "life" a sense that brings super-scientifically to consciousness what it concerns: the enormous atheoretical importance of that which allows itself to be brought into no concept. One *feels* it in Nietzsche immediately also without logically understanding it. This is indeed, not itself science, but scientifically meaningful because it points to the boundary of scientific thinking. Therefore everyone who confuses concepts with the reality of life can also learn much philosophically from Nietzsche.[16]

Rickert insists that the word "life" in Nietzsche is no technical term: it has no "theoretical or scientific linguistic meaning," he notes. The word "life" in Benjamin's phrase "bare life" is also no technical term and indeed is no term at all even if the condition it names is fundamentally and singularly terminal. The capacity of words and in particular written words to convey this paradoxical quality is the subject of a highly interesting footnote to the passage just cited, in which Rickert argues that Nietzsche, technically speaking, does not belong to philosophy: he is not classifiable as one of the "great philosophers" (Plato, Aristotle, Plotinus, Augustine, Descartes, Spinoza, Leibniz, Kant, and Hegel are invoked). Instead, Rickert calls Nietzsche among the "most astute writers that Germany possesses."[17] Rickert compares Nietzsche to "cultural phenomena such as that of Rousseau" and raises the question of whether Nietzsche should be understood as a "European event"—the category that Benjamin, following Valéry, later applied to Baudelaire. For Nietzsche, specifically as a "writer" (as distinct from "the great philosophers"), the word "life" has the "enormous atheoretical importance" of what cannot be a matter of conceptual knowledge. Rickert clearly marks the Kantian aesthetic context of these comments when he stresses that one "feels" *life*, rather than knowing it conceptually. Since this feeling of *life* involves being affected specifically by the written word, it raises the possibility of a philology of life that is an alternative philosophy of life.[18]

Rickert, however, does not pursue this philological possibility suggested by the terminology of *Lebensphilosophie*. Instead, he continues laying the groundwork for what Benjamin later describes as the occupation of the "house of poetry" by developing the value-philosophy (*Werte-Philosophie*) that established the dominance of "cultural sciences" (*Kulturwissenschaften*) in the field of academic literary history in Germany during the first decades of the twentieth century—elevating value over life (*GS* 3: 285; *SW* 2: 460). In an article foundational to this project published while Benjamin and Heidegger were students in Freiberg, Rickert describes the goal of value-philosophy in a way that anticipates his critique of the philosophy of life seven years later.[19] A properly philosophical "science of values," he argues, must respond to "the riches of life": it must "extend philosophically to the whole, for we stand before material which is essentially inexhaustible and with which we can never be finished."[20] Values are realized, Rickert proposes, through a philosophical process of "completion" (*Voll-Endung*), an endless and progressive striving toward the goal of uncovering the meaning of life. In this sense, the striving is to end all striving—striving to bring striving to a full stop (*eine Voll-endung*) with the realization of value.[21] This *Voll-Endung* or full stop must be sought in the transcendental sphere, beyond the immanence of time and *mere* history or life[22]: "Therefore philosophy has to take up into a transhistorical system in a different way the material that is to be found in the available cultural goods. It must connect the accidental element that can never be removed from the merely historical [*bloß Geschichtlichen*] with the necessity of the structural order [*Rangordnung*] and indeed in such a way that there is still a place for the openness of historical life in the closed structure of values that has emerged from this connection."[23] This combining of the accidental and the historical with the necessary and the transhistorical strives for an "open system" that enables value-philosophy to be understood as the progressive completion of "the philosophy of life."[24] Within the context of the system of values, Rickert distinguishes between two classes of goods that are subject to temporal *Voll-Endung*.[25] There are those completed in the future (*Zukunftsgüter*), and those completed in the present (*Gegenwartsgüter*). "With regard to the tendency to completion," Rickert notes, "the past can play no role as the theater for the realization of values." Rickert explains: "As temporal beings, we must always defer completion to the future, and therefore be content with a stage in a process that is preliminary. On the contrary, should the completeness be achieved in the present, then we must renounce the whole and limit ourselves to a part."[26] These two temporal regions of completion are hierarchical: future goods are of "higher worth" than present goods because, whereas the former include the "possibility of drawing closer to completed totality," the latter bear "the curse of finitude" (*der Fluch der Endlichkeit*).²⁷ This hierarchy, which Rickert goes on to formulate in gendered terms as the masculinization of infinitude (future goods) and the feminization of finitude (present goods), is attacked by Heidegger at the end of a series of lecture courses on life, and in particular on the concept of "factical life," delivered in Freiburg from 1919 through 1922 (precisely during the years when Benjamin was completing his study of life in Goethe's work). The series begins in the summer semester of 1919 with Heidegger's phenomenological critique of *Werte-Philosophie* culminating in reservations expressed over Rickert's account of the philosophy of life.²⁸ Unlike Heidegger, Benjamin left no systematic critique of the position taken by value-philosophy on the "*mere* life" of the philosophy of life. However, such a critique is legible in the complex philological program that he began developing during his student years. This critical project, which is focused on language rather than value, refuses to synthesize the opposition between the immanent and the transcendental, between *mere* life and the completed life. This is the life that is to be discovered in the image of the work of art in Benjamin's early literary criticism.

For Benjamin, the discovery of this life comes to rest fundamentally on the question of literary critical method. This is the subject of the "preliminary remarks" framing his interpretation of two poems by Friedrich Hölderlin in an essay that is contemporaneous with "The Life of Students" (*GS* 2.1: 105; *SW* 1: 18). Benjamin begins with the distinction between aesthetic and philological commentaries. The former have applied their "best energies" to the foundation of individual genres—especially tragedy; the latter have been employed as commentaries on works that lie outside of classical drama. Benjamin introduces his essay as an aesthetic commentary on a nonclassical work. However, there is a wrinkle: the aesthetic commentary turns on a philological question. The work under investigation is approached as a matter of two *versions* (*Fassungen*) of a poem by

Hölderlin. The aesthetic commentary is unthinkable in this case, it turns out, without the philological concept of multiple versions of a single work. Yet the goal of the inquiry is not the establishment of the authentic single version of the work—the traditional aim of philological investigations—but rather the exposition of the "inner form" of what makes many versions possible (*GS* 2.1: 105; *SW* 1: 18). Rather than stabilizing the text under consideration along the lines of a conventional philological operation, Benjamin's method assumes the transcendental task of disclosing the highly dynamic sphere that constitutes the "precondition" of the poem in all of its extant versions—"and others," as he significantly adds (*GS* 2.1: 106; *SW* 1: 19). This a priori condition of possibility of the poem is what he calls *the poetized* (*das Gedichtete*). As the precondition of the poem, however, the poetized constitutes the "limit-concept" (*Grenzbegriff*) not only of the poem but also of life (*GS* 2.1: 106; *SW* 1: 19). Benjamin writes: "Thus, the poetized emerges as the transition from the functional unity of life to that of the poem" (*GS* 2.1: 107; *SW* 1: 19–20). As its vocabulary conveys, the method is clearly related to neo-Kantianism, not only Rickert and its Southwestern branch but also the so-called Marburg school of Hermann Cohen and Ernst Cassirer.[29] Yet the specific structure or coherence given to life by the poem and to the poem by life—what Benjamin characterizes as "unity"—radicalizes the functional priority of relation over substance in a way that diverges from orthodox neo-Kantianisms. The unifying point of transition (*Übergang*) from life to the poem is not understood as leading to the completion of a transcendental task. Rather than a transcendental idea, an image of life is made by the poem and is made of the poem by the critical commentary. The latter results from an effort, on the one hand, to grasp the a priori precondition of the poem and, on the other, to take hold of the linguistic details of the work. The dexterity, or more precisely the ambidexterity, of the method must correspond to that of the poet who knows how to turn the poetized into the necessarily limited structure of the poem, without completely reducing the former to the latter. It demands, in other words, a critical commentary that maintains a tension between the aesthetic and the philological operations rather than synthesizing them.[30] To follow the poet, the method must remain in the thick or, as Benjamin says, "in the middle of all relations," including the relation between the transcendental and the immanent dimensions delineated by the structure of the poem. In neo-Kantian terms, this means that the transcendental remains intensively and irreducibly related to the immanent, instead of overcoming or completing it. In the terms of the alternative philology of life pursued by Benjamin, it means that the image of life emerging (transcendentally) from the (immanent) material structure of the poem both cannot be identified with *and* cannot do without that material.

In this sense, the a priori condition of possibility of the poem is discovered as a matter not of a fundamental, isolatable substance or ground in any conventional sense but of articulated layers, like the historical material that philology encounters as *Geschichte* according to Benjamin's 1921 letter to Scholem analyzed above. Or, more succinctly, the relation of the poem to the poetized (what we might seek to capture scripturally with a single word as *das Gedicht*[*ete*]) is equivalent to the relation of history to layering (what Benjamin leaves indefinite in his letter as [*die/das*] *Geschichte*). Indeed, as he wrote the letter on philology, Benjamin was in the midst of a study of Goethe's *Elective Affinities* that contains a statement making this connection between the poetized and history explicit. It begins with an allusion to Goethe's remark to Carl Friedrich von Reinhard (on December 31, 1809) about the status of the poetized in that novel and leads to a comment by Benjamin. "That which has been made poetic (*das Gedichtete*)," says Goethe, "asserts its right just as that which has happened (*das Geschehene*)." "Such a right," Benjamin adds, "is here indeed owing . . . not to the poem, but to the poetized (*dem Gedichteten*)—the mythic material layer of the work" (*der mythischen Stoffschicht des Werkes*) (*GS* 1.1: 146; *SW* 1: 314).[31] It is important to note that the right of the poetized—as Goethe might say, what entitles it to enjoy a status equivalent to that of an event that takes place historically—derives from a mythic material layer and not from a mythic material ground. The key difference is that a layer, unlike a ground, implies an irreducible relation to another layer, and thus collectively to what Benjamin calls "layering" (*Geschichte*) in his letter to Scholem on philology. In this sense, the right of the poetized as derived from mythic material layering is decidedly unlike the mythic foundation of the juridical law subjected to critique in Benjamin's "Toward the Critique of Violence"—an essay that is also precisely contemporaneous with both the letter on philology and the essay on Goethe's *Elective Affinities*. The poetized of Hölderlin's poem does not simply present the mortality of the poet as an imperfect manifestation of a life that is perfected and immortalized through myth. Rather, as inflected by the poetized, the life of the poet embodies, at the deeper layers of meaning disclosed especially by the later version of the poem, a sense of being alive that does not definitively exclude death. Rather than seeking to establish life on a fundamental mythic ground as ultimately immortal (as in the Christian myth of redemption or in the "secularized" myth of the state that pretends to immortalize the individual living being—the student, for example—as part of a political collective), the poetized defines life "at its deepest layer" as a matter of mythic layering: as the dense and irreducible convolution of "the mythic elements straining against one another" (*GS* 2.1: 108; *SW* 1: 20). This deeply layered structure of the poetized along with the transformations it generates is what connects art to life in the poem, as Benjamin explains in his remarks on the way the feeling of life enters the poem:

> One could say that life is, in general, the poetized of poems. Yet the more the poet tries to convert without transformation the unity of life into a unity of art, the plainer it is that he is a bungler (*Stümper*). We are used to finding such bungling defended, even demanded, as "the immediate feeling of life," "warmth of the heart," "sensibility." With respect to the significant example of Hölderlin, it becomes clear how the poetized creates the possibility of judging poetry according to the degree of coherence and greatness of its elements (*durch den Grad der*

Verbundenheit und Größe seiner Elemente). Both characteristics are inseparable. For the more a slack extension of feeling replaces the inner greatness and structure of the elements (*die innere Größe und Gestalt der Elemente*) (which we designate approximatively as "mythic"), the more meager the coherence (*Verbundenheit*) becomes and the more readily there comes into being either an endearing, artless natural product or some concoction alien to art and nature. Life, as the ultimate unity, lies at the basis of the poetized. But the more prematurely the analysis of the poem—without encountering the structuration of perception and the construction of an intellectual world (*Gestaltung der Anschauung und Konstruktion einer geistigen Welt*)—leads us to life itself (*das Leben selbst*) as the poetized, the more the poem proves, in a strict sense, to be more material, more formless, and less significant. Whereas, to be sure, the analysis of great works of literature will encounter, as the genuine expression of life, not myth but rather a unity produced by the force of the mythic elements straining against one another. (*GS* 2.1: 107–8; *SW* 1: 20)

According to this theory, life enters the poem at the hands of the poets by way of a sphere of mythical relations, and not by way of myth itself. Otherwise it is the "mere life" of a certain philosophy of life (the phrases "the immediate feeling of life" [*unmittelbares Lebensgefühl*] and "warmth of the heart" [*Herzenswärme*] can both be found in Dilthey and are invoked as specimens of the philosophy of life) and its insertion into the work reveals a lack of dexterity on the part of the craftsman.[32] A "bungler" (*Stümper*), according to Grimm's dictionary, is one "who in his craft (*Handwerk*), art and science understands and accomplishes little or nothing, ranging broadly from what is clumsy (*ungeschickten*) in one matter to what reveals an inferior mental disposition." The contrast is clearly to the poets who bring their "skilled hands" (*schickliche Hände*) at the end of "Timidity." The question is of the specific character of the "transformation" that takes place at the hands of the poets—the ambiguous structural limitation that grips and is gripped by the poem. From the perspective developed by Benjamin, it is certainly not the completion of "mere life" as qualified by myth. On the contrary, the poetized resists the imposition of mythic qualification and value—this is what Benjamin calls "mythic violence" in his essay on force. And yet the manipulation of life by the poets is "designated approximatively as 'mythic,'" Benjamin observes. This is precisely what the later version of Hölderlin's poem makes clear—namely, that the earlier version is dependent on a mythic determination of life and death and that this marks an approximative or provisional step toward the relations of the irreducibly deeper mythic layers of meaning made possible by the poetized. This is where the philological aspect of the method explicitly resurfaces.

The philological comparability of the two poems and the fact that "they have come down to us" as versions (*Fassungen*) of a poem derives from the aesthetic "sphere of relation"—itself "ungraspable" (*nicht erfaßbar*)—in which the truly skilled poets work. "Timidity" remains related to "The Poet's Courage" as a stronger to a weaker version of the poem. The former results from a powerful transcendental movement that, however, does not arrive at complete transcendence. Otherwise the poetized would cease to be a limit-concept. "The Poet's Courage" is thus not replaced by "Timidity"; the earlier and the later versions persist and have a right to exist as "two poems by Hölderlin" that are alike and related by way of the poetized—as more or less partial and limited manifestations of what by definition cannot appear as poems. Indeed, as we have seen, the method in question demonstrates less the meaning of the later stronger version of the poem, as one would expect in a more conventional approach, than "the binding precondition of the early draft" (*GS* 2.1: 111; *SW* 1: 24). This precondition is revealed by the "revolution of the structure" that "forces its way" from the earlier to the later version of the poem, making possible the existence of these poems "and others" (*GS* 2.1: 106; *SW* 1: 19). The critical commentary must focus specifically on the powerful connections which take hold of life and of which life takes hold along the way. Or, as Benjamin writes, "the method requires from the start setting out from what is connected, in order to gain insight into the articulation" (*GS* 2.1: 111; *SW* 1: 24). This statement suggests that the method and in particular its way of approaching the singular limitation of life in the poem is philological in two senses. First, the method takes as its point of departure the divergent ways the language and syntax of the two versions of the poem fasten onto a concept of life unlimited by perception, myth, or fate—through the application of an immortalizing mythic fate to the death of the poet in a context where space and time remain a "duality" (in "The Poet's Courage") and through the imposition of a more ambiguous poetic fate on the cosmos under the conditions of spatiotemporal interpenetration or "unity" that expose the "mythic elements" as straining against one another (in "Timidity") (*GS* 2.1: 110; *SW* 1: 23). In the former the connections are made by way of comparison and analogy to mythology; in the latter they are produced out of what is described as an electrochemical chain or force field of the image in which myth breaks down.[33]

But the specific linguistic and syntactic connections of the two poems with which the method begins are not the only philological elements in the commentary: the aesthetic "insight" (*Einsicht*) into what Benjamin calls the "articulation" (*Fügung*) of the poem is also philological. This word—*Fügung*—is precisely the one selected by Norbert van Hellingrath, the editor of the famous Hölderlin edition so admired by Benjamin, to categorize what is taken to be the singular characteristic of Hölderlin's verse, namely, "*harte Fügung.*" By choosing this phrase, which might be translated literally as "rough articulation" or "rough joining," Hellingrath placed Hölderlin's poetry in the middle of the major philological controversy over *asyndeton* in Pindar initiated in the German context during Hölderlin's time by August Boeckh, who was possibly the most influential student of Friedrich Wolf.[34] As its etymology conveys, *asyndeton* signifies a rough connection or even a disconnection between words. Boeckh, and in turn his student Ludolf Dissen in his 1830 edition of Pindar, sought to correct what they viewed as textual errors caused by the "*horror vacui*" of scribes who inserted punctuation and bits of language, in particular the connective adversative particle *dé* ("but" or "now") in Ancient Greek, to fill in perceived gaps between the words in Pindar's verse.[35] The movement of the method, it turns out, from the connections and the disconnections in the two poems takes place along philological lines. The aesthetic commentary does not transcend philology. Rather, the method imposes the interpenetration of aesthetic and philological elements straining against one another in the poem's rigorously articulated structure. This intensive process is suggested by the statement that the method requires *setting out* from the linguistic and syntactic connections in order to *see into* the articulation of the poem (*Die Methode verlangt, von Verbundnem von Anfang an "auszugehen," um "Einsicht" in die Fügung zu gewinnen* [*GS* 2.1: 111; *SW* 1: 24; my emphasis]). Aesthetic insight, in other words, requires an indispensable methodological detour by way of philology: precisely the sort of "detour" or "indirection" (*Umweg*) that Benjamin later identifies with method at the beginning of his study of the German play of mourning.[36] By tracing a movement that reverses the outside and the inside of the poetic structure, the method retraces the dynamic action of the image in the poem, in particular as manifested in the unfolding of the image of fate over the god at the hands of the poets in the final strophe of "Timidity," according to Benjamin.[37] In this way, the method may be said to reveal the image that is the nonobjective object of the philologico-aesthetic commentary: the image of the poem.

In keeping with this account of the shift in the linguistic connections which take hold of life and of which life takes hold, the movement from "Poet's Courage" to "Timidity" is toward not greater transcendental completion but rather more intensive interpenetration of the aesthetic and the philological dimensions of the poem. A good example of this is the substitution in the second stanza of the poem of the word *gelegen* (that which is opportune or, literally, that which is laid out or laid down) for *gesegnet* (blessed) in the fifth line that is addressed to the poet[38]:

> *Was geschiehet, es sei alles "gesegnet" dir* ("Dichtermut,")
> [Whatever happens, let it all be "blessed" for you]
> *Was geschiehet, es sei alles "gelegen" dir* ("Blödigkeit")
> [Whatever happens, let it all be *opportune* (or literally: "laid out" for you)] [my emphasis]

The word *gesegnet* (blessed) is the participle of the verb *segnen* (to bless). According to Grimm, *segnen* "goes back to the Latin *signare* (*cruce*), most commonly to the protective, consecrating sign of the cross that is made with the hand invoking God." Similarly, the English verb to bless, according to the Oxford English Dictionary, means "to make 'sacred' or 'holy' with blood . . . to consecrate by some sacrificial rite which was held to render a thing inviolable from the profane use of men." To the extent that it is encountered by the poet as blessed, life as poetic material has been consecrated and removed from profane use through a blood sacrifice. The same is true of the life—and the death—of the poet who is, as Benjamin puts it, "analogically" compared to the dying god (Phaeton) and is immortalized in the image of the setting sun in the first version of the poem (*GS* 2.1: 110; *SW* 1: 23). Each poetic sign from this mythic angle is made in the image of the immortalizing sign of the cross. The semiotic connections of "The Poet's Courage" point to the transcendental precondition of the poem from the perspective of the duality of man and god—the duality expressed by the mythic sacrifice of the mangod on the cross. The linguistic and syntactic connections of the second version, on the other hand, expose a unifying sphere where man and god are bound together, indeed where everything that occurs is bound together in the matrix of the poetized. This is the life that is opportunely laid out and indeed that is laid down for— and ultimately by—the poet as the intense unity of "what happens." Thus, the poet of "Timidity" is urged to "step nakedly into life" without protective gear to shield against the mortality with which this life is united. At one level, the "foot" of line 2 is indeed the body part standing for the mortality and animality that is exposed to earthly existence (it is connected in this sense to the "game animal" [*Wild*] of line 9). Yet, from the perspective that Benjamin developed six years later in his essay on the critique of force, the life into which this foot nakedly steps is not the mere mortal or "bare life" of a finite individual living being (*zoé*), much less the qualified life (*bíos*) of the collective biopolitical order. Rather, the life into which the poet is exhorted to step is closer to what Benjamin seeks to clarify by way of contrast to the existence of individual and collective "living beings" (*die Lebenden*) in his 1921 essay—namely, life as "being alive" (*die Lebendigen*) (*GS* 2.1: 200; *SW* 1: 250). The distinction between "mythical" and "divine" or "revolutionary" force is in this sense what Benjamin makes out of the difference between the life of "living beings" (*die Lebenden*) and the life of "being alive" (*die Lebendigen*) in "Timidity." While the life of the former (*die Lebenden*) is comprised of "[man's] situations (*Zustände*), his physical, humanly vulnerable life," that of the latter (*die Lebendigen*) "consists identically in earthly life, death and afterlife (*Erdenleben, Tod und Fortleben*)"—what Benjamin calls "the immutable aggregate situation of 'human being'" (*den unverrückbaren Aggregatzustand von "Mensch"*) (*GS* 2.1: 201; *SW* 1: 251). The life of "being alive" is composed of an interweaving of these elements that persist and consist in an irreducible relation to one another as life. Earthly existence, mortality, and living on are densely interrelated in the life into which the poet is urged to step in "Timidity." The going of the poet's "foot"—so the exhortation in the first strophe of the poem goes—is thus not simply that of life or of death on earth, although it does consist partially of a relation between the two that is more unified in the later than in the earlier version of the poem. For all of its vitality and mortality, this "foot" also claims to be poetic and thus in a certain sense not only to go (and ultimately to be gone) but also to *go on*. At this point it becomes clear that the "foot" at the beginning of the poem is inseparable from the "hands" at the end. If the former *goes on* the true, the latter come "with art," not to immortalize life but to draw into and to draw out of its mortality that which lives on ("the heavenly"), not as myth, but as "the mythic elements straining against one another" (*GS* 2.1: 108; *SW* 1: 20).

In a recent essay Hans Jürgen Scheuer provides an illustration of what Benjamin evocatively calls this "dislocation" or "shifting of the mythological" (*Verlagerung des Mythologischen*) in the development of the poem (*GS* 2.1: 116; *SW* 1: 28).[39] In a detailed analysis of the drafts of what would become "Timidity," Scheuer extends the methodological thrust of Benjamin's approach by illuminating the process through which the Orphic, Phaetonic, and Odyssean myths are successively layered onto the death of the poet as Hölderlin's poem takes shape and undergoes transformation, borrowing passages from Ovid and Homer. Ultimately, Scheuer concludes, "instead of being treated as a mythological subject [the theme of the death of the poet] is increasingly recognized as the *structural* problem of the ode."[40] Building on Ulrich Gaier's observation that "the last version of the poem ('Timidity') is no longer an ode about the poet but rather an ode about poetry," Scheuer adds: "And this poetry . . . bears within it—in its design and in not merely reproducing knowledge acquired from mythology manuals—the fragility and instability of the torn, dismembered body of the poet."[41] In support of this turn in the later version of the poem toward the structural problem, Scheuer discerns the superimposition of yet another classical source on "Timidity"— namely, Horace's famous characterization (in *Satires* 1.4: 62) of the transformation of poetic verse into critical prose as the literal dismemberment of the metrical body of the poem into the prosaic periods delineated in Latin specifically as *membra*—in the movement from the "foot" (l.2) to the "heart" (l.7) the "tongues" (l.13) and the "hands" (l.24).[42] From this perspective the enjambments that produce the flowing together of the middle strophes (3–5) of "Timidity"—an effect intensified by the revisions leading up to the last version of the poem—drives the prosodic feet of the traditional Asclepiadic ode to the metrical limit that separates poetry from prose, resulting in a "form" that Scheuer describes as *"no longer* strophic and *not yet* prose."⁴³ By way of this exposure to the prosaic, Hölderlin's poem may be understood to submit the going of the poet and of the poem to the Horatian test of genuine poetic construction as outlined in *Satire* 1.4: the capacity of the poetic composition to withstand translation into (critical) prose. The prosaic test can be passed, according to Horace, when the components of the poem are decomposed and in their very capacity for decomposition demonstrate the fortitude of the work to be recomposed into a poetic composition (and to go on). It is this persistent fragility or infirmity (*Blödigkeit*) of the poem in the face of its prosaic translation that is affirmed by the rough articulation of Hölderlin's "Timidity," according to Scheuer, based on the example of Horace. The shifting of the mythological determinations of the death of the poet that gives way to the structural dismemberment and reconstitution of the poem illustrated by Scheuer's analysis is described by Benjamin in formal terms: "The poet [in the last two verses] is no longer seen as a form; he is now only the principle of form, that which limits" (*GS* 2.1: 125; *SW* 1: 35). The structure (*Aufbau*) of the poem thus presents itself as evidence of the transcendental force of form over matter—of the capacity of the poetic structure to become a medium through which life lives on apart from the earthly life and death of living beings, including the life and death of the poets from whose hands this structure emerges. In this sense, although the poets are not immortal, their hands in "Timidity" are said to be like those of "the Creator" in the passage Benjamin cites from Schiller (*GS* 2.1: 125; *SW* 1: 35). From this perspective Hölderlin's poem is proof of the aesthetic "insight" of Schiller's words that liken the effect produced on its reader to a condition that is "pure and complete" (*rein und vollkommen*), which is to say, a condition that is "fully free" (*völlig frei*) and "inviolate" (*unverletzt*): in short, as Schiller goes on to write in this passage, "emancipated from the passions."⁴⁴

But the essay does not come to an end at this point. Instead, there is a pause—a caesura—as Benjamin turns to consider what has been, he writes, "deliberately avoided in the course of the investigation"—namely, "the word 'sobriety'" (*GS* 2.1: 125; *SW* 1: 35). This word is from Hölderlin's "Half of Life."[45] It describes the effect of the "sacredly sobering water" as the poetic swans of the first half of the poem give way to the "speechless" walls of the second.[46] Winfried Menninghaus has made us aware of the extent to which this poem foregrounds a Sapphic strain in Hölderlin's poetry that has been underappreciated due to the excessive emphasis on Pindar in the reception of his work beginning with Hellingrath.[47] As context Menninghaus cites Friedrich Schlegel's observation that Pindar's poems express a "public sentiment."[48] They are "choric poetry," Schlegel argues, even if "they are not sung by the chorus: in them a public voice speaks, not that of an individual."[49] By contrast, from Herder to the German romantics and Hegel the Sapphic voice is associated with the individual rather than the collective. Moreover, if Pindar's is a poetry of power, and perhaps above all a poetry that proclaims the memorializing power of poetic speech itself, Sappho's verse tends to mix power and weakness. Hölderlin touches on this aspect of her poetry when he writes that "Sappho portrays her sentiments with the weightiness of Alcaeus speaking of slaughter and tyrants."[50] Menninghaus finds the Sapphic expressed in Hölderlin's "Half of Life" by the prominent use of the five-syllable formula of the Adonic consisting of a dactyl followed by a trochee (—⌣ ⌣/—⌣) that was "invented" by Sappho in her lament for the death of Adonis (*ô ton Adônin*).[51] The phrases "*trunken von Küssen*," "*nüchterne Wasser*," "*Schatten der Erde*," as well as the poem's final words, "*klirren die Fahnen*," and indeed its title, "*Hälfte des Lebens*," all bear the stamp of the Sapphic Adonic which is, Menninghaus observes, "the metrical signature of the poem."[52]

By invoking "Half of Life" and specifically the "sobriety" that is central to this poem, Benjamin may be understood to suggest at the end of his essay that yet another mythic layer is to be applied to the death of the poet in "Timidity"—namely, that of Sappho's lament for the demise of Adonis (as Menninghaus points out, the phrase "*nüchterne Wasser*" itself takes the form of the Adonic). Thus, to the Homeric, Ovidian, and Horatian mythic contexts "dislocated" in the poem is now added the Sapphic. If there is no end to the layering and shifting of mythic relations discovered by Benjamin in the poem, this is because his commentary adheres to the paradoxical philological principle set forth by Wolf of the irreducibly interpolated character of the work. The relation of the modern poem to ancient Greek myth is interpreted in Benjamin's essay along the lines of the theory spelled out by Hölderlin in his famous 1801 letter to Casimir Ulrich Böhlendorff that was among those considered by Benjamin in 1931–32 for inclusion in a collection that would reveal "a secret Germany" (*GS* 4: 945; *SW* 2: 466).[53] This complex theory turns on the difference in poetry between what can be captured or appropriated (*das Fremde* [the foreign]) and what must be freely used (*das Eigene* [the own]).[54] For the ancients this is the difference between a sobriety that is foreign to them and a pathos that is their own; for the moderns "it is reversed" (*ist's umgekehrt*).[55] "Most difficult," according to Hölderlin, is the "*free* use of the *own*" ("*freie*" *Gebrauch des* "*Eigenen*"), which for the modern poet means the free use of sobriety. What makes this use of the own so difficult is that it excludes appropriation. The use of the own is free from the capture that Hölderlin attributes to Homer, who "plundered . . . Junonian sobriety," and also presumably free from what Benjamin characterizes as the "seizing" (*ergreifen*) of the god at the end of "Timidity" (*GS* 2.1: 122; *SW* 1: 32). Sobriety for the moderns, and not for the ancients, calls for and allows for a use of the own that rigorously excludes appropriation and ownership. If the Greeks mastered pathos less—because it was not foreign to them—the same or rather the reverse must be true "with us," Hölderlin writes, when it comes to sobriety. "We" are thus related to the Greeks by the common inability to appropriate *the* own, what we cannot even call *our* own: pathos for them and sobriety for us. Since the capacity for capture in both cases can never extend beyond what is foreign, ancient and modern poetry are ultimately both complementary or, philologically speaking, interpolated with respect to *the* own and to what therefore cannot ever be *their* own. This is where Hölderlin's poetic project intersects with and diverges from the romantic philology that Friedrich Schlegel derived from Wolf's study of Homer, as we will discuss in more detail in the next chapter on Benjamin's dissertation on German romantic criticism. Ancient Greek poetry is at once irreducibly complementary for the modern poet and irreducibly interpolated for the modern philologist. Yet from a Kantian perspective shared by Hölderlin and Schlegel, neither the modern poet nor the modern philologist is relieved of the transcendental task of delineating the a priori condition of possibility—the poetized—of Greek poetry. However, as Benjamin points out, this effort must "stand beyond all exaltation in the sublime" to the same degree that the Greeks stood beyond the "oriental pathos" of which their poetry was the complement: sobriety itself must not become exalted as sublime (*GS* 2.1: 126; *SW* 1: 35). The only way open is, in Hölderlin's words, the study of "the artifice (*méchané*) of the ancients."[56] The sobriety of such study, Benjamin argues, marks Hölderlin's later works:

> They (*Sie*) arise from the inner certainty with which those works (*diese*) stand in his own intellectual life, in which sobriety now is allowed, is called for, because this life is in itself sacred, standing beyond all exaltation in the sublime. Is this life still that of Hellenism? That is as little the case here as that the life of any pure work of art could be that of a people; and as little the case, too, that what we find in the poetized might be the life of an individual and nothing else. This life is shaped in the forms of Greek myth, but—this is crucial—not in them alone; the Greek element is sublated in the last version and balanced against another element that (without express justification, to be sure) was called the Oriental. (*GS* 2.1: 125–26; *SW* 1: 35)

The "life" described by Benjamin in this passage may be understood to emerge out of the dynamic tension between the speakers of "Timidity" and its addressee. This is the dimension of the poem disclosed, but not explicitly considered, by Benjamin's invocation of the phrase "sacredly sobering" from "Half of Life" at the end of his essay. From this perspective, the exhortations and assertions of the poets in "Timidity" appear as manifestations of the claims of poetic power that are subject to sobering limitation in the second half of "Half of Life." The poet addressed in the former poem, on the other hand, is as speechless as the walls in the second half of the latter. It is as if the tense interaction between the Pindaric and the Sapphic elements underlined by Menninghaus in "Half of Life" were transposed into the relation between the choric speakers and the silent protagonist of "Timidity."

Although it is stamped by Greek myth, specifically as transmitted by Sappho's verse, the silence addressed in "Timidity" is not mythic, Benjamin insists. To avoid this erroneous impression, he deliberately defers the introduction of the potentially mythologizing key word "sobriety" (derived from the Adonic phrase "*nüchterne Wasser*" in "Half of Life") until the commentary has demonstrated how it is to be understood—namely, as precisely what the modern poets cannot make *their* own. In another essay from this same period, "The Metaphysics of Youth," which explicitly refers to Sappho, the silence marked out by Benjamin with the word "sobriety" is described as "the inner border" of a singular "dialogue" or "conversation" (*Gespräch*) involving a speaker and a "listener" (*Hörende*) (*GS* 2.1: 95 and 91; *SW* 1: 9 and 6).[57] The listener, Benjamin asserts, "is the silent one. The speaker receives meaning from him; the silent one is the untapped source of meaning (*ungefasste Quelle des Sinns*)" (*GS* 2.1: 91; *SW* 1: 6). Like this listener, the mute addressee of "Timidity" gives meaning to what the speakers of the poem say *and also* to what Benjamin says (drawing on what the speaker of another poem says) about what the addressee of "Timidity" does not say. In this sense, silence gives an unmythological signification to the words of the poets as well as to the words from "Half of Life" interpolated by Benjamin into the commentary on "Timidity." In both cases, the word "sobriety" receives meaning from the silence of the poet or, more precisely, from the silence that is built into or outlined by the poem, as a sort of negative impression, and that in fact erases the figure of the poet as it develops from "Poet's Courage" (*Dichtermut*) to "Timidity" (*Blödigkeit*). Ultimately, like the word "timidity" in what becomes the poem's title, the word "sobriety" inserted by Benjamin designates not a quality of a substantial entity (for example, an individual silent poet addressed by the speakers of the poem) but rather a paradoxical condition (specifically, an unconditional condition) emerging from the limiting set of relations—the "mythic connections" (*mythischen Verbundenheiten*)—shaped by the poem (*GS* 2.1: 126; *SW* 1: 35). The word "sobriety" can now be understood, therefore, as arising from the "inner certainty" or "inner border" that separates and joins the poem (what the speakers say) to the precondition or "the poetized" of the poem (the silence built into and marked out of it). According to this same logic and diverging from the classic philological position of Wolf and his followers (including to a certain extent Schlegel), the "sobriety" of the "life" that supports and is supported by Hölderlin's late poems is not "that of Hellenism," not "that of a people," and not "that of an individual"—not even that, we might add, of a poet much less of Hölderlin (*GS* 2.1: 125–26; *SW* 1: 35).[58] Instead (retranslating the ambiguous and exceptionally precise sentence at the beginning of the passage just cited): "These (late works) (*Sie*) derive from the inner certainty with which these (words) (*diese*) [sacredly sobering] stand in the own intellectual life (*im eigenen geistigen Leben stehen*) in which sobriety is allowed, is called for because this life is in itself sacred" (*GS* 2.1: 125; *SW* 1: 35). Rather than being qualified—consecrated or blessed—as sacred through sobriety, the life in question precisely because it is "in itself sacred" permits and commands the sobriety of using freely what cannot be owned. By somewhat awkwardly excluding the possessive plural pronoun—*ihrem* (their)—from the phrase "*im eigenen geistigen Leben*" (in the own intellectual life), which would assign the life to the words "sacredly sober," Benjamin's commentary adheres strictly to Hölderlin's text. This striking formulation indicates that the words "sacredly sober" stand securely at the inner boundary between the modern poet and the inappropriable *own* set forth in the letter to Böhlendorff. The "intellectual life" that arises at this inner boundary is not "that of Hellenism," not "that of a people," not "that of an individual" or of a poet, and also, strictly speaking, not that of a condition that could be captured and appropriated by the words "sacredly sober" or indeed by any other words. What can be expressed by words such as these and what can be adumbrated in the poem is a life, Benjamin writes (retranslating again), that is "nothing but its own" (*keines als sein eignes*).[59] The possessive pronoun "its" (*sein*) in this phrase can and must be read to exclude all forms of possession, save one: that of an exceptional transcendental possessability recuperating absolutely everything that is otherwise owned illegitimately—that of a messianic revolutionary power. For Hölderlin such transcendental possession and repossession were rooted in passages from Kant's *Metaphysics of Morals* and *Religion within the Boundaries of Mere Reason*.[60] Benjamin's approach to this possibility of an ultimate force of possession that cancels all others—what Kant calls "supreme ownership" (*Obereigentum*) and what Benjamin will later call "divine" or "revolutionary" force (*Gewalt*)—was shaped by his radical reworking of some of these same Kantian texts. It is linked to what he characterizes as "the messianic realm or the idea of the French Revolution" in "The Life of Students," with which we began (*GS* 2.1: 75; *SW* 1: 37). At the end of the commentary on Hölderlin, the possibility of such an unpossessable own life is extended from the theological and the political realms explicitly to the aesthetic sphere of what Benjamin calls "the life of a pure work of art" (*das Leben eines reinen Kunstwerks*) (*GS* 2.1: 126; *SW* 1: 35). From this perspective, the analysis of the dislocations of Greek myth in the poem—those shaping the mythic interpolations not only of the Pindaric speakers but also of the silent Sapphic addressee—turns into a philology of life.

2
THE CONCEPT OF CRITICISM IN GERMAN ROMANTICISM

The philology of life that was under development in Benjamin's early essay on Hölderlin can be seen subtly and even surreptitiously at work in what might appear to be his most conventional and certainly his most professionally successful (indeed, his only professionally successful) piece of academic literary criticism—his doctoral dissertation on German romantic literary criticism, which was written in 1918–19 and published as *The Concept of Criticism in German Romanticism* in 1920. In keeping, it would seem, with the conventions of such a formal academic exercise, the dissertation—a literary critical study of the romantic concept of literary criticism—begins by reflecting on the limitations of its method and scope. This is not merely a matter of academic decorum: Benjamin's project, as we will see, is indeed all about self-limitation (*Selbstbeschränkung*). The emphatic care given to the limits placed on the project in the introductory paragraphs titled "Delimitations of the Question" (*Einschränkungen der Fragestellung*) contributes to the sense of disciplinary rigor that would have been expected of a Ph.D. thesis submitted to the University of Bern in 1919 (and indeed Benjamin's dissertation exceeded expectations and was awarded the citation of *summa cum laude*). Yet the stress on the limitations that lend coherence to the work also points to the obstacles standing in the way of a true understanding of what is most important about German romantic criticism from Benjamin's critical point of view. In this sense, the constraints placed on the dissertation, as Benjamin underlines in its opening pages, restrict the thesis to the limited critical contribution only of "materials" (*Materialien*) to be used toward the definition of the essence of German romanticism and preclude inquiry into the determination of its aesthetic "point of view" (*Gesichtspunkt*) (*GS* 1.1: 12; *SW* 1: 185). "This point of view," Benjamin states, "may be sought in romantic messianism" (*GS* 1.1: 12n3; *SW* 1: 185n3). This statement, contained in a footnote and thus relegated to the margins of the dissertation, is related to the "point of view" developing in Benjamin's own broader critical project during these student years. It raises the possibility that the restrictions imposed on the dissertation, which seem to be a matter of scholarly prudence and convention, might also have the effect of obscuring its author's own critical point of view. This is the thesis explored in this chapter—namely, that Benjamin's philological study of the romantic concept of literary criticism is designed simultaneously to outline and to underline the limitations of academic literary criticism from an aesthetic perspective that remains largely hidden in the dissertation. Or as Samuel Weber has elegantly put it in response to a comment by the eminent Germanist Peter Demetz: "Benjamin's 'professionally done' dissertation [as Demetz describes it] was thus intended to lead its readers to the limits of its explicitly treated subject-matter and point them beyond, in the direction of an 'esoteric' dimension that transcends the purview of traditional scholarly discourse."[1] In this sense, Benjamin's dissertation may be said to delimit romantic literary criticism in a way that is characteristic of all of his critical work on German literature throughout his early years. In this chapter, I will specify the critical engagement of Benjamin's dissertation with the authoritative sources of German studies in this period and then suggest how the "esoteric dimension" of this work contributes to the philology of life that we discerned in his earlier work.

Not a history of the concept of criticism, not a study of the place of romanticism in the history of philosophy, also not an investigation into romanticism from the perspective of the philosophy of history or an attempt to represent the "historical essence of romanticism," this dissertation is to be understood, as Benjamin insists in its first sentence, as "a problem-historical investigation": "The present work is conceived as a contribution to a problem-historical investigation . . . (*problemgeschichtlichen Untersuchung*)" (*GS* 1.1: 11; *SW* 1: 116). The term somewhat awkwardly translated as "problem-historical"—*problemgeschichtlichen*—inscribes Benjamin's critical project in the broader debate, spurred by the work of Max Weber and neo-Kantians such as Rickert and his teacher, Wilhelm Windelband, surrounding the question of the scientific status of the human and cultural sciences that emerged in the German university of the later nineteenth century.[2] *Problems*, anchored in communal commitments and thus collective values, allow cultural material to be raised above the status of mere empirical facts and enable the historical study of the human sciences to attain what Max Weber, drawing on neo-Kantianism, did not hesitate to call "objectivity" (*Objektivität*).[3] This was the proposition developed especially by Rickert on the basis of Windelband's work.[4] The neo-Kantian background on which Benjamin's dissertation draws in order to frame its approach is clearly visible in both of the two main parts of the study: the first being devoted to reflection, the second criticism. With respect to the section on reflection, which starts with Fichte, Benjamin cites Windelband's exposition of what will become the key source of the objection leveled by the German romantics at the author of the *Wissenschaftslehre*: the latter's emphasis on "unconscious representation" (*bewußtlose Vorstellung*) in the self-limitation of the "I" by the "non-I" in reflection. Benjamin quotes from the extensive account of this logic in Fichte provided by Windelband in the second volume of the fifth edition of the influential *Geschichte der neueren Philosophie in ihrem Zusammenhange mit der allgemeinen Kultur und den besonderen Wissenschaften,* which appeared in 1911.[5] "It will prove important for the relation between the Fichtean and the early romantic theories of knowledge," Benjamin observes, "that the formation of the 'non-I' in the 'I' rests on an unconscious function of the latter" (*GS* 1.1: 23; *SW* 1: 124). This remark is immediately followed by two quotations from Windelband, with the second one concluding that Fichte sees "the only way out for the explanation of the given content of consciousness in the fact that the latter stems from a representing of a higher sort, a free unconscious act of representing" (*einem freien unbewußten Vorstellen*) (*GS* 1.1: 23; *SW* 1: 124).[6] By contrast, Benjamin notes, "the romantics shudder at limitation through the unconscious" (*GS* 1.1: 36; *SW* 1: 132).

With respect to the second of the two main parts of the dissertation, which focuses on criticism, Rickert's philosophy makes a less conspicuous appearance but at a similarly crucial juncture. Unlike the reflecting "I" that is limited by the unconscious representation of the "non-I," the reflective medium of the work of art is not limited but infinitely *completed* through the intervention of criticism. "Completion" translates the German *Vollendung*. Benjamin quotes Novalis on such completing critical interventions: "They represent the pure, completed character of the individual work of art (*Sie stellen den reinen, vollendeten Charakter des individuellen Kunstwerks dar*)" (*GS* 1.1: 70; *SW* 1: 154). Yet the noun "completion" (*Vollendung*) employed by Benjamin invokes Rickert, who made this term the key to his value-philosophical system, as we have seen. Moreover, the ambiguity of *Vollendung* on which Rickert insists—as both consummation and consumption, completing and complete ending—is attributed by Benjamin to the romantic concept of criticism: "Entirely in contrast with the present-day conception of its essence, criticism in its central intention is not judgment (*Beurteilung*) but, on the one hand, completion (*Vollendung*), expansion (*Ergänzung*), and systematization of the work and, on the other hand, its dissolution or resolution in the absolute (*Auflösung im Absoluten*)" (*GS* 1.1: 78; *SW* 1: 159).[7] The broad outlines of the dissertation, then, as delineated specifically by the concepts of reflection and criticism within the framework of the "problem-historical investigation," suggest a link between romantic theory and neo-Kantian philosophy. However, Benjamin does not explicitly develop this connection. Although the findings of the dissertation with regard to the romantic concept of criticism have important implications for the neo-Kantian theory of "objectivity" in the cultural and human sciences, Benjamin remains interested in other connections.

These connections start to become evident in the first sentences of the second of the two introductory sections of the dissertation titled "The Sources" (*Die Quellen*). From the outset these evocative words are defined not only as "textual sources in the narrower sense" but also indeed primarily as *the theory* from which they may be understood to derive:

> Friedrich Schlegel's theory will be presented (*dargestellt*) in what follows as the romantic theory of criticism. The right to designate this theory as the romantic theory rests on its representative character. Not that all the early romantics declared themselves in agreement with it, or even took notice of it: Friedrich Schlegel often remained unintelligible even to his friends. But his apprehension (*seine Anschauung*) of the essence of criticism is the final word of the romantic school on this matter. He made this problematic and philosophical object most his own—although certainly not his alone. Along with Friedrich Schlegel's writings, only those of Novalis come into consideration as textual sources in the narrower sense for this presentation (*diese Darstellung*), whereas Fichte's earlier writings present indispensable sources, not for the romantic concept of criticism itself but for its comprehension. The justification for bringing in Novalis's writings along with those of Schlegel is the complete unanimity of both as regards the premises and consequences of the theory of criticism. Novalis was less interested in the problem itself; but he shared with Schlegel the epistemological presuppositions

on the basis of which the latter treated this problem, and together with him he upheld the consequences of this theory of art. (*GS* 1.1: 14–15; *SW* 1: 118–19)

The theory in question is emphatically *dargestellt*: presented, represented, or produced in the sense of the chemical process to which Benjamin compares romantic criticism in the final sentences of the second half of the dissertation (*GS* 1.1: 109; *SW* 1: 178). The stress is on the presentation, representation, or production of a theory that was not "laid down" (*niedergelegt*) by Schlegel and that remained unnoticed by the romantics. Strictly speaking, Schlegel can make no exclusive claim to this theory: he can only be said to "have made it most his own—although certainly not his alone" (*seinem eigensten gemacht—wenn auch gewiß nicht zu seinem einzigen*) (*GS* 1.1: 14–15; *SW* 1: 118). The theory is not given directly in the writings of Schlegel or of any of the romantics; it must be presented, represented, or produced in the dissertation, specifically as the romantic theory of criticism. Schlegel's theory of criticism requires a critical operation to present it. "For an understanding of [Schlegel's] concept of criticism," Benjamin goes on to assert later in this section, "the explication and the isolation, the pure presentation (*die reine Darstellung*), of this epistemological theory is indispensable" (*GS* 1.1: 16; *SW* 1: 119). The "right" (*Recht*) to present this unwritten theory as the romantic theory of criticism is based not on the endorsement of it by the romantics, or even on its independent existence in the writings of Schlegel alone or in combination with those of Novalis from this period, but purely on "its representative character" that is presented "in what follows." The theory ascribed to Schlegel, in other words, is presented in this passage and in the dissertation as the precondition of the romantic theory of criticism as it is manifested in the writings of the romantics, including especially those of Schlegel.

Another source acknowledged in this introductory statement is Fichte, whose early writings are also indispensable, not for the romantic theory of criticism itself but for an understanding of it.

Understanding romantic critical theory as a philosophical problem presupposes, first of all, that art is a manifestation of thinking and in particular of the capacity of thinking to reflect on itself—what Kant called "reflective judgment."[8] As noted, this is the focus of the first main part of the dissertation. According to Fichte, such reflection discloses the purely formal dimension of thinking. It reveals that thinking involves in addition to content also form. Science for Fichte includes knowledge not only of things but of the way things are known. This reflexive knowledge (of knowledge) makes the action or form of thinking into its content. The dizzying reversibility of form and content in pure reflection draws thinking into a cycle of potentially endless thinking about itself (as Benjamin notes with regard to a citation from Schlegel's *Lucinde*, "thinking can find an end least of all in reflective thinking about itself' [*GS* 1.1: 18; *SW* 1: 121]). But Fichte understood reflection to be meaningful only to the extent that it is limited by a self-positing "I" for which thinking becomes an object (and thus a "non-I") of reflection. This self-positing act, prior to all thinking of things (including the thing that thinking becomes for the "I" in reflection), limits reflective thinking. Without this particular limitation, reflection for Fichte "means nothing" and "leads into the void" (*GS* 1.1: 29; *SW* 1: 128). The act by which the "I" posits itself before things can be thought—what Fichte describes as "the one action of the human mind not contained under all those others"— is, as Benjamin points out, "the only single case of the fruitful application of reflection, namely, of that reflection that occurs in intellectual intuition" (*GS* 1.1: 29; *SW* 1: 128). In other words, it is ultimately through the thesis of an original and single reflexive act of positing in which the "I" is both subject and object (the "I" positing the "I") that Fichte seeks to reassert the Kantian claim of a thinking that produces its object. In this case, the object of the intellectual intuition is what Benjamin calls "second-level reflection" (the thinking of thinking) or what is also described as "the canonical form of reflection" as it "was recognized by Fichte" (*GS* 1.1: 30; *SW* 1: 129).

The German romantics were fascinated by the infinite potentiality of reflection that was outlined by Fichte in his early writings and that he proposed to overcome with the thesis of the self-positing "I." This fascination led Schlegel to an even more dynamic theory of self-limitation in reflection, specifically, the self-limitation of art in the form of the work. As the work of art, reflection undergoes a peculiar and even mystical mode of limitation that takes it beyond the boundaries of the account of the determination of the "I" offered in the *Wissenschaftslehre*. It is here, Benjamin observes, that the romantics "part company" with Fichte (*GS* 1.1: 19; *SW* 1: 122). This crucial "point of departure" (*Trennungsort*) is what Benjamin insists on calling the romantic *philosophy* of reflection, emphasizing that the divergence from Fichte is not simply slippage from philosophy into the realm of art—not a matter of "the artist's turning away from the scientific thinker and philosopher" (*GS* 1.1: 20; *SW* 1: 122).[9] But this philosophy involves a mode of self-limitation, in particular in the case of the work of art, that does not stand apart from interpretation and representation in the manner of the "I" that posits itself in Fichte. As taken up in critical reflection the work is understood to limit itself in a way that resists becoming an object and that turns into a reflexive process or what Benjamin calls a "medium of reflection." This medium, however, appears nowhere in Schlegel's writing. The concept of the work of art as a "medium of reflection" (*Reflexionsmedium*) is introduced or presented by Benjamin to designate what goes unnamed in Schlegel's text—it is not to be found explicitly in the "textual sources in the narrow sense" (*GS* 1.1: 36; *SW* 1: 132). Nevertheless, the "medium of reflection" is said to be subject to *citation* in the dissertation:

> The whole of Schlegel's theoretical philosophy is to be designated comprehensively with this term [i.e., medium of reflection] and in what follows it will be cited not infrequently with this expression. It is therefore necessary to explain it and to secure it more exactly. Reflection

constitutes the absolute and constitutes it as a medium. Although Schlegel himself did not have the expression "medium" available to him, he placed the greatest value on the constantly uniform connection (*Zusammenhang*) in the absolute or in the system, both of which are to be interpreted as the connection (*Zusammenhang*) of the real, not in its substance (which is everywhere the same), but in the degrees of clarity of its unfolding. (*GS* 1.1: 36–37; *SW* 1: 132–33)

If with regard to the overarching thesis of the dissertation the theory that is not given directly anywhere in Schlegel's writings is to be presented, represented, or produced as the romantic theory of criticism, when it comes to the key question of reflection—the focus of the first part of the study—the expression "medium of reflection" that appears nowhere in Schlegel's writings is nevertheless to be "cited" as "the whole of [his] theoretical philosophy." The verb "to cite" (*zitieren*) in this passage, like the verb "to present" (*darstellen*) in the earlier one, dramatizes the productive capacity of criticism on which the romantics themselves insisted. However, the word "medium," according to Benjamin, signifies the continuous and uniform connection of an integrated relational system—what the romantics call "the absolute." The definition of the medium as involving a certain kind of connection (*Zusammenhang*) underlined by Benjamin in this passage proves crucial to his interpretation of the romantic concept of the work of art and ultimately indicates where his method differentiates itself from Schlegel's. This word can be translated as "connection" and "context," but it is difficult to capture its range of significations with one English word. *Zusammenhang* derives from the verb *zusammenhängen*, which literally means "to hang together." As a noun, it signifies not just context but also composition, coherence, or perhaps structure. For the romantics, as we have seen, the composition, coherence, or structure of the work limits art in a way that makes possible its completion in criticism. To explain the crucial importance of the term *Zusammenhang* for an understanding of the meaning of reflection for the romantics, Benjamin alludes to

Hölderlin—more precisely, to Hölderlin's gloss on his translation of a fragment from Pindar and to the phrase "infinitely (exactly) connected" (*unendlich [genau] zusammenhängen*) (*GS* 1.1: 26; *SW* 1: 126). Ultimately, as we will see, Hölderlin's use of this phrase will have to be distinguished from the romantic theory that it illuminates.

As a "medium of reflection," the work of art gives rise to a mode of self-limitation that breaks out of the subject-object formation of Fichte's self-positing "I". The medium does not become an object of reflection. This occurs in what Benjamin calls "third level of reflection": the stage at which "the thinking of thinking"—the "canonical" form of reflection according to which the form of thinking becomes its content (in Fichte)—turns into the thinking of "thinking of thinking" (*GS* 1.1: 30; *SW* 1: 128). Benjamin acknowledges the risk he is running by deciding to introduce a formulation that could appear "sophistical." But describing the specific mode of connectedness characteristic of the romantic "medium of reflection" demands that one venture onto what may be shaky philosophical ground and employ language that might seem overly rhetorical. Nevertheless, Benjamin observes, "if one enters into the discussion of the problem of reflection, as the context requires (*wie sie der Zusammenhang erfordert*), then of course subtle distinctions cannot be avoided" (*GS* 1.1: 30; *SW* 1: 129). The difference between the "canonical" form of reflection and that of the romantics is that the latter involves a mode of limitation or "connectedness" that disintegrates or decomposes the relation of subject to object, of form and content, that still obtains in the second-level reflection according to Fichte's thesis of the self-positing "I". The shift is suggested by the German: with third-level reflection *Setzen* (positing) is subjected to *Zersetzung* (de-positing) (*GS* 1.1: 30; *SW* 1: 129). This leads to what Benjamin characterizes as "a peculiar ambiguity": reflection in the original or proper sense, according to which thinking becomes the object of thought, turns into both subject and object in third-level reflection. Reversibility becomes "ambiguity." The specific mode of self-limitation or connection that characterizes the medium of reflection and that produces the ambiguous relation of subject and object is once again to be captured by a citation: "If one starts from the expression 'thinking of thinking,' then on the third level this is either the object of thought, thinking (of thinking of thinking), or else the thinking subject (thinking of thinking) of thinking. The rigorous original form of second-level reflection is assailed and shaken by the ambiguity in the third-level reflection" (*GS* 1.1: 30–31; *SW* 1: 129). The textual mirroring of canonical reflection in a citation produces the "medium of reflection" as an image—what Benjamin at one point describes as an "image-object" (*GS* 1.1: 72; *SW* 1: 155). The form of this expression is not simply a matter of limitation in the conventional sense: it is also the means of overcoming limitation. The citation makes the "thinking of thinking" appear within and as the dynamic and ambiguous outlines of the "medium of reflection." Thinking in this context can no longer be rigorously and exclusively identified as either a subject or an object: the mirror image or citation of reflection suspends the subject-object relation. The reflection does not turn the thinking (of thinking) from a content into a form in the canonical sense. At issue is something other than conventional formal limitation. This is why Benjamin describes it as the "dissolution of the rigorous form of reflection" (*diese Auflösung der strengen Reflexionsform*): "Reflection expands without limit or check (*schrankenlos*), and the thinking given form in reflection turns into formless thinking which directs itself toward the absolute" (*GS* 1.1: 31; *SW* 1: 129). The phrase "medium of reflection," which does not translate the German *Reflexionsmedium* exactly, cites the ambiguity of Schlegel's theory of reflection: it should be read as a subjective and as an objective genitive. Or, as Benjamin notes, "on the one hand, reflection is a medium, on the strength of its continuous context (*kraft ihres stetigen Zusammenhanges*); on the other hand, the medium in question is one such that reflection moves within it" (*GS* 1.1: 36n60; *SW* 1: 189n63). As a subject, reflection contains the medium, and at the same time, as an object, reflection is contained by the medium. The movement of reflection is thus within and beyond the limits of the medium. This new, alternative form of containment or connection is associated with life by the romantics: "through its form the work of art is a lively center of reflection" (*ein lebendiges Zentrum der Reflexion*) (*GS* 1.1: 73; *SW* 1: 156). In this sense, the concept of the medium of reflection introduced by Benjamin is the source of the "messianism" he attributes to the German romantics: the medium is what allows the work to be saved through criticism. For Schlegel, according to Benjamin, the dynamic process of critical preservation made possible by the medium of reflection remains nevertheless grounded in a "self": "For Fichte, consciousness is 'I'; for the romantics it is 'self'" (*GS* 1.1: 29; *SW* 1: 128). Schlegel's "first, axiomatic presupposition is that reflection . . . is in itself substantial and fulfilled" (*GS* 1.1: 31; *SW* 1: 129). As Samuel Weber has noted, "Reflection, for Schlegel, qua Medium is ultimately and originally self-identical and self-contained, because it is there from the very beginning as expressed in the term *Urreflexion*—Original or Primary Reflection."[10] In a way that is ultimately to be differentiated from Benjamin's method in the dissertation with regard to the "medium of reflection" (and also the theory of criticism as such), the romantic concept of criticism, as Weber puts it, "looks back to an original beginning in which the process is already grounded."[11] What the medium saves above all for the romantics is a self. In this respect, the critical action of presentation and of citation in the approach taken respectively to romantic theory and to the "medium of reflection" in the dissertation is decisively different from the romantics' own account of reflection as the conservation of what was already there from the beginning—namely, a self. On this point Hölderlin proves crucial to the critical perspective on romanticism that Benjamin develops, largely in the background, in his study.

But the divergence of Benjamin's critical practice from the one under investigation in the dissertation does not prevent him from recognizing the achievement of the romantics, in particular with regard to their elaboration of an objective theory of art. In this the romantics surpass the critical approach that was being taken to their work in the conventional *Germanistik* of Benjamin's day. This is illustrated by the example of a 1913 study of Friedrich Schlegel by the Bonn Germanist Carl Enders to which Benjamin alludes. Enders attributes to the Schlegel family responsibility for overcoming the dogmatism of neoclassical aesthetics and awakening the "modern critical spirit" based on a "respect for the unique sovereignty of the productive creative power of the artist and thinker" (*GS* 1.1: 70–71; *SW* 1: 154). What Enders does not mention, Benjamin observes almost in passing, is that for Friedrich Schlegel—the member of the family most responsible for this achievement—the "critical spirit" overcomes not only the aesthetic dogmatism of the neoclassical canon but also what Benjamin characterizes as "the boundless cult of creative power understood as the mere expressive force of the creator" (*schrankenlosen Kultus der schaffenden Kraft als bloßer Ausdruckskraft des Schöpfers*) (*GS* 1.1: 71; *SW* 1: 154). In this way, according to Benjamin, Schlegel surpassed both neoclassical rationalism (the rule-based aesthetics of Gottsched) and the cult of *Sturm und Drang* that continued to affect literary criticism in the nineteenth and twentieth centuries (as Enders's approach to Schlegel illustrates). Overlooked by the latter is that with Friedrich Schlegel the "critical spirit" secures a position for literary criticism that elevates it above the "skeptical tolerance" accorded to it by what Enders calls in the cited passage "the exclusive sovereignty of the productive creative force of the artist and the thinker" (*GS* 1.1: 70; *SW* 1: 154).[12] Schlegel, Benjamin argues, "fixed the laws of the spirit into the work of art itself (*die Gesetze des Geistes in das Kunstwerk selbst gebannt*) instead of making the latter into a mere by-product of subjectivity" (*GS* 1.1: 71; *SW* 1: 154). In this sense, the "fundamental concept" (*Grundbegriff*) of German romantic criticism is that of the work as medium of reflection—the concept that was identified and added by Benjamin. With his concept of the work of art as a "center of reflection" Schlegel "secured, from the side of the object or the image (*Objekte- oder Gebilde-Seite*), that very autonomy in the domain of art that Kant, in the third *Critique*, had lent to the power of judgment" (*GS* 1.1: 72; *SW* 1: 155). For the romantics, in other words, the objectivity of art and of art criticism derives from the work itself as a medium of reflection. This theory of aesthetic objectivity constitutes the great critical achievement of early German romanticism, according to Benjamin.

Yet Benjamin's underlying concern in the dissertation is the development of a critical perspective on romantic objectivity. This objectivity, as we have seen, derives from the "immanent structure" (*immanente Aufbau*) of the work and in particular from the former's capacity to release reflection from the latter (*GS* 1.1: 71; *SW* 1: 155). This is not a matter of the subjective power of the critic to provide a judgment of the work. It is an objective reflection. The objectivity of the work of art for the romantics consists therefore in a formal structure that both limits and allows for the extension of reflection. Criticism *re*-flects the formal inflection of the work and in this sense "breaks down" or "decomposes" (*zersetzt*) the form of the work. Yet, critical *re*-flection does not simply overcome limitation in the manner of the creative artist championed by *Sturm und Drang*. Instead romantic criticism is drawn into an objective process of *extending* a reflexive medium that is formally *limited*. "In order for criticism ... to be the suspension of all limitation," Benjamin observes, "the work must rest on limitation" (*GS* 1.1: 73; *SW* 1: 156). The work is objective, from this point of view, in a way that resembles the object of neo-Kantian cultural and human science. It is an expression of collective philosophical values, specifically, the transcendental idea of art.[13] The work of art for the romantics is a dynamic image-object of infinite critical reflection. Through criticism the objective character of the work affirms its capacity to live on as art.

When it comes to poetry, according to romantic theory, this living on takes the form of prose. The objectivity of the poem as a medium of reflection is prosaic. This is the romantic thesis laid out by Benjamin in the final pages of the second of the two main parts of the dissertation—just before the "esoteric afterword" on early romantic aesthetic theory and Goethe that was added as an appendix.[14] With this closing argument Benjamin begins to introduce more explicitly a critical perspective on the romantic concept of the medium of reflection as he drives his discussion onto the same ground on which his commentary on "Timidity" ultimately lands. This becomes evident when he inserts Hölderlin's "proposition on the sobriety of art" into the analysis of the romantic theory of the prosaic character of poetry:

> This fundamental conception [of the idea of poetry as prose] founds a peculiar relation within a wider romantic circle, whose common element, like that of the narrower school, remains undiscoverable so long as it is sought only in poetry and not in philosophy as well. From this point of view, one spirit moves into the wider circle, not to say into its center—a spirit who cannot be comprehended merely in his quality as a poet in the modern sense of the word (however high this must be reckoned), and whose relationship to the romantic school, within the history of ideas, remains unclear if his particular philosophical identity with this school is not considered. This spirit is Hölderlin, and the thesis that establishes his philosophical relation to the romantics is the proposition on the sobriety of art (*der Satz von der Nüchternheit der Kunst*). This proposition is the essentially thoroughly new and still immensely influential fundamental idea of the romantic philosophy of art; what is perhaps the greatest epoch in the Western philosophy of art is defined by this proposition. The way this proposition connects (*zusammenhängt*) with the methodical procedure of the romantic philosophy of art—namely, reflection—is obvious. In ordinary usage, the prosaic—that in which reflection as the principle of art expresses itself to the highest degree—is indeed a metaphorical designation of the sober. As a thoughtful and calm attitude reflection is the opposite of ecstasy, the mania of Plato. (*GS* 1.1: 103; *SW* 1: 175)

As Benjamin goes on to cite the key words from Hölderlin's "Half of Life"—the "sacredly sobering"—the framework of the poet's 1801 letter to Böhlendorff that we considered at the end of the preceding chapter could not be clearer. The romantic concept of criticism is, it seems, ultimately to be understood from the same critical perspective that illuminates the transformations of what becomes "Timidity." This means that the paradoxical proposition on sobriety introduced by Benjamin at the end of his commentary on Hölderlin's poem also applies to the romantic theory of the work of art. The objectivity of the work is thus to be apprehended in its connection with what Hölderlin calls "the free use of the own," which for the moderns involves the free use of sobriety and what the romantics metaphorically designate as the prosaic.[15] The insertion of Hölderlin's proposition on sobriety into the examination of the romantic concept of the prosaic character of the work of art serves to clarify the chief contribution of the romantics to the philosophy of art. At the end of a long citation from Hölderlin's commentaries on Sophocles, Benjamin adds a footnote that maps out the philosophical terrain on which his analysis of the romantic concept of criticism has arrived:

> Although in these words [on the sobriety of poetry] Hölderlin hits definitively upon tendencies in Schlegel and Novalis, what is otherwise asserted with regard to them in this study does not hold for him. What was certainly, on the one hand, a powerful tendency in the founding of the romantic philosophy of art, but, on the other hand, one that is little developed or clarified—and therefore, where explicitly postulated was only the most advanced outpost of their thinking—this was Hölderlin's realm (*Bereich*). Hölderlin oversaw and mastered this realm (*Diesen Bereich übersah und beherrschte Hölderlin*), whereas for Friedrich Schlegel and indeed also for Novalis, who saw into it more clearly, it remained a promised land. Apart from this central idea of the sobriety of art, the two philosophies of art are, therefore, scarcely to be compared directly (*unmittelbar*) to one another, just as their promulgators had no relation personally to one another. (*GS* 1.1: 105n280; *SW* 1: 198n287)

Hölderlin's proposition on sobriety, it turns out, allows us to clarify the "epistemological presuppositions" of the romantic philosophy of art that, as Benjamin asserts at the beginning of his study, had not been laid down explicitly by Schlegel when they became operative in his writings of the later 1790s (*GS* 1.1: 15; *SW* 1: 119). By injecting Hölderlin's later writings into the dissertation, Benjamin is able to "release and present separately" the epistemological presuppositions that are so tightly bound together in the "extralogical, aesthetic determinations" of the fragments and essays that appeared in the *Athenaeum* at this time (*GS* 1.1: 15; *SW* 1: 119). Hölderlin's writings of the later period allow for the excavation of the philosophy of art that Schlegel failed to produce and that Benjamin is able to elucidate through the "explication and isolation" carried out in the dissertation.[16] In keeping with the proposition on sobriety, the "realm" in which Benjamin locates the epistemological presuppositions of Schlegel's theory of art excludes appropriation and ownership: it is the inappropriable domain of "the own" in the letter to Böhlendorff. Romantic aesthetic theory is thus revealed as touching on and overlapping with the nexus of myth and transcendental force that we encountered in Benjamin's commentary on Hölderlin.[17] The introduction of this "realm" into the discussion of the romantic concept of the work of art opens up the field of force in which, in the context of the dissertation, "the pure problem of art criticism comes immediately to light" (*GS* 1.1: 110; *SW* 1: 178). In this space, Benjamin goes on to argue in the "esoteric" appendix, Schlegel and Goethe represent opposing critical poles, with the criticizability of the form of the work (its idea) on the one hand, and the uncriticizability of its content (its ideal) on the other.

Uwe Steiner has emphasized the extent to which the completion of Benjamin's study of romanticism was shaped by his reading of Goethe, in particular the "maxims and reflections" collected in what the former described as the "unsurpassable rigorously philological Weimar edition."[18] Yet the underlying influence of Hölderlin in Benjamin's critical program and in particular the relational theory of force developed out of the reading of "Timidity" remains evident in the allusions to sobriety that punctuate (1) the discussion of the prosaic at the end of the second part of the dissertation and (2) the dramatic closing sentences of the appendix on the romantics and

Goethe (*GS* 1.1: 109 and 119; *SW* 1: 178 and 185). The proposition on sobriety continues to sound the key note. The turn from the romantics to Goethe at the end of the dissertation is in this sense more fundamentally the return of Hölderlin.[19] Indeed, the light shed on the romantic concept of prose by the thesis on sobriety also illuminates the traces of an initiative undertaken by Schlegel precisely between the 1795 essay "On the Study of Greek Poetry" and the *Lyceum-* and *Athenaeum-fragments* of the later 1790s—namely, the philological fragments composed in 1797 after the move from Jena to Berlin. Benjamin sees the development in Schlegel's thinking during this period—his "coming to himself"—as starting from a position on the irreconcilability of the work to the unconditional and an insistence on the irreducibly historical relation to antiquity that is close to Goethe's position in "On the Study of Greek Poetry" in 1795. This leads to the development of the romantic concept of the medium of reflection according to which the work can be reconciled with the unconditional through the intervention of criticism in the *Lyceum-* and the *Athenaeum-fragments* that began to appear in 1797 and 1798 (*GS* 1.1: 114; *SW* 1: 181). The philological fragments composed in 1797 fall precisely in the middle of this development and hover between the position of Goethe and the early Schlegel of the Jena period, on the one hand, and that of Schlegel during the period of his collaboration on the *Athenaeum* in Berlin, on the other. From the perspective of these reflections on philology, the opposition between Wolf and Winckelmann on the study of antiquity—what Schlegel calls the two "pillars" (*Stützen*) of his "philosophy of philology"—corresponds to the polar relation of Schlegel to Goethe proposed by Benjamin at the end of the dissertation.[20]

Schlegel's philological fragments, however, were not available to Benjamin. They appeared for the first time in 1928, nine years after he submitted his dissertation.[21] But the role of a sobering or prosaic element in the "continuance" or the life of the work of art is the central question animating Schlegel's interest in the philological discoveries published by Wolf in his *Prolegomena to Homer* in 1795.[22]

Although Schlegel initially rejected the main thesis of the *Prolegomena*,[23] after intensive study he came to accept the claim that "we no longer have the Homeric songs in their original form but rather completely transformed by rhapsodes, interpolators, and grammarians."[24] The progression during the Jena years is from "On the Study of Greek Poetry" in 1795, which responds mainly still to the historical problem of antiquity as posed by Winckelmann, to "On Homeric Poetry" in 1796, which begins by announcing the critical program for a comprehensively new historical approach to Greek verse based on Wolfian principles.[25] The latter resulted in the appearance of *History of the Poetry of the Greeks and the Romans* in 1798. The impact of Wolf on Schlegel, which is openly declared in the first footnote to "On Homeric Poetry," informs statements such as the following from *History of the Poetry of the Greeks and the Romans*: "It can no longer be a question of what is Homeric in these old songs and what is not. Under the pressure of this doubt Homer disappears from our research (*Nachforschung*) like the father's shadow from the embrace of Aeneas."[26] Before completing this Wolfian study, and immediately upon his arrival in Berlin during the summer of 1797, Schlegel composed the two notebooks containing fragments on "the concept of philology" that, instead of appearing in Niethammer and Fichte's *Philosophische Journal* or in the *Athenaeum* (as he proposed in letters from this period), were left unpublished until 1928.[27] The traces of these philological fragments are clearly evident in some of the *Lyceum-* and *Athenaeum-fragments*.[28] But what remained somewhat obscure before the publication of the notebooks on philology, and indeed what has been underappreciated generally since they were published, is the significance within Schlegel's intellectual development of the decisive question posed by Wolf's study: If the *Prolegomena* demonstrates the capacity of the Homeric text to accumulate foreign material at the hands of the rhapsodes and interpolators such that these imperfections cannot be eliminated definitively from the work, in what sense may modern scholars and poets reasonably speak of a critical, genuinely historical encounter with the ancient Greek poem and with antiquity as such?[29] This is the question to which Schlegel began to develop a response in the wake of his reading of Wolf. For Schlegel the irreducibly interpolated character of the Homeric text becomes paradigmatic for the interpenetration of work and criticism in romantic aesthetic theory. Like the philological activity of editing and interpolating that have produced and that continue to produce the *Iliad* and the *Odyssey*—from Aristarchus to Wolf—criticism for Schlegel is the historical enactment of the literary work. However, there is a key difference between the philology of the notebooks and literary criticism of the *Athenaeum*: the Homer and the Homeric poem of Wolf's study exclude not only the subjective grounding of an individual poet (an "I" that can be posited to limit and anchor the work) but also the objective grounding of a self-consistent poetic text (a uniform and continuous medium that is in itself substantial and full). Schlegel's philology can thus be reconciled neither with Fichte nor with the romantic theory of criticism elaborated in the *Athenaeum-fragments*. The historical experience of what Schlegel would later call the "classic"—the ancient and the modern work of art—is fundamentally different from that of philology. It is no longer an encounter with what is already substantially there from the beginning. The historical experience of the philological encounter with the text involves the dynamic action exemplified by Benjamin's presentation and citation of romantic theory. When Schlegel asserts that "the purpose of philology is history" (*Der Zweck der Philologie ist die Historie*), he is alluding to a historical experience that he sets aside in order to pursue the theory of criticism explicated and isolated by Benjamin in his dissertation.[30] Accordingly, the historical character of the concept of the literary work in the romantic philosophy of art is not the extension but rather the overcoming of the philological object. Benjamin's definition of philology as history in his 1921 letter to Scholem in this sense resonates with Schlegel's notes toward a "philosophy of philology."[31] Although Benjamin could not have read the philological fragments, his designation of philology as history is consistent with the point of view derived by Schlegel from Wolf. Benjamin's ambiguous definition of philology as *Geschichte* associates historical experience with the irreducibly layered texture of the Homeric poem according to Wolf.[32]

From the perspective of Schlegel's pursuit of an objective aesthetic theory, Wolf's *Prolegomena* suggested a way to navigate between the Scylla of neoclassicism and the Charybdis of *Sturm und Drang* while at the same time tracing a critical path that, as Schlegel strikingly declared, corresponded to the one laid out in philosophy by Kant.[33] Although the main evidence of Wolf's impact on Schlegel was not available to Benjamin, his exposition of the key components of the romantic concept of criticism, on the basis of the texts contained in J. Minor's 1906 edition of Schlegel's early prose writings, makes connections that illuminate the significance of philology within the romantic program.[34] It suggests the possibility, for example, that the development of the concept of the work as a medium of reflection together with the theory of prose as the medium through which the work is presented or produced in criticism might have served as a resolution to the fundamental philological problem discovered by Wolf in the *Prolegomena*—namely, the difficulty of reconciling the irreducibly interpolated texts that have come down to us as the *Iliad* and the *Odyssey* with the Winckelmannian ideal of Homer's poetry. For Schlegel, as noted, the challenge was how to reconcile Wolf with Winckelmann—the letter of philology with the spirit of classicism. However, Benjamin's insertion of Hölderlin's proposition on the sobriety of art into the analysis of Schlegel's theory of the prosaic accentuates precisely the irreconcilability of this problem by undercutting the concept of the work as a medium of reflection—in the neo-Kantian terms adopted in Benjamin's account, as a "transition" or "continuum" between the conditional and the unconditional (*GS* 1.1: 114; *SW* 1: 181). The sobering effects of the doctrine of free use articulated in the letter to Böhlendorff restrict the work from acquiring the absolute transcendental force attributed to it in what became the romantic theory of criticism, in particular as articulated in the *Athenaeum-fragments*. The introduction of Hölderlin's proposition on the sobriety of art into the analysis of the romantic theory of prose discloses or produces a rift between the concept of criticism and the idea of the work of art as a medium of reflection and, by extension, a conflict in Schlegel's critical project between the impact of Wolf and the interpretation of Fichte. It suggests that the philological project undertaken and left unpublished by Schlegel in 1797, rather than being an intermediate step toward the mature concept of criticism presented in the *Athenaeum-fragments*, could have led further in the direction of the more "powerful tendency in the founding of the romantic philosophy of art" associated, from Benjamin's point of view, with Hölderlin.[35]

By elevating philology to transcendental philosophy and bridging the gap separating modernity from the ideal unity of antiquity, Schlegel prepares the way for criticism to constitute the work of art as a continuum: as a medium of reflection. In order for the prosaic character of the work—its criticizability—to become a medium it must shed the contingency of its limitation and shape: "The overcoming of contingency, of the torso character of works, is the intention in Friedrich Schlegel's concept of form. In relation to the ideal, the torso is a legitimate shape; it has no place in the medium of forms. The work of art cannot be a torso; it must be a mobile transitory moment in the living transcendental form (*in der lebendigen transzendentalen Form*). By limiting itself in its own form, it makes itself transitory in a contingent shape, but in that fleeting shape it makes itself eternal through criticism" (*GS* 1.1: 115; *SW* 1: 182). The life of the work in criticism is understood by Schlegel as the "overcoming" (*Aufhebung*) and transcending of the "contingency" (*Zufälligkeit*) of a rigorous shape—what Benjamin goes on to describe as a "pure (and, as such, rigorous) form" (*reinen [und als solcher strengen] Form*)" (*GS* 1.1: 117; *SW* 1: 183). The contrast is between Schlegel and Goethe. For Schlegel, the works of art form a totality that progressively and continuously fulfills the infinite idea of art. For Goethe, the works of art consist in a multiplicity that repeatedly and in each instance expresses the ideal unity of art. The former, according to Benjamin, is a matter of "pure form," the latter of "pure content": "This infinity is that of pure form; this unity is that of pure content" (GS 1.1: 117; SW 1: 183). As Benjamin points out—with a nod again to neo-Kantianism—form and content in this discussion are to be understood not empirically as independent, self-consistent "substrata" in the work but rather functionally as "relative distinctions in it" (GS 1.1: 117; SW 1: 183). The relation between the romantics and Goethe stands for the functional relation between the idea of art (its pure form) and the ideal of art (its pure content). From the perspective being developed in the dissertation, the romantics and Goethe are seen to take up these positions within a field or sphere that is under the supervision of Hölderlin (and that remains beyond the purview, strictly speaking, not only of the aesthetic theories of the romantics and of Goethe but also of this academic study of romanticism).[36] Benjamin makes this clear in the last substantive annotation to the dissertation elucidating the key term in this philosophical discussion of form and content, namely "pure":

> There is, of course, an equivocation here in the term "pure." In the first place, it designates the methodical dignity of a concept (as in "pure reason"), but it can also have a substantively (*inhaltlich*) positive and, so to speak, morally tinged meaning (*sittlich gefärbte Bedeutung*). Both of these meanings figure above in the concept of "pure content," . . . whereas the absolute form can be designated as "pure" only in the methodical sense. For, its concrete (*sachliche*) determination—which corresponds to the purity of the content—is presumably rigor (*die Strenge*). And this the romantics have not brought out in their theory of the novel, in which the entirely pure, but not rigorous, form (*reine nicht aber strenge Form*) was raised to the absolute. Here, too, is a sphere of thought in which Hölderlin surpassed them. (GS 1.1: 117n315; SW 1: 200n323)

Benjamin's note is somewhat cryptic. It may be suggesting that the difference between pure form and pure content corresponds to the distinction between the exclusively methodical focus of the *Critique of Pure Reason* on the one hand, and the combining of method and substance in the critique of pure practical reason prepared by the *Groundwork for the Metaphysics of Morals* on the other. The note seems to refer to this Kantian framework for an understanding of the "equivocation" in the term "pure" as it applies differently to form and content in this context. But Benjamin leaves no doubt as to the source of the "rigor" that is presumed to be the differentiating factor in this contrast between romantic pure form and Goethean pure content—namely, Hölderlin and, more precisely, the poet's translation of the reconstruction of the first eight lines of a choral song attributed to Pindar. Present in the Goethean concept of pure content but lacking in the romantic concept of pure form is "the rigorous mediacy" (*die strenge Mittelbarkeit*) that is "the law" (*das Gesetz*) in Hölderlin's translation of and gloss on Pindar's Fragment 169, entitled "The Highest" (*Das Höchste*).[37] The word in Pindar's text translated by Hölderlin as *das Gesetz* is the ancient Greek *nomos*. Of course, there has been great and extensive disagreement about the precise signification of this word in Pindar's fragment and the nature of the law to which it refers, beginning in antiquity with Callicles and Herodotus through the modern and just as tendentious interpretations of Carl Schmitt and Giorgio Agamben. Clearly Benjamin had been developing an interpretation of Hölderlin's translations and glosses and the issue they raise in his philosophy.[38] For Benjamin, from the early commentary on Hölderlin to the essay "Toward the Critique of Violence," the *nomos* of Pindar's fragment—*das Gesetz*—is to be understood as what the Italian classical philologist Marcello Gigante in his commentary on this text characterizes as "absolute divine justice."[39] The rigor of the mediacy that is the law in this fragment is attributed in the gloss to an insuperable force of limitation and of the setting of boundaries that invalidates every claim to overcome it. The *nomos* of the fragment derives from the verb *nemo*, which has been interpreted as ultimately signifying the appropriation of land.[40] From this perspective, with the rigor of the "pure content" we are on the ground of the "supreme ownership" of what Hölderlin calls "the own"—of a mediacy that can only be used freely and that cannot be appropriated precisely because it is not foreign but innate. The "pure form" of romantic theory does not recognize "the rigorous mediacy" of this "law" as "the highest."[41] For Schlegel, Benjamin concludes, "the absolutizing of the created work, the critical procedure, was . . . the highest" (*das Höchste*) (*GS* 1.1: 119; *SW* 1: 185).

If the romantic absolutization of pure form fails to capture the rigor of pure content in Goethe's aesthetic theory, Goethe's determination of pure content with the concept of the "primal image" leaves unsolved the romantic problem of pure form. Indeed, when Goethe tries to solve the problem of form with the solution to the problem of content he falls into a mythological thinking reserved for the ancients (we will return to this point in Benjamin's critical commentary on *Elective Affinities* in the next chapter).[42] The irreconcilable tension between these two positions is maintained right up to the final sentence of the dissertation as the "dazzling brilliance" produced by the romantic vision of the work of art as part of a totality (as idea) "extinguishes" Goethe's conception of it as belonging to a multiplicity (in relation to an ideal): the "brilliance" of the romantic absolutizing of the work "extinguishes the multiplicity of works" (*GS* 1.1: 119; *SW* 1: 185). Key to note once again is the clearly marked presence of Hölderlin: the light source of the effect of the romantic critical procedure on Goethe's vision of art is said to be "sobering" (it is *das nüchterne Licht*) (*GS* 1.1: 119; *SW* 1: 185). Thus, Hölderlin's thesis of the sobriety of art runs underneath the discussion of the romantics and Goethe and in particular the analysis of the idea of pure form and the ideal of pure content in the final pages of the dissertation—not as a self-consistent, substantial ground but as a sphere or field of inscription, transcription, and translation. The decisive concept of rigor derives from Hölderlin, or to be precise, from Hölderlin's translation of and gloss on a fragment reconstructed by philologists and attributed to Pindar. Important to emphasize is that the "rigorous mediacy" that is "the law" of this sphere also applies to this "law." By invalidating every claim to appropriate it, the law of "rigorous mediacy" refuses to provide a ground on which to distinguish finally and authoritatively between what is given in it and what is made of it. In this sense, the *law* emerging at the end of Benjamin's discussion of the aesthetic theories of the romantics and of Goethe recalls the *life* at issue in the final paragraph of his commentary on Hölderlin—"the life of a pure work of art" (*das Leben eines reinen Kunstwerks*) (*GS* 2.1: 126; *SW* 1: 35). The "rigorous mediacy" of this work consists in the way it is "infinitely (exactly) connected," as Hölderlin writes in his gloss on Pindar's "The Infinite."[43] By linking these two fragments and glosses, Benjamin's argument in the course of the dissertation suggests that the "law" of the one is affected by the "connection" in the other. More explicitly, the "law" of Pindar's one fragment ("The Highest") is related to the "connection" of Hölderlin's gloss on the other ("The Infinite"). The connection in the gloss concerns the "life" in the fragment and the way in which this life goes beyond itself in writing: in poetry, translation, and commentary. The poem asserts, in other words, its capacity to outlive itself: "so myself / Circumscribing, beyond / Me live" (*so mich selbst / Umschreibend, hinaus / Mich lebe*).[44] It is therefore fitting that this word—*zusammmenhängen*—added by Hölderlin in his gloss on Pindar's fragment bears the Sapphic metrical signature of the Adonic that rigorously undercuts even while making this assertive connection.

3
"GOETHE'S ELECTIVE AFFINITIES"

Benjamin opens his essay "Goethe's Elective Affinities" by reflecting on the discrepancy between its appearance and its meaning. The essay appears to be a commentary, but it is meant to be a critique: "It could appear as a commentary; yet it is meant as a critique" (*Sie könnte als Kommentar erscheinen; gemeint jedoch ist sie als Kritik*) (*GS* 1.1: 125; *SW* 1: 297). According to Benjamin, the appearance of a commentary comes from the way in which the essay approaches its object—namely, through detailed analysis of the subject-matter (*Sachgehalt*) of Goethe's work. The critical meaning, on the other hand, is expressed by its inquiry into the truth-of-the-matter (*Wahrheitsgehalt*)—what the work means.[1] This opening reflection is itself critical in the sense that it focuses on the truth content of the essay: what Benjamin calls the "fundamental law of literature" (*Grundgesetz des Schriftums*). But this law is determined by the *relation* between the meaning of the work (the truth-of-the-matter) and the way it means (the subject-matter), between what it wants to say and what it says: "The relation between the two determines that fundamental law of literature according to which the more significant the work, the more invisibly and the more inwardly (*desto unscheinbarer und inniger*) the truth-of-the-matter is bound up with its subject-matter" (*GS* 1.1: 125; *SW* 1: 297). Thus, the law that is the truth of the essay is a law of relation, specifically, of the relation between the appearance of the work (what it says) and its meaning (what it wants to say).[2] The critic—the meaning notwithstanding—must begin with the former because to the extent that a work endures, Benjamin proposes, the latter "remains hidden" (*GS* 1.1: 125; *SW* 1: 297). For the critic, then, commentary is a "precondition" (*Vorbedingung*) and this is precisely demonstrated by the essay (*GS* 1.1: 125; *SW* 1: 297). Already in the first paragraph the irreducible tension between its appearance and its meaning prevents Benjamin from saying directly what he wants to say about criticism. He is compelled therefore to resort to similes in his critical prologue. Immediately after the appearance of the word "precondition" (*Vorbedingung*) to describe the way the subject-matter of the work presents itself to the critic—following a caesura at the very middle of the paragraph (as it happens in the twenty-second line of its forty-four lines in the version that appeared in the *Neue Deutsche Beiträge* in 1924)—Benjamin permits himself to insert a comparison: "One may compare [the critic] to a paleographer in front of a parchment whose faded text is covered by the outlines of a more robust writing that refers to this text" (*GS* 1.1: 125; *SW* 1: 297–98). This comment raises the question again of the appearance of what presents itself to the critic and what allows "the fundamental critical question" (*die kritische Grundfrage*) to come to light (*GS* 1.1: 125; *SW* 1: 298). At this point we are presented with a dense and enigmatic formulation of the fundamental question facing the critic: "whether the semblance (*Schein*) of the truth-of-the-matter is due to the subject-matter, or the life (*Leben*) of the subject-matter is due to the truth-of-the-matter" (*GS* 1.1: 125; *SW* 1: 298). A key to the enigma of the relation between the truth-of-the-matter and the subject-matter—and to "the fundamental law of literature" determined by this relation—is the ambiguity of the two words *Schein* and *Leben* in this sentence. The English translator,

Stanley Corngold, tries to highlight the ambiguity of the first by proposing to translate *Schein* as "semblance/luster," thus raising the question: does *Schein* describe the subject-matter of the work negatively as the mere appearance (the semblance) or positively as the shining appearance (the luster) of its true meaning? There appears to be no analogous pair of English words available to capture the similar ambiguity in *Leben*, which is translated simply as "life." Yet there is a parallel question: does *Leben* describe the truth-of-the-matter under consideration in the work negatively as the mere life or positively as the enduring life of its subject-matter? The question of the "immortality" (*Unsterblichkeit*) of the work is decided by this ambiguous relation between the subject-matter and its true meaning as they separate themselves from one another and from an initial state of unity in the course of its "history" (*Geschichte*) (*GS* 1.1: 125; *SW* 1: 298).

The ambiguity of *Schein* and *Leben* over which the critic presides like a paleographer over the fate of an ancient text leads Benjamin to his second "simile"—the equation of the critic with the alchemist: "If, for the sake of a simile, one wants to view the growing work as a burning funeral pyre, then the commentator stands before it as a chemist the critic like an alchemist. Whereas, for the former, wood and ash remain the sole objects of his analysis, for the latter one the flame itself preserves an enigma: that of being alive (*das des Lebendigen*). Thus, the critic inquires into the truth whose living flame (*lebendige Flamme*) continues to burn over the weighty pyre of what has been and the light ashes of what has been lived through (*des Erlebten*)" (*GS* 1.1: 126; *SW* 1: 298). If the distinction between commentary and critique in this simile carries forward the parallel difference between philological and aesthetic commentaries from "Two Poems by Friedrich Hölderlin" (*GS* 2.1: 105; *SW* 1: 18), the comparison of the commentator and the critic to the chemist and the alchemist recalls the analogy of the critical "presentation" (*Darstellung*) of the romantics to a chemical process in *The Concept of Criticism in German Romanticism* (*GS* 1.1: 109; *SW* 1: 178). The relation between the chemist and the alchemist, like the one that obtains between the commentator and the critic or between philological and aesthetic commentaries or indeed between the appearance and the meaning of the essay on Goethe, is neither complementarity nor mutual exclusivity.[3] As the composition of the essay shows the relation is more complex. Presenting the truth contained Goethe's "elective affinities" and carrying out the critical task requires going into the details of the subject-matter and appearing as a commentary. Yet the interpenetration of critique and commentary must start with the true philological details of the work rather than with what Benjamin later calls the "first falsehood in almost all modern philology," namely, that of the author's life (GS 1.1: 155; SW 1: 320). This emphasis on the primacy of the objective character of the work in the investigation of the "elective affinities" and on a true philology that is "determined by linguistic and material research" (*durch Wort- und Sacherforschung*) also builds on the study of the romantic concept of criticism (GS 1.1: 155; SW 1: 320). Thus, the conventional writing on literature to which Benjamin alludes in the first sentence of his essay conveys the misleading impression that detailed commentary is necessarily in the interest of false philology, and not of true philology— the philology that is the subject of Benjamin's February 14, 1921, letter to Scholem cited above (and written as "Goethe's Elective Affinities" was being completed). As the essay on Goethe will demonstrate, the enigmatic life of "what is alive" in the work from the perspective of truly critical philology is decidedly different from the biographical details of the author's life as it is portrayed in "almost all modern philology."

". . . there is more in it than anyone is capable of grasping in a single reading" (. . . *es steckt darin mehr, als irgend jemand bei einmaligen Lesen aufzunehmen im Stande wäre*) (6: 644).[4] This is how Goethe is reported to have described his *Elective Affinities* to Eckermann on February 9, 1829, reaffirming a point he made twenty years earlier as the work was going into production.[5] The same could be said of Benjamin's essay on Goethe's novel, in which both of these remarks are cited (*GS* 1.1: 146; *SW* 1: 313).[6] This is due to the extraordinary density of the subject-matter through which the true meaning of the work is released. Because its meaning remains hidden as long as it lasts, the work of art must be approached by way of its appearance—its "concrete realities" (*Realien*) (*GS* 1.1: 126; *SW* 1: 298). This is true first of all, Benjamin asserts at the beginning of the second paragraph of his essay, for the author of the work and for the contemporary public for whom its meaning (its truth) is "most deeply sunken" into its appearance (its subject-matter). But this is the case as well for all later critics confronted by the most enduring, which is to say the greatest, works. For Goethe and his contemporaries, the subjects available for art had become particularly "impoverished," according to Benjamin. Nothing in this sphere in the "age of criticism," as Kant called it, is self-evidently meaningful—there was "never a time more foreign than Goethe's to the thought that the most essential contents of existence [*die wesentlichsten Inhalte des Daseins*] are stamped on the world of things " (*GS* 1.1: 126; *SW* 1: 298). For Goethe as for Hölderlin, Benjamin suggests, the contrast is to the situation of Pindar.[7] Thus, Goethe's project becomes the renewal of the "subject-matter" for art, more precisely, of artistic matter as the common denominator and connection between subject-matter and truth available for works of art as "preserved in life and language" (*GS* 1.1: 126; *SW* 1: 298). If Schlegel discovered in antiquity the idea of the *form* of the modern work of art—its criticizability as a medium of reflection—Goethe's classicism was predicated on finding in the works of the ancients the *content* that could serve the artist in the wake of enlightenment and after Kant. This is the argument that Benjamin begins to make at the end of his dissertation and that he pursues further in his essay on Goethe. In the context of this renewal project, marriage in *Elective Affinities*—Benjamin's (and Goethe's) starting point—becomes a matter not of a causal-mechanical nature as regulated by law in the sense of rights as in Kant's *Metaphysics of Morals*, much less of a sentimental love as in Mozart's *Magic Flute*, and least of all of a "mishmash" of commonplaces offered by Mittler in the novel. Rather, marriage is to be apprehended transcendentally as a "synthetic intuition."

Yet, although marriage in *Elective Affinities* testifies to Goethe's new way of apprehending the realities of modern life, ultimately it is not the true subject-matter of the novel. "The object of *Elective Affinities*," Benjamin argues, "is not marriage" (*GS* 1.1: 131; *SW* 1: 302). This is the highly compressed proposition that is formulated in the next two paragraphs of the commentary, which provide a fine example of the genuinely philological "linguistic and material research" (*Wort- und Sacherforschung*) to which Benjamin alludes at the beginning of the second part of the essay (*GS* 1.1: 155; *SW* 1: 320). Following this argument requires paying close attention therefore to his manipulation of the linguistic matter, beginning with the word "subject-matter" (*Sachgehalt*):

> How clearly the most sublime spirits of the enlightenment had a sense of the matter (*Gehalt*) or an insight into the subject (*Sache*), yet how incapable even they were of raising themselves to the intuition of the subject-matter (*Sachgehalt*), becomes compellingly evident with regard to marriage. It is marriage, as one of the most rigorous and objective articulations of the content of human life, that in Goethe's *Elective Affinities* attests, also for the first time, to the author's new perspective that is inflected by the synthetic intuition of the subject-matter ("*bekundet*" *zugleich am frühesten, in den Goetheschen Wahlverwandtschaften, sich des Dichters neue, auf synthetische Anschauung der Sachgehalte hingewendete Betrachtung*). (*GS* 1.1: 127; *SW* 1: 299)

As the English translator underlines by including the key German words in parentheses, a true understanding of the subject-matter (*Sachgehalt*) of marriage from this new perspective involves the genuine apprehension of the subject (*Sache*) and the matter (*Gehalt*). Both must be understood in a way that differs from what had become conventional in the enlightenment, including within a certain dimension of Kant's critical philosophy. Put simply, the *subject* must be seen as something more than mere appearance and the *matter* as something more than indivisible substance. Also, Benjamin explains, apprehended in this way the content (*Gehalt*) will never be derivable from the subject (*Sache*): never be derivable as an independent matter related to a subject (*niemals ableitbar ihr Gehalt sich zur Sache verhält*) (*GS* 1.1: 128; *SW* 1: 299). The *Sachgehalt* is to be differentiated, in other words, from a *Sachverhalt* (state of affairs) in Husserl's sense, even if the reworking of *Sache* underway in this passage has parallels to the phenomenological exposition of *Sachverhalt*: "Kant's definition of marriage in *The Metaphysics of Morals* . . . is the most sublime product of a *ratio* that, incorruptibly true to itself, penetrates infinitely deeper into the state of affairs (*Sachverhalt*) than sentimental ratiocination. Of course the subject-matter itself (*der Sachgehalt selbst*), which yields only to philosophical intuition (*Anschauung*)— or, more precisely, philosophical experience (*Erfahrung*)—remains inaccessible to both" (*GS* 1.1: 127; *SW* 1: 299).[8] With regard to marriage in the novel, Benjamin goes on to propose, "the matter of the subject" (*der Gehalt der Sache*), "must be grasped as the seal (*Siegel*) that presents it [the subject]" (*das sie [die Sache*—KM] *darstellt*) (*GS* 1.1: 128; *SW* 1: 299). *Siegel* in German, like its English cognate "seal," can signify both the impression made in a receptive material like wax to authenticate a document as well as the instrument that makes the impression.[9] Yet the seal to which Benjamin compares the true subject-matter of marriage can be derived neither from the object bearing the seal's impression (wax, for example) nor from the one making it (*Petschaft* in German, translated into English as "signet"). The true experience of the seal has nothing to do with a substance or a subject affected by an impression or an object. It is specifically not subject to the "epistemological mythology" that Benjamin attributes to Kantian philosophy in his programmatic statement from 1918 on "the coming philosophy" (*GS* 2.1: 161; *SW* 1: 103). Thus, as Peter Fenves has perceptively noted, Benjamin's image of the seal as an illustration of the higher, philosophical experience of marriage reworks Kant's image of the "monogram" of pure imagination in the first *Critique*.[10] In a gloss on this image, Rudolf Makkreel observes: "In its most common usage a monogram is a configuration of letters or initials that stands for a name. Similarly, the figurative synthesis of imagination can be explicated in linguistic as well as in mathematical terms."[11] Benjamin's manipulation of the *Sachgehalt* handles the word itself as a monogram or a seal. The philosophical experience of marriage presented by the subject-matter is comparable, he suggests, to an encounter with language, more precisely, with writing or letters—specifically, "divine" letters. This experience is like being affected by a word in which the subject (*Sache*) and the matter (*Gehalt*) are inseparable (or infinitely separable) from one another—beyond all relation of subject and object. This inseparability is conveyed by the German word *Sachgehalt* in a way that can be presented by neither of its component parts alone (and that cannot be presented adequately in English by a single word). Benjamin's discussion drives the two elements together and overlays one with the other such that the reading of the single word may be understood to correspond to the philosophical experience not of the *Sache* or the *Gehalt* but of the *Sachgehalt*.[12] From this new perspective, the true subject-matter of marriage, Benjamin asserts, is "continuance in love" (*Bestehen der Liebe*)—specifically, eternal continuance as indicated once again by the word *Ehe* (marriage), which is etymologically related to *ewig* (eternal), as in the title of Kant's "Toward Eternal Peace" (*Zum Ewigen Frieden*) (*GS* 1.1: 130; *SW* 1: 301). Benjamin appears to draw on this connection, and also to play on the phonetic overlap of *Ehe* (marriage) and *eher* (sooner), when he observes that "in truth marriage (*die Ehe*) is justified never in law (that is as an institution) but solely as an expression of continuance in love, which by nature seeks this expression sooner in death than in life" (*von Natur im Tode eher suchte als im Leben*) (*GS* 1.1: 130; *SW* 1: 301). In this sense, the content of marriage "is graspable only in the philosophical experience of its divine imprint, evident only in the blessed intuition of the divine name" (*erfaßbar allein in der philosophischen Erfahrung ihrer göttlichen Prägung, evident allein der seligen Anschauung des göttlichen Namens*) (*GS* 1.1: 128; *SW* 1: 300). Only from this new transcendentally "divine" perspective does it become possible to distinguish the true eternal fidelity (*Treue*) from its merely "natural moment" (*Sexualität*), true decision (*Entscheidung*) from mere choice (*Wahl*), and a series of higher and lower orders of experience and of life at work in Benjamin's reading of Goethe's novel. Continuance in love, it turns out, is expressed most purely not by the juridical institution of marriage but by the experience (the "synthetic intuition") of the work of art or of what might be called the aesthetic phenomenon as that which remains truly alive. The image of the seal and specifically of the experience of sealing that is said to imprint marriage with "the divine name" runs throughout what Benjamin later described as the "dialectically rigorous" tripartite structure of his essay as it moves from "the mythic as thesis" in part 1 to "redemption as anti-thesis" and "hope as synthesis" in parts 2 and 3.[13] This image of the "divine imprint" appears explicitly again at a key point in the allusion to the biblical "book of life" in the final third part of the essay, as we will see (*GS* 1.1: 189; *SW* 1: 346).

Yet marriage is ultimately not the subject-matter of Goethe's novel, Benjamin insists. Rather, its "imprint" (*Ausprägung*) as a "juridical norm"—the mark of the lower order of the legal letter—was needed to reveal myth as the origin of marriage as a legal institution and thus as the true subject-matter of the work. The approach taken to the mythic origins of marriage is informed by the theory of juridical versus revolutionary or divine force in "Toward the Critique of Violence." From this perspective, the dissolution of marriage as a juridical matter in the *Elective Affinities* lays bare and is imposed by the decline of myth: "the mythic is the subject-matter of this book: its content (*Inhalt*) appears as a mythic shadowplay in the costumes of the age of Goethe" (*GS* 1.1: 140–41; *SW* 1: 309). The novel, in other words, narrates the "disappearance" of myth masquerading as marriage (*GS* 1.1: 131; *SW* 1: 302). To return to Benjamin's initial terms: if myth appears as the novel's subject-matter, the decline of myth is its true meaning. This thesis of the decline or decay (*Verfall*) of myth in *Elective Affinities* in the first part of the essay outlines the space within which Benjamin's justly famous and influential essays on modern aesthetics of the 1930s unfold: the decline of myth corresponds to that of the craft of storytelling (and the rise of the novel), of the aura of the work of art (and the advent of the technical reproducibility of the artwork), and of experience as *Erfahrung* (and its substitution by *Erlebnis*). As I have been suggesting and as we will see again in a key passage from part 2 of the Goethe essay, this thesis derives from Hölderlin's proposition on sobriety and on the inappropriable character of what is paradoxically proper to the moderns. In this sense, the subject-matter for Goethe is implicated in the problem of what Hölderlin calls the "free use" of the "own." According to this thesis, the decline of myth as "preserved in life and language" is the *publica materies* of postclassical literature that cannot be made into the *private juris* of the modern writer.[14]

By not referring exclusively to the two-volume publication that first appeared in Tübingen in 1809, the title "Goethe's Elective Affinities" announces the precise scope of Benjamin's essay. It is not limited to the novel. Indeed, in the first edition of the essay in two installments in 1924–25 (the only version published in Benjamin's lifetime), the word translated by the phrase "elective affinities" (*Wahlverwandtschaften*) is not marked as the title of a literary work. Rather, throughout the essay "elective affinities" is treated consistently as a plural noun.[15] Moreover, in a way that seems to differ from his dissertation on romanticism—at least at first glance—Benjamin's study of Goethe has a wide range of sources. This includes, in addition to a number of other literary, aesthetic, and natural-philosophical works by Goethe and a generous sample of his letters and conversations, also a significant list of contemporary reviews and letters as well as more recent critical studies (see the appendix). Benjamin's essay thus presents itself as an investigation of a problem that extends beyond the scope not only of Goethe's novel but also of his own writings: it is not just Goethe's problem but also a *Goethe problem* that is at issue in the essay.[16] Yet in order to get at this problem,

Benjamin repeatedly insists, we must approach it strictly by way of the novel as a literary work. With this he returns to the stress in his dissertation on the primacy accorded by the romantics in their theory of literary criticism to the objective character of the literary work as an "immanent structure" (*immanente Aufbau*) (*GS* 1.1: 71; *SW* 1: 155). The abundant set of materials on which the Goethe essay draws is consistently understood on the basis of a critical reflection on the work—even when the material in question is nowhere to be found in the novel itself. An example of this is the role of biography—the explicit subject of the first section of the second part of the essay devoted to "criticism and biography," according to Benjamin's outline of the composition (*GS* 1.3: 836). Although "the biographical ... does not enter at all into commentary and criticism," yet it must be understood to have its "place" in the essay on the basis of the "hidden spheres" that it shares with the work (*GS* 1.1: 141; *SW* 1: 309). Or, as Benjamin notes a few pages later, although it is "wasted effort to try to gain an understanding of elective affinities from the author's own words on the subject," the reverse is not the case: the problem of "elective affinities"—as treated in the context of the novel—does yield an understanding of the author's own words on the subject (*GS* 1.1: 145; *SW* 1: 313). In this case, for example, we see that these statements were designed not to correct foolish misinterpretations but to prevent all critical interpretation and to keep hidden the true meaning of the problem of "elective affinities" as it is addressed in the novel. This principle and Benjamin's method of exposing it are illustrated by his critique of "the fable of renunciation" invented by Goethe both to provide a moralizing defense of his work and to cover up its deeper meaning. After citing a conversation with Friedrich Wilhelm Riemer in which Goethe is reported to have laid out the core of the novel as consisting in the conflict between sensuality and morality, Benjamin abruptly and forcefully rejects this account on the basis of what he calls the "moral content (*moralische Gehalt*) of this work that lies at much deeper layers (*viel tiefern Schichten*) than Goethe's words lead one to suspect" (*GS* 1.1: 144; *SW* 1: 312). The truth of this moral content of the work not only invalidates Goethe's own words as reported by Riemer, it also validates words tenuously attributed to Goethe by Bettine von Arnim in which the claim of moral "renunciation" (*Versagung*) gives way to the acknowledgement of sheer "neglect" (*Versäumnis*).[17] In both cases, but to opposite effect, the content of the work as an "immanent structure" is the sole criterion for the verification of the words about the novel, regardless of the relative authoritativeness of the documentary sources according to conventional standards of editorial evidence.

What is the meaning of "elective affinities" from the perspective of the novel's content? In chapter 4 of part 1, Charlotte explicitly poses this critical question: "What is essentially meant here by affinities?" (*Wie es eigentlich hier mit den Verwandtschaften gemeint sei?*).[18] The immediate response to her question comes from the Captain, who cites a scientific theory that he remembers reading about some ten years ago and that, for all he knows, may have already fallen out of fashion—an observation that prompts Eduard to bemoan the ephemerality of modern learning in general as compared with that of "our ancestors."[19] Indeed, the very conversation about these "affinities" in the novel belongs to a social and literary fad of late eighteenth-century salon culture that was still current in Goethe's day.[20] None of the characters involved in this conversation seems to be able to say definitively what these "affinities" mean. Charlotte refers them to relations among humans. This "error" (*Fehler*), as she calls it, nevertheless takes the term back to its original meaning as this was understood at the time and as it is presented in volume 13 of Grimm's dictionary, which appeared as Benjamin was completing his essay on Goethe.[21] The "correct" meaning in the context of the conversation, in other words, is metaphorical—the "affinities" are an anthropomorphic projection of relations among humans onto the natural world, Eduard suggests. Yet of course within the narrative the attractive relations among natural elements assume the character of a primary meaning that may be transferable to human relations. The logic of the novel thus reverses the relation between the primary and the secondary meanings of the "affinities," making the supposedly original signification of the term a question of metaphor. More precisely, the novel raises the question of the primary meaning of the "affinities" and refrains from providing a definitive response to it. This is also the case in the conversation in which they are introduced into the novel as a question. Instead of saying what the "affinities" mean, the novel offers what one commentator has described as "a multiplication of hypotheses . . . not so much in order to explain a phenomenon as above all to represent it in its complexity."[22]

The question of "elective affinities" is also approached in Benjamin's essay as one of meaning. As is hinted by the first sentences of his essay, this is a question, specifically, of how they appear and what they mean in the novel. For Benjamin this is fundamentally, in other words, a matter of language. To say that "the characters are under the spell (*unter dem Banne*) of elective affinities," he observes, is to utter "a judgment, not on their actions, but on their language" (*GS* 1.1: 134; *SW* 1: 304). Under the sign of "elective affinities," Benjamin claims, Goethe "conjures" (*beschwört*) a world dominated by myth (*GS* 1.1: 140; *SW* 1: 309). In this mythic world, the novel's characters are locked into a "single structure of guilt and expiation" (*einem einzigen Zusammenhang von Schuld und Sühne*)—a structure analyzed by Benjamin in the context of the mythic origins of civil law (*Recht*) in "Toward the Critique of Violence" (that was composed alongside the essay on Goethe) (*GS* 1.1: 138; *SW* 1: 307). Within this structure, Ottilie's fate is to be understood as a mythic sacrifice of an innocent that expiates the sins of the guilty. Yet, Benjamin's argument continues, this mythic world with its structure of guilt and expiation is conjured and presented as such in the novel. There is a countermovement discernible in the work according to which this entire structure becomes subject to a greater force that lifts the spell of its mythic world. This countercurrent involves a transformation in the meaning or the "truth-of-the-matter" of "elective affinities" in the novel. Benjamin's argument in these pages (*GS* 1.1: 138–40; *SW* 1: 307–9) requires the discovery in the novel of the traces of a countermovement—what he considers a revolutionary or divine force in his essay on violence—in the very language of the mythic structure that is in decline. It may appear "sophistical," as Benjamin acknowledges in his argument about the shift in the structure of the romantic "medium of reflection" from positing to de-positing (from *Setzen* to *Zersetzung*) in his dissertation, but entering into the logic of this countervailing force affecting the "elective affinities" in Goethe's novel makes "subtle distinctions" unavoidable (*GS* 1.1: 30; *SW* 1: 129). Thus, for example, in the detailed explication of the logic of divine or revolutionary force in "Toward the Critique of Violence," Benjamin insists on shifting the meaning of the crucial prefix in the German term for "expiation," namely, *Entsühnung*. As it is conventionally employed, the prefix *Ent-* in *Entsühnung* has the semantic function of completing the meaning of the root word *Sühne*, which already signifies "expiation." Grimm's dictionary lists the verb *entsühnen* as a synonym for *sühnen*. In "Toward the Critique of Violence," however, *Sühne* and *Entsühnung* operate as antonyms, and the prefix *Ent-* negates, rather than completes, the meaning of the root word (see *GS* 2.1: 199–200; *SW* 1: 249–50). This negation, in what Peter Fenves and Julia Ng in a new English edition of the essay on violence translate as "de-expiation," is at work in Benjamin's interpretation of the meaning of Ottilie's fate in Goethe's novel.[23] It is this countervailing movement—analogous to the one that marks the transition from Hölderlin's "The Poet's Courage" to his "Timidity"—that must be seen as informing the "rigorous dialectic" outlined by Benjamin in the framework of topical page headings he prepared for the integrated book edition of his essay that never appeared in his lifetime.[24] In the language of "The Critique of Violence" the movement from "The Mythic as Thesis" in the first part of the essay to "Redemption as Antithesis" to "Hope as Synthesis" in the second and the third parts must be understood according to a logic of de-expiation that deactivates the mythic economy of guilt and atonement.

If the characters in the novel are unable to say precisely what "elective affinities" means in social and natural terms, they are also unable to understand what these words signify in the higher transcendental sphere that leads from myth to redemption and hope. Echoing the interpretation of Hermann Cohen to which Benjamin refers, the characters are said to be "deaf to God and mute before the world" (*GS* 1.1: 134; *SW* 1: 304). In a chapter from his *Aesthetic of Pure Feeling* that is indispensable for an understanding of Benjamin's essay, Cohen formulates this as a conflict in the novel between *Leben* and *Erlebnis* (life and lived experience) or between "the eternal right of love and the earthly right of marriage."[25] The linguistic conditions of the mythic order conjured by Goethe in the novel are thus marked by what Benjamin calls a "poverty of naming" (*die Kargheit der Namengebung*) that "belongs ... most intimately to the essence of an order whose members live out their lives under a nameless law, a fatality that fills their world with the pallid light of a solar eclipse" (*gehört vielmehr innigst zum Wesen einer Ordnung, deren Glieder unter einem namelosen Gesetze dahinleben, einem Verhängnis, das ihre Welt mit dem matten Lichte der Sonnenfinsternis erfüllt*) (*GS* 1.1: 135; *SW* 1: 305). The extreme scarcity of names in the narrative is cited as evidence of this law. Indeed, one of these names, Benjamin notes, is not even genuine—namely, "Eduard." This name is "inauthentic" (*unecht*): "it is arbitrary, chosen (*gewählt*) for its sound" (*GS* 1.1: 135; *SW* 1: 305).[26] This is the explanation explicitly provided in the novel. Yet at this time and in this novel, with its elaborate allusions to *La Nouvelle Héloïse*, the name the baron chooses for himself of course contains an unmistakable ring of Rousseau's Edouard Bomston. Goethe and his contemporaries would have been very aware of this resonance in the fashionable name.[27] But in keeping with the logic outlined by Benjamin at the beginning of his essay there is also something buried in this "inauthentic" name that may have been hidden from the contemporary public if not entirely from the author himself—an element that does not explicitly surface in Benjamin's essay on Goethe but that is implied in the appendix to his dissertation on romanticism. It subsists in the novel as a connection to romantic theory that has come to light in more recent criticism and that has emerged out of Benjamin's comment on the "poverty of naming" in the novel.[28] It is taken up in an important essay by Norbert Oellers published in 1982. Oellers points out that "Eduard" may be understood to translate the baron's given name, "Otto," based on the common root *ot* signifying "property, happiness."[29] Building on Oeller's thesis, Gabrielle Bersier has made the case for an interpretation of "Eduard" as a parodic allusion to Friedrich Schlegel, whose *On the Language and Wisdom of the Indians*, a philological study of what the romantic repeatedly designates as the "affinities" (*Verwandtschaften*) among the roots common to the Greek, Latin, German, and Persian languages.[30] We know that as Goethe began to compose his novel he read Schlegel's study which appeared in 1808, one year before *Elective Affinities* was published.[31] From this perspective, "Eduard" and the impoverished onomastic network in the novel—according to which all four of the principal characters (and also the child that results from their fantastic union) bear the name "Otto"—may be seen to invoke a theory of language based upon the spiritual meaning of root words and syllables such that, as Schlegel writes, "every root truly is what the name says and is like a living germ" (*jede Wurzel wahrhaft das, was der Name sagt, und wie ein lebendiger Keim*).[32] In this sense, according to Belsier, Goethe's novel may be read as "transforming the organic-spiritual principle of root affinity into the polar-chemical principle of elective affinity" and subjecting it to a reflexive and enigmatic romantic parody.[33]

Yet as a translation of the given name "Otto"—supposedly based on the etymological root *ot*—the adopted name "Eduard" is in fact implicated in the activity described in the novel's opening sentence—namely, grafting. Here is the first sentence: "Eduard—this is the name we will give to a rich baron in the prime of life—Eduard had been spending the best hour of an April afternoon in his nursery grafting newly obtained shoots onto young roots" (*frisch erhaltene Pfropfreiser auf junge Stämme zu bringen*) (HA 6: 242; EA 19). If "Eduard" is to be understood from an etymological perspective as an Anglo-Saxon name grafted onto an older Germanic root, the husbandry of the baron reverses this order: he grafts onto "young roots" (*junge Stämme*). By reversing the relation between the old and the new, Eduard's grafting thus violates not just conventional horticultural practice but also the philological root principle of Schlegel's 1808 treatise on Indo-European—the very principle that also informs the romantic's earlier programmatic essay from 1795, "On the Study of Greek Poetry," in which the cultivation of modern letters through the study of ancient verse is compared to "the grafting of a new branch onto the damaged roots" (*ein frischer Zweig auf den schadhaften Stamm gepfropft*).[34] In this sense, the name "Eduard" does not simply convey the spiritual meaning of "Otto" in a straightforward way. Instead, according to the paradoxical logic of the baron's grafting, the palindrome "Otto," the original name onto which "Eduard" would be grafted, literally reverses the root *ot* that is shared by all of the principal characters in the novel and that is borne ephemerally by the child "Otto." Thus, rather than providing a simple starting point (for example, of the baron's authentic given name) for a genetic pattern leading to a simple end point (for example, of the name given to the doomed child), "Otto" is an ambiguous turning point around which the plot of the novel develops. Indeed, instead of supplying a spiritual substance or meaning that can be translated into the names of the characters, the name "Otto"—which begins and ends with a graphic zero—fails to say anything at all except that fundamentally it means nothing.[35] "Otto" in this sense is less a name that says what its root truly means than a rootless unname that stammers nonsensically across the names of the characters in the novel. It expresses the impoverished language of the principal characters in the novel. "Otto" marks the decline of the mythic name that places them under the spell of what Benjamin describes as a "nameless law" (*einem namenlosen Gesetze*) (*GS* 1.1: 135; *SW* 1: 305). As "subject-matter" the name "Eduard," the first word uttered by the narrator of the novel, signifies the disappearance from the start of the mythic origins of language—the spiritual "affinities" among its roots.

The grafting of "Eduard" in the opening scene may also contain an allusion to written language and thus may suggest a connection between the meaning of "elective affinities" and writing. The very clearly calculated presentation of the baron engaged in this particular horticultural operation at the beginning of the chapter must be linked within the logic of the novel to the introduction of the "elective affinities" that appear in the "book" from which he reads at the beginning of chapter 4 and that are then framed and discussed in explicitly alphabetical terms at the end of that chapter.[36] Plato of course associates grafting with writing in the famous scene from the *Phaedrus*. From a perspective that overlaps in at least one important respect with the theory of language that informs Benjamin's approach to Goethe's novel and to his philological method in general Jacques Derrida made this figure an explicit focal point in the influential series of essays on writing in philosophy and literature that appeared in the late 1960s and early 1970s.[37] What Derrida describes as the effects of the "grafting operation" (*l'opération de greffer*) of writing in Plato's dialogue are also explicitly thematized in the early chapters of *Elective Affinities*.[38] Writing in this sense is depicted, in conventional terms, as a hazardous medium that serves, at the beginning of the novel for example, not to stabilize the newly established household (as Charlotte proposes in her offer to share in the copying of Eduard's journals) but rather to disrupt this apparently fragile domestic idyll (as a result of the letter of invitation that the baron decides to send to the Captain). But the role of language in this context is presented with greater precision in the key scene in which the "affinities" are introduced into the novel in chapter 4. The conventional association of writing with exposure and publicity is certainly part of this scene: Eduard's reading material is exposed to the gaze of Charlotte, who is able to read it herself "over his shoulder"—an act of insubordination from the perspective of the baron.[39] But at that point the question of the "affinities" has already been posed. Charlotte's rebellious act of reading is triggered by something that she *hears*—more exactly, something that she "*hears read*": "You will certainly excuse my error when I confess what happened to me in this moment. I heard you read of affinities" (*Ich hörte von Verwandtschften lesen*).⁴⁰ The question of the "affinities" is raised by an occurrence that combines speech and writing; it is an act of language that cannot be assigned exclusively to writing in the conventional way. This is the possibility that Derrida considers repeatedly in his interrogation of the thematization of writing in the philosophical and literary tradition—for example, as grafting. Derrida asks in effect: What if grafting raises a question that is not restricted to the institution or technique of writing, even if the verb *to graft* (like the French *greffer*) bears an etymological relation or affinity to the Ancient Greek root meaning *to write* (*grapheion*)? Indeed, might the etymological connection, which the German verb *pfropfen* does not share, be understood as the very attempt to contain a drifting tendency in language that is not limited to writing? And then, what if this writing-character is not reserved for language in the strict sense but is instead extended to communication in the broadest possible sense and thus to "experience"? This is the question posed by Derrida near the end of his essay "Signature Event Context":

> Are these predicates, along with the entire system joined to them, reserved, as is so often believed, for "written communication," in the narrow sense of the word? Are they not also to be found in all language, for example in spoken language, and ultimately in the totality of "experience," to the extent that it is not separated from the field of the mark, that is, the grid of erasure and of difference, of unities of iterability, of unities separable from their internal or external context, and separable from themselves, to the extent that the very iterability which constitutes their identity never permits them to be a unity of self-identity?⁴¹

With this series of questions Derrida's critique of the writing-character of language as the basis of all "experience" overlaps with what I am calling Benjamin's philology of life. This proposition of the language-character of experience is announced most explicitly in Benjamin's programmatic essay on language from 1916 ("On Language as Such and on the Language of Man") and is carried out in the works under consideration in this study and indeed in all of his work. The specific point of overlap between Derrida and Benjamin in this regard is a critique of the phenomenological account of experience, in particular that of Husserl, from the perspective of language.

Seen in the light of recent onomastic scholarship the grafting of "Eduard" provides an illustration of what Benjamin describes as the process according to which the "truth-of-the-matter" under consideration in the work is released through the historical reception of its "subject-matter." However, it also suggests that the "poverty of naming" in Goethe's novel may be understood as a commentary on romanticism and, in particular, on the impoverished content of the romantic theory of the work of art as a medium of reflection. This is where Benjamin's essay on Goethe returns to the question that forms the basis of his critique—and, according to him, of Goethe's implicit rejection—of the romantic concept of literary criticism, namely, the question of the content (*Gehalt*) of the literary work. Approached from the perspective of the novel, Benjamin argues, the true content of "elective affinities" is life, specifically, the life to which the words attributed to Goethe by Bettine von Arnim allude. Whether indeed Goethe said or wrote these words, they nevertheless point to his experience of what is inevitably "missed" or "neglected" (*versäumt*) and what fails to be captured in one's own life in the conventional sense of an *Erlebnis*. From this angle, the second part of Benjamin's essay takes up the question that dominated literary criticism throughout the nineteenth century and that was reformulated in the early twentieth-century German context in the terms of *Lebensphilosophie*—namely, the question of the relation between the life and the work of the author (what Proust summarized and dismissed with the formula *l'homme et l'œuvre*).[42] Benjamin's explicit target in the essay is the literary criticism of the George school and in particular Friedrich Gundolf's study of Goethe that had been published in 1916. According to Benjamin, Gundolf and the followers of George in general turn the author into a "mythic hero" and treat his life as his greatest accomplishment (see especially *GS* 1.1: 156–58; *SW* 1: 321–23). In Gundolf's book, Goethe's misleading "fable of renunciation" may be understood to take the mythic form of a heroic "task" (*GS* 1.1: 157–58; *SW* 1: 322). What Benjamin discovers in Goethe's novel is not the redemption of a "mythic life" of heroic renunciation and self-sacrifice that saves "humanity"; it is, rather, the hope of redeeming a life consisting of missed opportunities (*GS* 1.1: 157; *SW* 1: 322). In keeping with the principle of romantic literary theory critical reflection on the work as an "immanent structure," not commentary on the author as a hero, leads to the life that concerns Benjamin in the essay. Yet it is important to stress that this is not a matter of aesthetic formalism: the life in question is consistently related to a content associated with Goethe in the critical presentation. Thus, from a methodological perspective Benjamin remains respectful of what he calls "the great modesty of authentic biographism"—even if, unlike commentary and criticism, biography does not have the capacity to grasp the true meaning of the "archive containing the documents (by themselves undecodable) of this existence" (*GS* 1.1: 161; *SW* 1: 324). The precise link between the work and the life of Goethe on which Benjamin insists throughout the essay is evident in the care with which he moves onto this well-ploughed critical terrain in the opening sentences of part 2. He begins with the proposition that works such as Goethe's novel do indeed have the capacity to illuminate "the life and the being" of the author. However, he specifies, the conventional critical perspective fails to apprehend this aspect of the work due to its adherence to the false first principle that the author's life is the basis of the work's "content" (*Gehalt*). The truth is that the more the work is explained on the basis of the life according to the common view the less the life is illuminated from the perspective of true criticism. The common view of "almost all modern philology" begins with the false premise of life as "lived experience" and makes the work "more accessible to lazy understanding" (*GS* 1.1: 155; *SW* 1: 320). For true philology, which is "determined by the study of word and material" and which "addresses itself to content and being, the work must by all means stand in the foreground" (GS 1.1: 155; SW 1: 320). True philology proceeds from the work to the life, not the reverse. The more criticism adheres to this approach, the greater the insight it is able to provide into the life that is the true content of the work. False philology goes in the opposition direction: toward a philology of "lived experience" rather than a philology of life, toward an *Erlebnisphilologie* rather than a *Lebensphilologie*.

The life of true philology can be understood, according to Benjamin, by reinterpreting the word *Gelegenheit* in Goethe's famous remark to Eckermann on the role of *Gelegenheitsgedichte* in his work.[43] *Gelegenheit* can be translated as "occasion" and *Gelegenheitsgedichte* as "occasional poems." To the extent that this word as applied to poetry conventionally signals the subordination of the poem to the occasion, the literary work to a particular event, Goethe's statement might appear to signal the priority of life over the work; yet it means precisely the opposite.[44] Poetry for Goethe became the occasion or the opportunity, another possible translation, for life. In this sense, life had to become "poetically full of content (*poetisch gehaltvollen*), full of subject-matter and opportunities (*Gelegenheiten*) for 'the poet'" (GS 1.1: 166; SW 1: 328). If in his youth Goethe had fled into the domain of literature in order to escape the emergencies of life, in old age he became subject to the law of this domain in which life turns into a matter of poetic opportunity. "Age," Benjamin argues, "made poetry master over his life" (GS 1.1: 165; SW 1: 328). Thus, Goethe's statement that all of his work constitutes "occasional poetry" means the precise opposite of what it appears to say from the perspective of a literary history that grants priority to life in the sense of "lived experience" over poetry.[45] It is not "lived experience" but poetic opportunity that "provides the content" of Goethe's greatest late works, according to Benjamin. *Elective Affinities* tells the story of such an opportunity and of how it is missed while at the same time claiming tentatively to redeem it. The tale is thus one not of marriage but of art—specifically, of life from the perspective of literature. This is the secret meaning or content of the work and indeed of the phrase "elective affinities." It is, in short, the "truth-of-the-matter" at issue in this work.

This thesis emerges out of the critical field of force within which Benjamin's philological project was unfolding during this time and to which I alluded in the preface. If the interpretation of *Elective Affinities* as the story of a failure (of *Versäumnis*) adheres to the romantic principle of the priority of the work of art as an "immanent structure" over the life of the author, the understanding of the role of "opportunity" in Goethe's literary production leads back to Hölderlin's proposition on the sobriety that is native to the modern poet. Benjamin makes this clear by citing the lines from "Timidity" in which the poet is told to let everything that happens be "opportune for you":

... only step
Naked into life, and have no care!
Whatever happens, let it all be opportune for you!
(*GS* 1.1: 166; *SW* 1: 329)

The gloss offered on these lines, which is also a gloss on Goethe's remark to Eckermann on the occasional character of his work, hints at the interpretation of "Timidity" that I began developing above. These lines describe, Benjamin says, "precisely the ancient vocation of the poet" (*GS* 1.1: 166; *SW* 1: 329). This assertion might appear to be a comment that affirms Goethe's receptivity to the ancient calling, yet it is meant as a critical reflection on his utterly different situation as a modern poet. To the extent that the "opportunity" in question exists as an "ancient vocation" it is precisely *not* the calling of the modern poet. Within the context of Hölderlin's poem, strictly speaking, it is presented in the form of an exhortation. In this sense, as I suggested in chapter 1, "Timidity" can be understood as an affirmation of poetic power on the part of a Pindaric chorus addressing a speechless modern protagonist. The "timidity" or "infirmity" of the latter consists precisely in an inability to answer the call and to seize the "opportunity" granted to the ancient poets. Under the conditions of modernity the "opportunity" that presented itself to the ancient poets has been revoked, according to Hölderlin's theory. The ancient poets were called, on certain occasions, to capture their native pathos with a sobering "artifice" that was foreign to them. "From Pindar to Meleager from the Isthnian Games to the hour of love," Benjamin notes, "the poet found only distinctly high, yet as such always worthy occasions for his song" (*nur verschieden hohe, als solche aber stets würdige Gelegenheiten für seinen Gesang*) (*GS* 1.1: 166; *SW* 1: 329). But the calling of the ancient poets has been revoked, and Goethe, Benjamin argues, "felt this absence with horror" (*GS* 1.1: 166; *SW* 1: 329). Under these circumstances and in order to reverse this revocation (and to renew the calling) Goethe turned not to religion like the romantics but to the possibility of the alternative "opportunity" that the invocation of Hölderlin is meant to illuminate: one that specifically cannot be seized.[46] By yielding to it, the silence of the poet addressed in "Timidity" becomes the "opportunity" or "occasion" for the poem. The "promise" (*Verheißung*) of such an "opportunity" or "occasion" for poetry that is neither seized nor missed—only "allowed" (*erlaubt*)—animated the late work of Goethe, according to Benjamin, starting with *Elective Affinities*: "If in the series of these works from his old age *Elective Affinities* is the first, then a purer promise (*Verheißung*), no matter how darkly myth holds sway in it, must already be visible there" (*GS* 1.1: 167; *SW* 1: 329).[47] The hope to which this "promise" gives rise is the focus of the third and last section of Benjamin's study.

The third part of the essay approaches Goethe's novel as dramatizing the possibility of such a renewed "opportunity." This brings Benjamin back to the question with which he began—namely, that of the relation between commentary and critique, subject-matter and its true meaning. Inquiry into this relation, which is, as Benjamin writes, "the rigorously determined origin of art," requires that the critic stand close to the work (*GS* 1.1: 172; *SW* 1: 333). This is the only way to reveal how its appearance (its subject-matter) is bound up with its hidden meaning (its truth). Because neither the poet nor the critic can say directly what this "relation" or "affinity" means, both are ultimately compelled to resort to similes or images—not in order to seize the meaning of the appearance but to allow it to appear. The renewed opportunity for modern poetry requires a redefinition of the content that appears in the work. As with the word *Gelegenheit* and as with so many of the major terms adopted by Benjamin in his writing ("dialectic" is, as we will see, another example), the *content* of the work of art is not quite what it seems.[48] Benjamin uses this term, especially in the essay on Goethe, in a way that might appear merely to draw on traditional Hegelian aesthetic theory. The belated reception of Benjamin's work, as mediated by the Frankfurt School and in particular as overseen by Adorno, tends to reinforce this sense (I will return to this point at the end of this study). But as with "dialectic," the use of the word "content" is not simply the application of a Hegelian term.[49] This becomes clear in the "image" to which Benjamin turns at the beginning of the third part of the essay to provide an illustration of the relation between the subject-matter and the truth-of-the-matter that is at issue in the work of art, but that cannot be directly presented:

> Yet an image . . . is perhaps be allowed (*erlaubt*). Let us suppose that one makes the acquaintance of a person who is beautiful and attractive but impenetrable (*verschlossen*), because he carries a secret within him. It would be reprehensible to want to pry (*verwerflich, in ihn dringen zu wollen*). Still it would surely be allowed (*erlaubt*) to inquire whether he has any siblings (*Geschwister*) and whether their nature could not perhaps explain somewhat the enigmatic character of the stranger. In just this way critique inquires into the siblings of the work of art. All genuine works have their siblings in the realm of philosophy. It is, after all, precisely these figures in which the ideal of philosophy's problem appears. (*GS* 1.1: 172; *SW* 1: 333)

In this image, the subject-matter of the work of art appears to the critic as a "beautiful and attractive" stranger and its truth is like an inviolable secret he is carrying. But how can inquiring into the stranger's "siblings" clarify his "enigmatic character"? Or, put more simply, what is essentially meant here by "siblings"? The word "siblings" translates the German *Geschwister*, which derives from the root word for "sister" (*Schwester*) and which extends its signification to include sisters and brothers and ultimately persons who are related: what in English are called "relations" and what in German is described as *Verwandtschaft*.[50] Charlotte in Goethe's novel uses this expression when the question of "elective affinities" (*Wahlverwandtschaft*) is introduced: "I heard you reading about relations (*Verwandtschaft*) and I thought right away about my relatives (*Verwandten*), a pair of cousins."[51] Benjamin's image thus appears to repeat Charlotte's "error" of anthropomorphism, in this case transposing the relation between criticism and the work of art onto a relation between human beings. But the interpenetration of aesthetic and social relations in Benjamin's image of "elective affinities"—like the interpenetration of social and natural relations in the presentation of this problem in Goethe's novel—complicates the question of primary and secondary meanings. Indeed, the similarity between Benjamin's image and Goethe's novel also extends to the role played by natural science in both presentations. Like Goethe, Benjamin finds in contemporary science a context that allows him to clarify the relation that he is pursuing in his investigation of "elective affinities," specifically, in the relation of the work of art to its content (of the subject-matter to its true meaning). This scientific context is introduced by the language of virtuality that appears at this point in his explication of the image of the secretive stranger. After emphasizing once again that the content of the work of art expressed in relation to the ideal realm or "system of philosophy" is as inviolable as the "secret" of the "stranger" in the simile, Benjamin insists that criticism is nevertheless allowed to enter into a relation with this definitively hidden element:

> Even if, however, the system [of philosophy] is in no sense ascertainable through inquiry, there are nevertheless images (*Gebilde*) which, without being questions, have the deepest affinity (*Affinität*) with the ideal of

the problem. These are works of art. The work of art does not compete with philosophy itself—it merely enters into the most precise relation to philosophy through its affinity (*Verwandtschaft*) with the ideal of the problem. And to be sure, according to a lawfulness grounded in the essence of the ideal as such, the ideal can represent itself (*sich darstellen*) solely in multiplicity. The ideal of the problem, however, does not appear in a multiplicity of problems. Rather, it lies buried (*vergraben*) in a multiplicity of works, and its excavation (*Förderung*) is the business of criticism. The latter allows the ideal of the problem to appear in the work of art in one of its manifestations. For criticism ultimately shows in the work of art the virtual possibility of formulating its truth content (*die virtuelle Formulierbarkeit seines Wahrheitsgehalt*) as the highest philosophical problem. . . . If, therefore, one is allowed (*erlaubt*) to say that everything beautiful (*Schöne*) is related somehow to the true, and that the virtual site (*virtueller Ort*) of the true in philosophy is determinable (*bestimmbar*), then this is to say that in every true work of art an appearance of the ideal of the problem can be discovered. Hence, it follows that from the point at which reflection on the foundations of the novel raises itself up to the intuition of its completion philosophy not myth is called upon to guide it. (*GS* 1.1: 172–73; *SW* 1: 334)

Throughout this passage the stress is on the *virtual* character of the content of the work of art. By demonstrating the formulatability or the determinability of its true meaning the work of art reveals its relation to or "affinity" with philosophy. In this way, the true meaning of Goethe's *Elective Affinities*—its foundation in philosophy rather than in myth—is comparable to the theory of the virtual conservation of matter in early twentieth-century science. Benjamin's analysis of the content of the work of art in his essay on Goethe's scientifically inflected novel draws on contemporary developments in the history of science and in particular on Émile Meyerson's historical critique of scientific paradigms from the perspective of "principles of conservation" (indeed the first footnote to Benjamin's study of the Baroque *Trauerspiel*, on which he began working immediately following the completion of the Goethe essay, is to Meyerson's 1921

Explanation in the Sciences [*GS* 1.1: 213 and 410n1]).[52] The word "virtual" in Benjamin's commentary on the image of the impenetrable stranger thus links the aesthetic question concerning the content of art—the element that makes possible the conservation of life in art—to long-standing natural-scientific inquiry into the principles governing the conservation of matter in the physical world.

This history is illustrated by the transformed signification of the word *Gehalt* in Benjamin's essay. Until the end of the eighteenth century, *Gehalt* described the amount of precious metal (gold or silver) contained in a coin (the Latin *valor* is given as an equivalent).[53] Hegel, apparently following Schiller and adapting this metaphor to aesthetic theory, employs *Gehalt* to describe the essential substance or kernel of truth in the work of art. As such, *Gehalt* defines what is essential in art from the perspective of philosophy, according to Hegel. In an illuminating essay on this topic, Georg Lukács speaks of what he labels Hegel's *Gehaltsästhetik*, declaring that this focus on the substance of truth—the *Gehalt* of the work of art—is itself the "hidden and fruitful kernel" (*verborgener und fruchtbarer Kern*) of Hegel's aesthetics.[54] It is from such a kernel, Lukács concludes, that a genuinely historical aesthetic theory will grow. The *Gehalt* of the work of art in Hegel, Lukács explains, does not "originate" out of the "individual activity of the aesthetic subject, the activity of the artist, or the recipient," but rather from the "independently existing objective social and historical reality."[55] Thus, for Lukács the individual artist cannot fully grasp this substantial content or *Gehalt* of his work: he is rather in the grip of this *Gehalt* when it becomes the subject of his work. The one who is in a position to grasp it, according to this view, is the philosopher of art. The Hegelian philosopher occupies the necessary vantage point from which to observe and identify the substance of truth that exists impurely in the work of art. This is also the standpoint from which the essential content of works of philosophy appear to this particular philosophical position, whether it be that of Hegel on the writings of his precursors or that of Lukács on the "essential kernel" of Hegel's aesthetic philosophy.

The divergence of Benjamin from such a perspective is suggested by the word "virtual" that surfaces in the phrase at the end of the essay on translation, which was completed while he was composing the essay on Goethe: "all great texts contain (*enthalten*) their virtual translation" (*virtuelle Übersetzung*) (*GS* 4.1: 21; *SW* 1: 263). For the translator, the *Gehalt* of an original work is not like a substance; it is not a purified intellectual essence to be extracted and inserted into a foreign language.[56] Rather, the content of the literary work involves a virtual element. Accordingly, in the years leading up to his study of Goethe, Benjamin develops a critical vocabulary stressing virtuality: communicability (*Mitteilbarkeit*), criticizability (*Kritisierbarkeit*), and translatability (*Übersetzbarkeit*).[57] This aspect of his terminology extends in the passage in question from the Goethe essay to the formulatability and determinability of the truth content in the work of art from the perspective of criticism. Like the image of the secretive stranger that it explicates, the scientific theory of virtuality provides Benjamin with a context that allows the true meaning of "elective affinities" (the problem) in Goethe's novel to come to light. Neither the image nor the theory captures this meaning, but they also do not simply miss it. The same is true of *Elective Affinities* (the work). Goethe's novel tells the story of what appears to be missed when it cannot be captured.

It turns out that Benjamin's image of the "impenetrable" stranger draws on an inconspicuous citation that occurs a few pages later in the third part of the essay. It is taken from the fifth edition of Julian Schmidt's *History of German Literature Since Lessing's Death* (1866). The quotation comments on the "impression" made by Ottilie: this "impression comes exclusively from her appearance; despite the numerous diary pages, her inner essence remains closed off. She is more reserved than any female figure of Heinrich von Kleist" (*GS* 1.1: 178; *SW* 1: 338).[58] The single key word that is translated here first as "closed off" and then as "reserved"—the same word that is translated as "impenetrable" in the parable of the secretive stranger—is *verschlossen*. This word can be translated as "impenetrable," "closed off," and "reserved." Ottilie is *verschlossen*, like the stranger in Benjamin's image.[59] Her impenetrability, moreover, is said by Schmidt to be greater "than any female figure of Heinrich von Kleist." Although Benjamin does not elaborate on it, this allusion seems to make a general connection between Goethe's Ottilie and Kleist's enigmatic heroines, who are indeed discussed by Schmidt in an earlier chapter of the book. But the comment Benjamin cites from Schmidt refers to a specific link, what earlier the latter emphatically calls a "relation" (*Verwandtschaft*), between Ottilie and the Marquise of O, and by extension between Goethe's novel and Kleist's novella that appeared one year before *Elective Affinities*: "Apart from the heaviness of the narrative, which was alien to him [Goethe], he must have found more of a relation (*Verwandtschaft*) in this novella than to any other literary work by Kleist, a relation (*Verwandtschaft*) with his work at this time, namely, the novella in *Wilhelm Meister's Apprentice Years* and *Elective Affinities*."[60] In other words, Schmidt identifies Kleist's heroine and his novella as a "relation" (*Verwandtschaft*) of Goethe's character and his novel. This genealogical link between Ottilie and the Marquise of O and between the works in which they figure is typical of what Benjamin viewed as the bourgeois literary histories of the nineteenth century. *History of German Literature Since Lessing's Death* is a leading example of this genre, having been republished in revised and expanded editions in a variety of formats no less than six times during a period when Schmidt coedited with Gustav Freytag *Die Grenzboten*, one of the most popular cultural and political journals in the German speaking world.[61] The publication model of Schmidt's multivolume literary history called for repeatedly refreshing the material and, as a result of this process, the passage cited by Benjamin on the relative "impenetrability" of the heroines of Kleist and of Goethe and the earlier one singling out "The Marquise of O" as a "relation" of *Elective Affinities* disappear from the relevant sections of the subsequent version of Schmidt's book that was published in 1890.[62] Although Goethe's novel and Kleist's novella are both discussed again in this later edition, evidently the "relation" between them, and between their "female figures," had not survived the test of time from the perspective of Schmidt's literary historical project and in particular within the context of its publication model. Yet Benjamin cites the edition of 1866, transforming and redeeming the comment that disappears from the later edition of Schmidt's book.[63] Specifically, Benjamin reframes Schmidt's comment with the "image" of the impenetrable stranger that is introduced at the beginning of this part of the essay. By way of the "image" the true meaning of what Schmidt said is allowed to appear— namely, that the greater "impenetrability" of Ottilie as compared with Kleist's heroines concerns a "relation," not in the context of literary history, but in "the realm of philosophy." To the extent that they appear in works of art, the Marquise of O and Kleist's other heroines have such "relations" as well, but these lie more deeply buried in Goethe's Ottilie and in his novel. The connection made in Schmidt's commentary between *Elective Affinities* and "The Marquise of O" cannot be one of "relation" (*Verwandtschaft*) as it is to be interpreted in Goethe's novel. This is reserved for philosophy.[64]

Schmidt's comment on *Elective Affinities* and all of the others by Goethe and his readers cited by Benjamin in the course of the essay are rescued in this way as they are drawn into the critical reflection on the novel as an "immanent structure." Under such conditions this material enters into relation with "the realm of philosophy," in particular the philosophy of art. But this remains strictly a matter of "relation." The sequence leading up to Schmidt's comment illustrates this principle. It comes after Benjamin has invoked and rejected the Platonic doctrine that "memory" (*Erinerrung*) is essential to beauty in his interpretation of Ottilie's appearance in the novel.[65] "Ottilie's existence does not awaken such memory," Benjamin argues, "in it beauty really remains what is foremost and essential" (*GS* 1.1: 178; *SW* 1: 338). The impenetrability on which Schmidt can at this point be understood to comment is related to, but resists being identified with, the Platonic doctrine of beauty. Benjamin's assertion, which makes the transition between the quotations of Plato and Schmidt, holds them apart—in relation to one another. If in Ottilie beauty refuses memory, this is first and foremost because she is an irreducible and impenetrable matter of appearance; or, precisely as Schmidt says, "her impression comes exclusively from her appearance" (*GS* 1.1: 178; *SW* 1: 338). By adhering insistently to an appearance that is related to but not identical with ideas—for example, of beauty—Benjamin's essay, strictly speaking, does not belong to the philosophy of art. Instead, the critical method developed in "Goethe's Elective Affinities," which oscillates between commentary and critique, responds to the rigorous appearance attributed to the image of Ottilie in the novel—an image that refrains from revealing its philosophical relations. In the last pages of the essay, this impenetrable appearance is defined in relation to the ambiguous character of *Schein* (semblance and luster) in aesthetic theory with which the opening paragraphs begin. In the case of Ottilie, Benjamin argues, Goethe leaves no doubt: it is the appearance of semblance without luster or, more precisely, with fading luster. Ottilie's appearance is like the setting of the sun, the fading of a light, and the extinguishing of a flame, as the verb forms in this passage suggest:

> That semblance (*Schein*) which presents itself in Ottilie's beauty is the one that goes under (*untergehende*). It is not to be understood, however, as if external need and force brought about Ottilie's decline (*Untergang*); rather, it is based in the kind of semblance itself that it must be extinguished (*verlöschen*), and that it must be extinguished soon. This semblance is quite different from the triumphant one of dazzling beauty, which is that of Luciane or of Lucifer. And whereas the figure of Goethe's Helena and the more famous one of the Mona Lisa owe the enigma of their splendor to the conflict between these two kinds of semblance, the figure of Ottilie is governed throughout by the single semblance that extinguishes (*verlischt*). . . . Hence, what appears in Ottilie is not the semblance of beauty as such, which manifests itself doubly, but solely of that of a fading (*vergehende*) beauty that is her own. Yet this semblance of course discloses insight into the beautiful semblance as such and [this fading semblance] makes itself known for

the first time in it [the beautiful semblance as such]. Therefore, to every view (*Anschauung*) that beholds the figure of Ottilie the old question arises whether beauty is semblance (*GS* 1.1: 193; *SW* 1: 349–50 [brackets added for clarification])

Ottilie fades without shining. Her appearance is not identical with the ambiguous semblance of beauty in the realm of the philosophy of art.[66] Yet it holds a relation to this idea, one that is impenetrable— more impenetrable, it seems, than Helena in *Faust Part Two* or the Mona Lisa, both of which bear the ambiguous semblance that discloses beauty as such and that reconciles the two kinds of semblance presented by Luciane and Lucifer, on the one hand, and Ottilie, on the other. If Helena is the ambiguous phenomenal appearance of beauty as such, Ottilie is the unambiguous phenomenal disappearance of a kind of beauty that fades. It is the difference, Benjamin argues, between the veil of Helena and the "living body" (*lebendige Leib*) of Ottilie (*GS* 1.1: 197; *SW* 1: 353). Within the context of the play, Helena's veil is presented to Faust by Mephistopheles as the luminous appearance of classical antiquity and as a mere semblance onto which the lover of Helena is urged to "hold fast."[67] From this perspective the "clouds" that appear to take hold of Faust at this point and transport him to the "ether" are to be contrasted with the sobering image of the "silent lightning" that is marked by the magic staff in Faust's hand at the end of the masquerade in Act 1. Within the context of the novel, Ottilie's "living body" expresses, less ambiguously than the veil of Helena, "a law" that applies to "all beauty that appears as semblance" (*alle scheinhafte Schönheit*) and that can "only adhere to being alive" (*am Lebendigen*). This law states that this kind of beauty disappears with life: "With the complete end of the one, the other too must pass away" (*GS* 1.1: 197; *SW* 1: 353).

At this point there is a break in the essay as Benjamin approaches the end of his reflections on the novel. It is marked graphically by a dash that occurs in the penultimate paragraph after the sentence that concludes the discussion of Ottilie's "living body," which reads: "The human body lays itself bare, a sign that the human being itself stands before God—" (*GS* 1.1: 197; *SW* 1: 353). As it happens, this dash appears at the very middle of the page in the second installment of the first edition published in the *Neue Deutsche Beiträge* in 1925 and at the very end of the page in the version that appears in the *Gesammelte Schriften* in 1974.[68] These are undoubtedly accidents that nevertheless appear fortuitous. But there can be no doubt about the significance of this break as deliberately marking the turn to the essay's conclusion. The English translator's decision to introduce a new paragraph at this juncture underlines this structural feature of the presentation (the new paragraph begins with the sentence: "Beauty that does not surrender itself in love must fall prey to death" [*GS* 1.1: 198; *SW* 1: 353]). The break clearly frames a concluding section that starts by reaching back to the beginnings of Benjamin's literary critical project, and in particular to the theme of youth as interpreted, for example, in "The Life of Students."[69] The fading beauty specific to the life just analyzed is now referred to youth. Ottilie, Benjamin asserts, is "the most youthful of all of the figures whom Goethe created"; like the students of the earlier essay, she is defined by a "readiness for death" (*Todesbereitschaft*) (*GS* 1.1: 198; *SW* 1: 353).[70] More precisely, through the figure of Ottilie, Benjamin argues, Goethe granted youth a "view" of life to which he refused to assent: "Never in a work did he give to youth what he granted it in Ottilie: the whole of life, in the way that, from its own duration, it has its own death. Indeed, one may say that if he was in truth blind to anything, it was precisely to this. If Ottilie's existence, in the pathos that distinguishes it from all others, nevertheless refers to the life of youth, then only through the destiny of her beauty could Goethe become reconciled with this view, to which his own being refused assent" (*GS* 1.1: 198; *SW* 1: 353).

The German verb aptly translated at the beginning of this passage as "to grant" is *zugestehen*. It signifies "to acknowledge" or "to concede." According to Grimm, the modern sense of this word derived from a juridical context to mean more generally "to acknowledge what another demands, desires, needs" or "to concede that something is true, correct, or there" (*einräumen, daß etwas wahr ist, zutrifft oder da ist*). In the noun form *ein Zugeständnis*, Grimm states, is "an acknowledgment of a debt" (*Eingeständnis einer Schuld*) or "a conceding of an opinion or fact" (*Einräumung einer Meinung oder Tatsache*).[71] Thus, in spite of the overlap between granting and giving, the meanings of these verbs diverge in the first phrase of this passage: Goethe never attributed to youth in a work what he conceded to it in Ottilie. Not attributed but conceded, according to Benjamin, is a singularly finite life: "the whole of life, in the way that, from its own duration, it has its own death" (*das ganze Leben wie es aus seiner eigenen Dauer seinen eigenen Tod hat*). Goethe, Benjamin continues, refused to accept such a life: "If he was in truth blind to anything, it was precisely to this." Blindness to the finitude of life is the source of what Benjamin describes earlier as "the mythic thinking" (*des mythischen Denkens*) and "the daemonic forces" (*der dämonischen Kräfte*) that manifest themselves in Goethe's work (*GS* 1.1: 150–51; *SW* 1: 317): "The author's aversion to death and to everything that signifies it bears all of the features of the most extreme superstition. It is well known that no one was ever allowed to speak in his presence of anyone's death" (*GS* 1.1: 151; *SW* 1: 317). The "fear of death" (*Todesangst*) was thus accompanied in Goethe by what Benjamin calls a "fear of life" (*Lebensangst*) (*GS* 1.1: 152; *SW* 1: 318). Yet, according to the interpretation being developed in the essay, the depiction of Ottilie is not ultimately shaped by "mythical thinking" and "daemonic forces." Her life is not determined by a "structure of guilt and expiation," and her death is not presented as a mythic sacrifice or as a tragedy. Instead, her singularly "whole" and finite life is conceded to youth. Goethe does not so much accept this life as acknowledge a certain blindness to it. "Ottilie" is in this sense the name for the blindness—if it is truly blindness and not an impaired "vision"—to which Goethe concedes.[72]

The word "destiny" in this passage clearly situates Goethe's concession in what Benjamin calls "the realm overseen by Hölderlin" in the dissertation (*GS* 1.1: 105n280; *SW* 1: 198n287). "Destiny" translates the German *Geschick* which invokes the contrast between the ancients and the moderns in the "Letter to Böhlendorff" cited by Benjamin at the end of his earlier essay on Hölderlin and also the "skilled hands" (*schickliche Hände*) he discusses in "Timidity."[73] Goethe's concession to youth is to be understood, from this perspective, as an expression of sobriety that deactivates the mythic economy of guilt and atonement that is mobilized around Ottilie's life. For Hölderlin, *Geschick* delineates a semantic field that includes "destiny" and "skill." Thus, to say that youth, specifically the disappearing beauty of its life, is granted *ein Geschick* is to suggest a destiny (or perhaps a destiny of lacking destiny in the sense of the Greeks) as well as a skill. It is therefore by acknowledging a destiny and a skill that Goethe allows youth to express its view of its own life in its own words, albeit with a certain sobering modification. As evidence of this concession, Benjamin calls upon what he describes as "a peculiar and to a certain extent source-like reference" (*einen eigenartigen und gewissermaßen quellenmäßign Hinweis*)—a letter from Bettine von Arnim to Goethe that is dated May 22, 1809 (*GS* 1.1: 198; *SW* 1: 353).[74] We know that the letter is dated to a time when Goethe was composing part 2 of *Elective Affinities*.[75] In it, von Arnim praises the failed nationalist uprising by the Tyrolians in the spring of 1809 against French occupation and exhorts Goethe to "secure immortality for the heroes" like the slain warriors in Valhalla (*GS* 1.1: 198; *SW* 1: 353).[76] Goethe responds to von Arnim's letter by inserting her description of the immortalization of the heroes into Ottilie's account of her own death in the diary entry at the end of the third chapter of part 2.[77] Benjamin finds the "affinity of mood" (*Stimmungsverwandtschaft*) expressed by Ottilie's words "striking": "For the affinity of mood of those short sentences is striking, striking in Goethe the thought of Valhalla, striking, finally, how directly (*unvermittelt*) it is introduced into Ottilie's note. Would it not be a sign of the fact that, in those gentler words of Ottilie, Goethe had drawn closer to Bettine's heroic demeanor?" (*GS* 1.1: 199; *SW* 1: 354).

It is surprising that Benjamin characterizes the introduction of von Arnim's letter into Ottilie's diary as "direct" or "unmediated" (*unvermittelt*)—employing a term, once again with a Hegelian inflection, that will become a crux in his later methodological disagreements with Adorno, as we will see. Clearly there is mediation involved in the transposition of the language of heroic pathos in von Arnim's exhortation into Ottilie's "gentler words" (*sanftern Wörter*). This is indeed an example of the effects of the work as an "immanent structure" on the material content that is drawn into its field. The sobriety of Ottilie's sentences permits von Arnim's words truly to express the youthful view of life and thus to become a "source" for the view that Goethe concedes to it in this passage. The immediacy described by Benjamin concerns the apparent spontaneity with which von Arnim's words are acknowledged—as they are mediated and reframed by the sobering perspective of Ottilie in the novel. This aspect of Goethe's compositional method resembles Benjamin's own in the essay, as I have been suggesting. In this case, the interpolation of von Arnim's letter into the novel is said to draw Goethe closer to the sobering view of life that Benjamin associates with youth in his early work.

But the spontaneity of Goethe's encounter with the youthful expression of life in von Arnim's letter is not to be mistaken with that of a "lived experience," as this is defined by the "philosophy of life" that informs the perspective of Friedrich Gundolf's influential study—a key target of the Goethe essay. With this, Benjamin returns in the final paragraph to the romantic thesis that was central to his dissertation—namely, the priority of the work over life in truly critical reflection on literature. The approach promulgated by Gundolf moves in the opposite direction: it starts with the life of the author and proceeds to the work. With regard to Ottilie, for example, this leads Gundolf to the nonsensical claim that her character is somehow not the "main content" (*der Hauptgehalt*) or the "essential problem" of the work and that she instead "derives from a unique lived experience of Goethe" (*stammt aus einem einmaligen Erlebnis*

Goethes).⁷⁸ As a result of this procedure, Gundolf entirely misses not only the encounter with the singular life of youth to which the name "Ottilie" refers in the novel but also the spell under which the name places Goethe, compelling him to "save someone passing away" and to "redeem in her a loved one" (*GS* 1.1: 199; *SW* 1: 354). With regard to the latter, the work was Goethe's only hope, as he acknowledged, according to Benjamin, in a conversation with Sulpiz Boisserée that at this point can be understood to "allude more deeply to the secret of Goethe's work than he might have suspected" (*GS* 1.1: 199; *SW* 1: 354). The conversation in question took place during a journey from Karlsruhe to Heidelberg on October 5, 1815. As the stars rose in the evening sky, Goethe spoke of the novel that had appeared six years earlier and of his "relationship to Ottilie, of how he had loved her, and how she had made him unhappy" (*GS* 1.1: 199; *SW* 1: 354).⁷⁹ Benjamin adds: "If it did not escape this reporter how, with the rising of the stars, Goethe's thoughts steered themselves toward his work (*auf sein Werk*), Goethe himself was quite probably hardly aware—a fact to which his language attests—how sublime beyond measure the moment was and how clear the warning in the stars. In such admonition, what had long ago faded away as lived experience (*Erlebnis*) persisted as traditional experience (*Erfahrung*)" (*GS* 1.1: 199; *SW* 1: 354). Thus, in Benjamin's account the meaning of Boisserée's report is expressed by way of the work—specifically, the stars that appear to Goethe in the sky over Heidelberg merge with the image from *Elective Affinities* in which the narrator reports with regard to Eduard and Ottilie: "Hope soared away over their heads like a star falling from the sky."⁸⁰ With this turn to the work as an "immanent structure," Benjamin returns to his study of romanticism.⁸¹ At the same time, with regard to the image of the falling star itself, Benjamin promptly inserts an explicit allusion to Hölderlin's discussion of the caesura in his "Remarks on Oedipus": "That sentence, which to speak with Hölderlin contains the caesura of the work and in which, while the embracing lovers seal their fate, everything pauses reads: 'Hope soared away over their hears like a star falling from the sky'" (*GS* 1.1: 199–200; *SW* 1: 354–55).[82] By drawing simultaneously on his commentary on Hölderlin and his study of romanticism, Benjamin fuses the major strands of his literary critical project up to this point in the final paragraph of the Goethe essay. But this summary is of course in no sense the end of the project, any more than the novel *Elective Affinit*ies was the end of Goethe's engagement with Ottilie, as the conversation with Boisserée six years after the publication of the novel demonstrates. This would run precisely counter to Benjamin's critical argument about the way that *Erlebnis* can turn into *Erfahrung*. Just as the stars and the falling stars repeatedly appear in the night sky, Goethe—and also Ottilie—returned in Benjamin's critical work.

Six years after the composition of the Goethe essay was complete, Benjamin, along with other leading men of letters, was invited to submit a "short autobiographical note" to the *Literarische Welt* in honor of Stefan George's sixtieth birthday (*GS* 2.3: 1429). Several now forgotten writers responded with enthusiastic appreciations of the authoritativeness with which George had led German literature into the realm of art. There was also Martin Buber, who credited George's collections of poetry with teaching him that poems joined together in a series could become "a dialogue"; and Bertolt Brecht, for whom George was an effete bourgeois "entirely meaningless for younger people."[83] But Benjamin made what must be considered the most memorable contribution. He was ambivalent about George. The ridicule directed at Gundolf in the Goethe essay may be understood to have had George as an ultimate target; yet Benjamin later on recalls waiting in great anticipation to catch a glimpse of the poet in the Schlosspark in Heidelberg during the summer of 1921 when he was working intensively on his Goethe essay and attending Gundolf's lectures at the university.[84] In the remarks offered to the *Literarische Welt* in 1928, and reworked in an essay published in 1933, Benjamin describes George's effect upon him as a "tremor" (*eine Erschütterung*).[85] Especially moving, Benjamin writes, were the poems found "at a particular, gripping moment (*eingreifended Augenblick*) in the mouths of those with whom I lived together (*verbunden*) at the time and once or twice in my own mouth" (*GS* 2.1: 622). The period during which George's poems came to life in this way for Benjamin started coming to an end, he explains, in early 1914 when the collection of poems, *Stern des Bundes* (*Star of the Covenant*), appeared "ominously on the horizon" (*unheilverkündend überm Horizont*) (*GS* 2.2: 623). This marked the beginning of the war and the suicide of a friend, the poet Friedrich Heinle, in August 1914. "Months followed," Benjamin continues,

> of which I can remember nothing. In these months, however, the poems that he had left behind entered into the few places in me where poems were still capable of taking effect decisively. They formed another figure (*sie bildeten eine andere Figur*). . . . Thus the effect of George on my life is bound to the poem in its liveliest sense (*So ist Georges Wirken in mein Leben gebunden ans Gedicht in seinem lebendigsten Sinn*). The way his dominion (*Herrschaft*) arose in me and the way it disintegrated played out entirely in the space of the poem and in the friendship to a poet (*im Raume des Gedichts und in der Freundschaft eines Dichters*). (*GS* 2.1: 623)

The months to which Benjamin refers in this passage were devoted to the composition of his essays on "the life of students" and on Hölderlin, with which we began. When he writes at the end of the Goethe essay of the "spell" cast over the author of *Elective Affinities* that compelled the latter to try to "save someone passing away"— someone "he had loved" who "had made him unhappy"—Benjamin is describing his own singular experience of the life of youth. The literary critical project on which he embarked from the early writings to the study of romanticism and the essay on Goethe can in this sense be described as a philology of that life.

CODA: THE AFTERLIFE OF PHILOLOGY

Embedded in Benjamin's note on philology and life from the later 1930s that is cited at the beginning of this book is a citation from Hugo von Hofmannsthal: "Read what was never written" (*Was nie geschrieben wurde, lesen*) (*GS* 1.3: 1238; *SW* 4: 405).[1] This line occurs at the end of Hofmannsthal's 1893 verse drama *Death and the Fool* (*Der Tor und der Tod*). It is spoken by Death and refers to fools like the play's protagonist, Claudio, who has just passed away in despair on what he calls "the stage of life" (*die Lebensbühne*). Death ridicules Claudio, in particular for engaging foolishly in a life of "interpreting" (*deuten*) and "reading" (*lesen*). Indeed, the rhyme in the line in question (of *lesen* with *Wesen*) suggests that reading is essentially foolish from the perspective of Death.[2] Benjamin's citation thus defies Death when he claims that the reader to which this refers is "the true historian." In keeping with remarks on Kafka made in a letter that Benjamin wrote to Scholem during this same period, the fool gets the last word.[3] If Death announces itself in the play as having "always only one meaning" (*stets nur einen Sinn*) Benjamin's insertion of this line into his note on the "dialectical image" opens it up to an alternative interpretation and suggests that, rather than simply a foolish waste of time, reading can become true history.[4] This different meaning of Death's line becomes possible, Benjamin proposes, when life is approached as a book and indeed as a specific book, namely, "the book of life" (*das Buch des Lebens*). According to one version of the traditional biblical image, this book has written in it the names of those who will be saved.[5] But the "book of life" in Benjamin's note saves what has *not* been written. Indeed, in this sense the philological "book of life" itself has never already been written, although it can be made out in the biblical text, Benjamin implicitly proposes, if the traditional image is transformed into a book with the dynamic capacity to save what has never been written in it.[6] The transformational reading of this book, Benjamin writes, is a "historical method" and the method is "philological." Important to notice is that he does not say that the philological method is historical, which would express the conventional view. What does it mean to say that history is determined methodologically by philology, rather than the reverse? These sentences do not include Benjamin's definition of "philology," but they do provide a succinct illustration of its method. This can be seen in the way that the proposition about philology makes the citation embedded in it, like the image of the "book of life," legible in a new way. The changed meaning of the citation is an effect of the philological operation. Specifically, the proposition that the historical method is philological makes Hofmannsthal's phrase readable as a methodological imperative of "the true historian" who is called upon to save an act of "reading" that is otherwise condemned to ridicule from the perspective of Death in the play. Saved in this sense is an act of reading from the perspective of life. This particular philological intervention may also be understood to rescue a line from a youthful work by the author who had published Benjamin's essay on Goethe over a decade earlier.[7] This late note on the dialectical image that was left among the sketches surrounding the posthumously published "On the Concept of History" encapsulates the philological method that is developed by Benjamin in the set of three overlapping case studies considered in the preceding chapters of this book. Repeatedly Benjamin can be seen taking phrases but especially words from the writing of one author and transposing them onto that of another in a way that allows the true meaning of both components to come to light. There is an element of artistry in this method that resembles Goethe's description of his compositional technique as involving the selection of "images that are juxtaposed to each other and that at the same time mirror one another" (*durch einandergegenübergestellte und sich gleichsam eineinander abspiegelnde Gebilde*).[8] But the effects of this philological procedure are also presented, as I have been emphasizing, in the language of force that is adopted from natural science.

Philology as an academic discipline—as a science or a history of language—enters into the romantic theory of the work of art through Friedrich Schlegel's encounter with Wolf's study of Homer, as we have seen. Wolf's insistence on the capacity of the Homeric text to appropriate foreign material provides the basis for the interpenetration of work and criticism in romantic aesthetic theory—what Schlegel calls the "criticizability" (*Kritisierbarkeit*) of the work. Hölderlin, who seems to have had no direct contact with Wolf, and Goethe, who was wary of the philologist's revolutionary interpretation of the Homeric poem, also base their theories of the modern work of art on a highly dynamic concept of ancient poetry that has affinities with the one that Wolf had adopted from the philological studies of the Bible developed during the second half of the eighteenth century.[9] Under the specific cultural conditions of German letters at the end of that century—one in which the university played a unique role—academic philology mingled with literary theory and practice, including to varying degrees that of Hölderlin, the romantics, and Goethe. Yet, in spite of the importance Benjamin placed on philology he pays almost no attention to Wolf or to the role of academic philology in this period.[10] Benjamin's concern is not with the historical development of philology or with philology as a historical discipline but rather with a historical method that is itself philological. The focus of this method in the set of critical studies considered above is precisely on the period when philology emerged in the German university as a science and a history of language. But Benjamin defines philology differently, as he makes clear in his 1921 letter to Scholem and as he continues to insist in the notes and fragments on history from the end of the 1930s. This alternative philology connects the early literary critical studies culminating in the Goethe essay with the reflections on history of the later period. What might appear to be a shift from a focus on literary works to an engagement with questions of history is part of an ongoing philological practice. In this sense the project consisting of the critical studies of Hölderlin, the romantics, and Goethe is to be understood as a historical reflection on what Benjamin at one point calls "perhaps the greatest epoch in the Western philosophy of art" (*GS* 1.1: 103; *SW* 1: 175). Starting from the dynamic concept of the work that the romantics theorized as a "medium of reflection," Benjamin develops his critical studies within a wider field in which these literary phenomena interact with one another, often in the absence of any explicit links connecting them other than the juxtapositions and mirrorings that take place in the philological investigations. In this way the specific nexus formed by the writings of Hölderlin, the romantics, and Goethe in Benjamin's project presents singular images of an epoch that is—and indeed that was—fading away.

The philological encounter with these literary and critical writings in Benjamin's early literary criticism is truly historical in view of the singular finitude of the specific phenomenon under consideration, which appears as a set of attempts to elaborate an aesthetic theory and practice that saves what is destined to pass away. By the same token, the later studies explicitly focused on questions of historical method continue to engage in literary critical practice, as is suggested in sentences leading up to the citation of Hofmannsthal in the note on the philology of life:

> If one wants to view history as a text, then what a recent author says about literary texts applies to it: the past has deposited images in them that can be compared to those captured by a light-sensitive plate. "Only the future has developers available who are strong enough to allow the image to appear in all of its detail. Some of the pages of Marivaux or Rousseau have a secret meaning that contemporary readers were not able fully to decipher." The historical method is a philological method based on the book of life. "Read what was never written," runs a line by Hofmannsthal. The reader one should think of here is the true historian. (GS 1.3: 1238; SW 4: 405)[11]

If history is viewed as a text—rather than, for example, as the progressive continuum of conventional historiography—then it can be seen to involve a receptivity to time that is characteristic of literary texts. Specifically, like literary texts, history when it is viewed as a text can be understood to have the capacity to capture time in the form of images. These images, moreover, are comparable to the inscription of light on a photosensitive plate described in the citation from volume 1 of André Monglond's *Le préromantisme français*. In the context of Benjamin's writings on art and technical reproducibility in the 1930s, the comparison to photography suggests that time enters into the text of history in a way that eludes conscious perception (GS 1.2: 476; SW 4: 254). Just as the texts of Marivaux and Rousseau have meanings indecipherable to their contemporary readers, the text of history has images of time that are only available to "the future." But the question is: what is the process or method that allows these images of time to appear in all of their detail, as Benjamin puts it in his translation of Monglond?[12] With regard to photography, it is a chemical process that brings out the inscriptions of light on the plate. In the case of history when it is viewed as a text, it is a philological method that allows the images of time to come to light. This is the clear suggestion of the associative chain that links the two parts of this paragraph in Benjamin's note, both of which are composed of a statement followed by a citation. As a result of the juxtaposition, the one illuminates and is illuminated by the other.

The imprint of this philological method with its focus on images of the dynamic time of "life" remains legible in Benjamin's later work on Baudelaire where it is developed in a more overtly political context.[13] This extension of the reflection on "life" that we have traced to Benjamin's earliest writings is made clear in the philosophical scaffolding he provided for Adorno and Horkheimer in the first section of the version that appeared in their *Journal for Social Research* in 1940 under the title "On Some Motifs in Baudelaire." This essay begins apodictically by situating the project in the context of the social conditions of mid-nineteenth-century capitalism and in relation to the development of *Lebensphilosophie*, providing as points of reference Dilthey's *Das Erlebnis und die Dichtung* and Bergson's *Matière et mémoire*—what are described as philosophical "attempts to grasp 'true' experience, as opposed to the kind that manifests itself in the standardized, denatured existence of the civilized masses" (*GS* 1.2: 608; *SW* 4: 314). From here, the first section of the 1940 essay goes on to introduce the conceptual distinctions between enduring "experience" (*Erfahrung*) and mere "lived experience" (*Erlebnis*), true "memory" (*Gedächtnis*) and factual recollection (*Erinnerung*). This sample from the much larger Baudelaire project was prepared from February to July 1939 specifically in response to Adorno's criticism of an earlier draft that he judged to be lacking in "theoretical interpretation."[14] This earlier version, which was written in the summer and fall of 1938 and which was eventually published in the 1960s under the title "Paris of the Second Empire in Baudelaire," bears the distinct stamp of the philological method to which the note on the dialectical image alludes (*GS* 1.3: 1135). It begins with a figure or a "type" (*Typus*), specifically, that of the "professional conspirator" as glossed by Marx in his commentary on the memoirs of the police informer and writer Lucien de la Hodde. The opening section of this earlier draft proceeds by approaching Baudelaire and his poetry through a series of citations, mainly from Marx, along with commentary on the "professional conspirators" under the Second Empire. These full-time revolutionaries, who devoted all of their activity to looking for opportunities to spark a revolt, are said to bring to mind the "physiognomy" of Baudelaire (*GS* 1.2: 513; *SW* 4: 3). "The metaphysics of the provocateur" that Benjamin finds expressed by this physiognomy is also characteristic of the philological method that is being extended into the investigation of the poet. From Benjamin's perspective, the mission that Baudelaire shares with the professional conspirator is what Marx describes as the opportunistic attempt "artificially to bring the revolutionary process to a point of crisis and to produce a revolution extemporaneously without the conditions for a revolution" (*GS* 1.2: 518; *SW* 4: 6). This improvisational political agitation corresponds to Baudelaire's efforts to make his poetry receptive to images of a time that disrupts the forces deployed in the Paris of the Second Empire to deny access to "'true' experience"— the singular temporal finitude that Baudelaire calls "modern life." Benjamin's philological method involves looking for openings in the poetry of Baudelaire, through which images of modern life may be released extemporaneously from the cognitive grip of "lived experience" (*Erlebnis*). The extent to which this project marks a continuation of the approach taken in the earlier literary criticism is suggested, not only by Benjamin's allusion to "the dialectical rigor" of the tripartite structure of the Goethe essay as a "model" for the study of Baudelaire (in a letter from April 4, 1938), but also by the philological method of textual juxtapositionings and mirrorings that was exemplified most completely in the approach taken to *Elective Affinities*.[15]

It is precisely this methodology that Adorno finds wanting in "Paris of the Second Empire in Baudelaire."[16] From Adorno's point of view, the "motifs are assembled but not worked through" (*versammelt aber nicht durchgeführt*); the ideas "are walled off behind impenetrable material layers" (*undurchdringlichen Stoffschichten*); the "dialectic lacks . . . mediation" (*Vermittlung*) (*GS* 1.3: 1094–95; *SW* 4: 99–101). Benjamin's response makes it clear that he perceived this criticism not as a set of recommendations for revising details in the presentation but rather as a fundamental rejection of the critical method that he had been perfecting for more than two decades, and in particular a rejection of the indispensable role played by philology in it. The rejoinder to Adorno reveals the poignancy and the complexity of the situation facing Benjamin during what turned out to be the last two years of his life. For the sake of his project, he can afford neither to dismiss nor to accept Adorno's criticisms, since accepting them would undermine its integrity and dismissing them would prevent its publication. Therefore, Benjamin frames and reformulates the criticisms from the perspective of what he calls its "overall construction" (*Gesamtkonstruktion*).[17] On one level, this refers to the schematic tripartite structure that he had developed for the larger study of Baudelaire during the late 1930s. According to this plan "Paris of the Second Empire in Baudelaire" was to have been the second part of a three-part composition—preceded by a section on "Baudelaire as Allegorist" and followed by one on "The Commodity as a Poetic Object."[18] However, Benjamin does not simply claim that the first part will supply what Adorno finds missing. Instead, within the "overall context" (*Gesamtzusammenhang*) of the project what Adorno describes as an absence of "theoretical interpretation" can be understood more correctly as a "lack of theoretical transparency" in the philological method. This lack of clarity is to be rectified to a certain extent in the first section of the work, not when the "theoretical interpretation" is provided, but rather when the "philological procedure" is named as such. The "lack of theoretical transparency," which is inherent in the philological presentation, has its basis in part, Benjamin observes, "in the risky experiment of writing the second part of the book before the first."

But Benjamin does not just defend the philological method that is especially prominent in this section: he turns it on Adorno's criticisms in a way that brings to light their true significance within the context of the "overall construction." This procedure is especially evident in the paragraph in Benjamin's letter that begins by citing a key phrase in Adorno's negative assessment of the approach taken to Baudelaire in the essay: *"staunende Darstellung der Faktizität."* The English translation of this phrase as "wide-eyed presentation of facticity" accurately captures the caustic tone of Adorno's critical comment.[19] However, the German word *staunende* ("wide-eyed"), from *staunen*, is the standard translation of the ancient Greek *thaumazein*, which refers to the authentically philosophical attitude in the Western tradition. It is usually translated into English as "wonder," as in the famous sentence from Plato's *Theatetis*: "Wonder is the only beginning of philosophy" (155d).[20] Benjamin pivots on this term in a way that transposes the traditional connection between wonder and philosophy into the philological context of his project: "When you speak of a 'wide-eyed presentation of facticity' you are thus characterizing the genuinely philological attitude."[21] Philological wonder had to be "sunken into the construction as such," Benjamin explains, not only for the sake of "the results" it produced. Yet while this attitude or bearing (*Haltung*) is essential and necessary to the project's construction, it is also essentially and necessarily limited. Thus, in keeping with the philological procedure in question, Benjamin allows Adorno's terms as a provisional description of the way in which this occurs, first as liquidation and then as dialectical sublation. Benjamin cites Adorno's declaration that the "non-differentiation between magic and positivism . . . must be liquidated" and then specifies the theoretical perspective from which this liquidation is seen to take place: "In other words, " Benjamin writes, "the author's philological interpretation is to be sublated by dialectical materialists in the Hegelian manner." The formulaic, citational character of the phrase describing the theoretical limitation or "mediation" of the "philological interpretation"—as it is "sublated by dialectical materialists in the Hegelian manner"—prepares the next step in Benjamin's argument, which also turns on a citation, this time from Adorno's study of Kierkegaard[22]: "Amazement (*Das Verwundern*), you write in your book on Kierkegaard, announces 'the deepest insight into the relationship of dialectic, myth, and image.'

I am tempted to call on this passage for support. Instead, I want to propose a correction to it.... I believe the sentence should read: amazement is an outstanding *object* of such an insight."²³ The "correction" proposed by Benjamin draws on a distinction he makes in his dissertation on romanticism and involves a shift in perspective from an attitude that provides insight into the way that dialectic, myth, and image are connected to a reflection on that attitude. In the "canonical" version of such a reflection the form of amazement or wonder would become its content (*GS* 1.1: 30; *SW* 1: 128). But the romantic theory of what Benjamin designates as the "medium of reflection" in his dissertation posits a higher "third level" reflection that disintegrates or decomposes the relation of subject and object, of form and content, giving rise to an "image-object" (*GS* 1.1: 72; *SW* 1: 155). The "genuinely philological attitude" becomes an "*object*" in the ambiguous sense of the romantic "medium of reflection" (as I have stressed, with this translation of Benjamin's term being understood as a subjective and as an objective genitive). The dynamic objectivity that the philological attitude shares with the romantic medium of reflection has what Benjamin calls the "semblance of self-contained facticity," but it is also contained and limited—not so much "liquidated" and "sublated," as it appears from Adorno's perspective, but historically "constructed." As Benjamin sees it, philology is the medium or the method through which the images deposited by the past are experienced as history. Like the romantic medium of reflection and like the Leibnizian monad to which he also alludes in this passage the philological attitude may thus be said to come "alive."²⁴ This means, moreover, that the wonder that is the only beginning for philology is also singularly finite and the "spell" that it casts "disappears"—precisely as it enters into the construction of a "historical perspective": "the semblance (*Schein*) of self-contained facticity that adheres to philological study and that casts its spell on the scholar disappears (*schwindet*) to the degree to which the object is constructed in historical perspective. The vanishing lines of this construction flow together in our own historical experience (*historischen*

Erfahrung). In this way the object is constituted as a monad. In the monad, everything comes alive (*lebendig*) that lay frozen in mythical rigidity as the textual record."²⁵ The semblance of philological study—what Adorno perceives as the "wide-eyed presentation of facticity"—"disappears" into our "historical experience." Pathos gives way to sobriety in the construction of the philological object. By insisting on the authenticity of the wonder that "casts its spell on the scholar" and that also "disappears," Benjamin makes the defense of his Baudelaire project a matter of saving the "philological attitude" (*philologische Haltung*), just as his essay on Goethe's *Elective Affinities* was a matter of saving the "attitude of the narrator" (*die Haltung des Erzählers*) (*GS* 1.1: 200; *SW* 1: 355). In this sense, Benjamin's late critical composition, which remained incomplete, came to focus on what might be called the life—or indeed the afterlife—of philology.

No one did more than Adorno after the Second World War to preserve the writings of Benjamin. The two-volume collection of *Schriften* edited by Adorno and his wife in 1955 is only the most obvious example of the key role he played in the reception of Benjamin's work. Even the essay on Baudelaire that Adorno rejected before the war was ultimately published by his student Rolf Tiedemann in 1969 (as it happened, the year of Adorno's death) (*GS* 1.3: 1135). Some indirect credit is due as well to Adorno for Tiedemann's authoritative and meticulously edited seven-volume set of Benjamin's *Gesammelte Schriften*, which started to appear in 1974. However, there has been considerable criticism of Adorno's oversight of Benjamin's legacy.²⁶ With regard specifically to the development of a distinctive philological method in Benjamin's early literary criticism and its extension into a broader cultural field in his later work, it is clear that the "theoretical interpretation" promoted by Adorno in his rejection of Benjamin's 1938 essay on Baudelaire is fundamentally inhospitable to the project. Adorno was already preparing a space for the reception of Benjamin's work that left no room for "the genuinely philological attitude." Benjamin's response, I have just suggested, is to reverse the roles and to try desperately to keep the door open to dialectical theory by applying the philological method to the terms of Adorno's criticisms.

The gap separating Benjamin's philological method from Adorno's dialectical theory is suggested by a passage in the latter's 1963 lecture on Hölderlin and specifically by the way it draws on former's early essay on the poet. Adorno presents his lecture as an intervention in a polemic between philosophy and philology and frames the question as a conflict between "the currently fashionable thought" of "philosophical interpreters" (Heidegger and his followers), on the one hand, and the tradition of philological literary criticism (Beissner, May, and Staiger), on the other. Adorno charges the former with turning Hölderlin into "clichés from the jargon of authenticity" and the latter with reducing the meaning of his poetry to a "reconstruction of what the author intended."[27] But while "philological science" deserves the respectful delineation of its limitations, according to Adorno, the pseudo-philosophical interpretation of Heidegger must be repudiated. The latter is Adorno's main target, in particular, its suggestion "that what the poet says is so, without mediation (*unmittelbar*), literally; this may explain the neglect of the poetized (*Gedichteten*) at the same time that it is glorified. The abrupt deaestheticization of the content palms off the indispensably aesthetic as real without regard for the dialectical disjunction between form and truth content (*dialektische Brechung zwischen Form und Wahrheitsgehalt*)."[28] As in the letter to Benjamin more than two decades earlier, Adorno's criticism of the Heideggerian interpretation of Hölderlin is that it lacks "mediation" and therefore neglects the aesthetic composition of "the poetized." In order to refute and to displace Heidegger's pseudo-philosophical approach to Hölderlin, Adorno returns to Benjamin's essay "Two Poems by Friedrich Hölderlin."[29] By drawing on Benjamin's critical commentary, Adorno proposes to develop a genuinely philosophical approach to that which is "indispensably aesthetic" in Hölderlin's poetry—namely, what Benjamin designates as "the poetized."[30] A key source in this effort is Benjamin's analysis of the peculiar "seriality" of Hölderlin's poetry that Adorno classifies as "parataxis." Paratactic presentation in Hölderlin's late verse, according to Adorno, "gently suspends the traditional logic of synthesis" and substitutes for it what he calls a logic of "aconceptual synthesis" (*begrifflose Synthesis*). The seriality of Hölderlinian poetry releases language from being "chained" to the traditional form of conceptual thinking according to which the particular is subsumed by the general concept in a synthetic judgment on the part of the subject. As it enacts an "aconceptual synthesis," Adorno argues, Hölderlin's paratactic verse runs counter to language understood as a "mimetic-expressive" medium:

> Benjamin captured this state of affairs descriptively in the concept of the series (*mit dem Begriff der Reihe*): "So that here, at the center of the poem, human beings, divinities, and princes are arranged serially, catapulted, as it were, out of their old orderings." What Benjamin links with Hölderlin's metaphysics as a balancing of the sphere of the living and the divine also names Hölderlin's linguistic technique. While, as Staiger correctly pointed out, Hölderlin's technique, which is tempered by Greek, is not lacking in boldly formed hypotactic constructions, still the parataxes are striking—artificial disturbances that evade the logical hierarchy of a subordinating syntax. Hölderlin is irresistibly drawn to such constructions.[31]

According to Adorno, the paratactic seriality of Hölderlin's poetry ultimately reverses the traditional interpretation of synthetic logic and elevates aconceptual language over the subject. But this disjunctive synthetic operation of language in Hölderlin does not, Adorno insists, go "beyond the subject"; rather, it mediates the subject: "Hölderlin's procedure gives an account of the fact that the subject, which misrecognizes itself as immediate and ultimate, is something thoroughly mediated" (*durchaus ein Vermitteltes*).[32] In this way, Adorno concludes, "language speaks for the subject . . . which can no longer speak for itself."[33] From this perspective the "truth content" of the poem is understood as the mediation of the subject by the aconceptual synthetic force of serial language as it breaks down subjective intention and conceptual form.

However, the passage on the seriality of Hölderlin's language that Adorno cites from Benjamin's essay belongs to a discussion not of synthesis and mediation but of life—specifically, of the radically changed "concept of life" (*Lebensbegriff*) that emerges from the specific linguistic force at issue in the serial presentation of the last version of Hölderlin's poem "Timidity" (*GS* 2.1: 111; *SW* 1: 24). Overthrown is less directly the "primacy" of the subject, than the conventional concepts of space and time as independent, self-consistent elements of experience. This overturning takes place by way of what Benjamin calls "spatiotemporal interpenetration" in the last version of the poem (*GS* 2.1: 112; *SW* 1: 25).[34] From this perspective in its initial form "The Poet's Courage" is governed by a "nonintuitive presentation of life" (*unanschauliche Lebensvorstellung*) consisting in the "lack of relation between events"—one that is replaced in "Timidity" by a new field of force in which everything is intensively and singularly interconnected (*GS* 2.1: 111; *SW* 1: 24). Benjamin emphasizes that the "impenetrability" of this force field is accessible only by feeling. The difference is specifically one of a radically changed feeling for life: a feeling for the singular mortality and finitude to which both humans and gods are subordinated in the second version of the poem.[35] In the first version of the poem, the life and in particular the death of the poet gives the feeling of a virtuous attitude (courage) toward a specifically human destiny (the finitude of life that is reserved for humans in the first version of the poem). The feeling of life expressed by the death of the poet in the first version takes place in a space and time, in which the relation between mortals and immortals has yet to be determined by the spatiotemporal interpenetration and finitude of the poetized—what Benjamin calls "life in poetry" (*Leben im Gesang*) by which both mortals and immortals are ultimately defined in the later version of the poem (*GS* 2.1: 113; *SW* 1: 26).

The difference between this focus on a changed "concept of life" and Adorno's stress on genuinely dialectical "aconceptual" synthesis when it comes to the serial or paratactic quality of Hölderlin's poetry becomes clear in the divergent approaches taken by Benjamin and Adorno to the first stanza of "Timidity" and in particular to the key lines "Therefore, my genius, only step / Nakedly into life, and have no care!" (*Drum, mein Genius! Tritt nur / Bar ins Leben, und sorge nicht!*). Adorno appears to take his cue from Benjamin: the passage from "Parataxis" focused on these lines culminates in an allusion to Benjamin's comments on "passivity" and "non-violence."[36] Yet the interpretation advanced elides what Benjamin regards as the decisive change instituted by the version of the poem that bears the title "Timidity." Adorno interprets the action of the poet in these lines as a mode of spirit "that defines itself as nature through self-reflection." Adorno elaborates:

> Genius would be consciousness of the nonidentical object. To use one of Hölderlin's favorite terms, the world of genius is *"das Offene,"* that which is open and as such familiar, that which is no longer dressed and prepared and thereby alienated: *"So komm! Dass wir das Offene schauen, / Das sein Eigenes wir suchen, so weit es auch ist"* ("So come, let us scan the open spaces, / Search for the thing that is ours, however distant it is") ("Brot und Wein").[37] The "thing that is ours" contains the Hegelian presence (*Dabeisein*) of the subject, of that which illuminates; it is not a primordial homeland.[38]

Adorno insists on giving priority to the "genius" of these lines, in order ultimately to subordinate it through mediation, and he interprets "bareness" as a quality of this figure: "If in '*Blödigkeit*' genius is called '*bar*' (naked), it is that naked and unarmed quality that distinguishes it from the prevailing spirit."[39] Significantly Adorno interprets "Timidity" by way of recourse to "Poet's Courage," citing the earlier version of the poem twice as revealing the meaning of the later version of the poem—precisely the reverse of Benjamin's procedure. Indeed, Adorno insists explicitly on the earlier version of the first stanza in which the genius "wanders forth defenseless / through life" that Benjamin singles out as governed by a preliminary "nonintuitive" concept of life that is overcome in "Timidity."[40] By contrast with Adorno, Benjamin stresses the transitive aspect of Hölderlin's phrase *"der Dichter tritt ins Leben, er wandelt nicht in ihm fort"* (the poet *enters into* life; he does not wander forth in it (*GS* 2.1: 116; *SW* 1: 28). Thus, the word *bar* is not an adjective assigning an attribute to the poet, as Adorno asserts, but rather an adverb modifying the action of the poet. Critical for Benjamin is the difference between life as a preexisting space and time and as a dynamic field of singularly finite movement (the shift is from the dative *in dem Leben* to the accusative *ins Leben*). In "Poet's Courage," Benjamin argues, "'life' lies outside poetic existence; in the new version it is not a precondition but the object of a movement accomplished with a mighty freedom: the poet *enters into* life; he does not wander forth in it" (*GS* 2.1: 116; *SW* 1: 28).[41]

The life into which the poet steps is one where everything passes away. It is the life (and death) that appears as Ottilie in Goethe's *Elective Affinities*. The poet of "Timidity," along with the people and the gods, enters into what Benjamin describes as the "infinite and at the same time limiting" life in the service of the poem—in a movement that transposes all into a sphere of "signs and writing" (*Zeichen und Schrift*) (*GS* 2.1: 121 and 116; *SW* 1: 32 and 28). From the perspective of Benjamin's philological method this is the sphere in which history can be viewed as a text. In this context philological wonder—the surprising effects of linguistic juxtapositionings and mirrorings—is the only beginning for historical experience. Adorno was wary of this sphere in 1938, and he does not enter into it when he returns to Benjamin's essay on Hölderlin in 1963, even though it surrounds the discussion of seriality in the latter. Unmediated occurrences become possible in such a context, and it is understandable from the perspective of historical materialism that one would harbor suspicion toward a philology that, like Marx's "professional conspirator," attempts "artificially" to improvise a revolution without the necessary conditions, which is to say, without "mediation" (*GS* 1.2: 518; *SW* 4: 6). Yet, if Adorno remains unable to make space in his critical theory for Benjamin's "philological attitude"—if a methodological gap persists between the dialectical theory of the one and the dialectical image of the other—the door has remained open for yet others to reassess the significance of Benjamin's philological method within his critical writings as a whole in no small part due to Adorno's efforts. The fundamental importance of this methodological development in Benjamin's work seems not to have been recognized by his contemporary readers, including even Adorno who nevertheless took it seriously enough to reject it explicitly as theoretically inadequate. It was also not appreciated in the initial critical reception of the writings that appeared in the two-volume *Schriften* in 1955 and in the collections edited by Hannah Arendt and Peter Demetz in the 1960s and 1970s under the titles *Illuminations* and *Reflections*. But the editorial labor led by Tiedemann, Adorno's student and later assistant, along with that of teams of scholars and translators working in several languages, have made it possible in the intervening decades to retrace the outlines of a distinctive and fundamentally important philological project in Benjamin's work starting in the early essay on Hölderlin, continuing through the dissertation on romanticism and essay on Goethe, and extending into the late work on Baudelaire.[42] It has now become possible, in other words, for the significance of what Benjamin calls "the genuinely philological attitude" and what I am calling the philology of life to come to light in his writings.

Other factors have also contributed to this possibility. I mentioned at the outset the renewal of interest in the question of life in the wake of Michel Foucault's work in the late 1970s on "biopolitics" and Giorgio Agamben's subsequent interpretation of Benjamin's remarks on "bare life" in that context. There has also been what Paul de Man described in 1982 as a "return to philology" in some quarters of literary studies in Europe and North America that has helped prepare the ground for an excavation of the philology of life in Benjamin's work.[43] To be mentioned as well is the impact more broadly of poststructuralist theories of language and in particular that of Derrida's work on the significance of language in the text of philosophy, which has some underlying parallels to Benjamin's intellectual project with regard to a critique of phenomenology from the perspective of a certain understanding of what I called the language-character of experience above in chapter 3. These intellectual developments, and others, have provided conditions for an appreciation of the links between philology and life in Benjamin's work. In the end, however, this called for the detailed reading of his early philological studies of Hölderlin, the romantics, and Goethe, which would not have been possible if Adorno had not rescued them from the wreckage of the war.

ACKNOWLEDGMENTS

I would like to acknowledge and thank the remarkable set of friends and colleagues who have shared their insights on Benjamin's work over the past three decades, in particular, Howard Eiland, Peter Fenves, and Samuel Weber. Gratitude is due as well to Susan Bernstein and Thomas Schestag who kindly read drafts of portions of this study while it was in preparation. I am grateful to the series editors at Fordham University Press, Jacques Lezra and Paul North, for their interest in this work. My sincere thanks also goes out to my colleagues in the Office of the Dean of the Faculty at Brown University who, with their diligence, skill, and good humor, gave me the peace of mind that allowed me to devote time here and there to this project over the past eight years. Most fundamentally, I thank my daughters, Sara and Emily, and my wife, Ourida, to whom this book is dedicated in memory of our time together during the plague years as it was being completed.

APPENDIX: SOURCES FOR BENJAMIN'S "GOETHE'S ELECTIVE AFFINITIES" (1924–25)

Note: Sources are based on Rolf Tiedemann's notes to *GS* 1.3: 858–67.

PRIMARY WORKS BY GOETHE CITED BY BENJAMIN

Goethe, Johann Wolfgang von. *Die Wahlverwandtschaften.*
———. *Dichtung und Wahrheit.*
———. *Faust. 2. Teil.*
———. "Fragment über die Natur."
———. *West-östlicher Divan.*
———. *Wilhelm Meister.*
———. *Winckelmann und Sein Jahrhundert in Briefen und Aufsätzen.*
———. *Zur Farbenlehre.*

SECONDARY WORKS CITED BY BENJAMIN

Abeken, B. R. "Ueber Goethes Wahlverwandtschaften," in *Goethe ueber seine Dichtungen.* Frankfurt am Main, 1901.
Bachofen, Johann Jakob. *Das Mutterrecht. Eine Untersuchung über die Gynaikokratie der alten Welt nach ihrer religiösen und rechtlichen Natur*, 2nd ed. Basel, 1897.
Baumgarten, Alexander. *Göthe. Sein Leben und Seine Werke.* Freiburg im Bresgau, 1885.
Bielschowsky, Albert. *Goethe. Sein Leben und seine Werke*, vol. 2. Munich, 1907.
Boll, Franz. *Sternglaube und Sterndeutung. Die Geschichte und das Wesen der Astrologie.* Leipzig/Berlin, 1918.
Cohen, Hermann. *Äesthetik des reinen Gefühls.* Berlin, 1912.
———. *Die dramatische Idee in Mozarts Operntexten.* Berlin, 1915.

Dante, Alighieri. *Inferno, Divina Commedia*. Trans. Stefan George. Berlin, 1921.
François-Poncet, André. *Les Affinités Électives de Goethe*. Paris, 1910.
George, Stefan. *Der siebente Ring*. Berlin, 1907.
Gervinus, G. G. *Über den Göthischen Briefwechsel*. Leipzig, 1836.
Gundolf, Friedrich. *Goethe*, 4th ed. Berlin, 1918.
Hebbel, Friedrich. "Vorwort zur 'Maria Magdalene,'" in *Werke in Zehn Teilen*. Berlin/Leipzig/Wien/Stuttgart, 1910.
Hölderlin, Friedrich. "Anmerkungen zum Ödipus" and "Hölderlin an Casimir Böhlendorf," in *Übersetzungen und Briefe. 1800–1806*. Munich/Leipzig, 1913.
———. "Blödigkeit," in *Gedichte. 1800–1806*. Munich/Leipzig, 1916.
Humboldt, Wilhelm von, an seine Frau 6. 3. 1809, in *Goethe in vertraulichen Briefen seiner Zeitgenossen*. Berlin, 1921.
Jacobi, Friedrich Heinrich, an J. F. Köppen 12. 1. 1810, in *Goethe in vertraulichen Briefen seiner Zeitgenossen*. Berlin, 1921.
Kant, Immanuel. *Die Metaphysik der Sitten*. Berlin, 1914.
———. *Grundlegung zur Metaphysik der Sitten*. Berlin, 1911.
———. *Kritik der* Urtheilskraft. Berlin, 1913.
Kloptock, Friedrich Gottlieb. "Die Grazien," in *Sämtliche Werke*. Leipzig, 1839.
Meyer, Richard M. *Goethe*. Berlin, 1905.
Mézières, A. W. *Goethe*. Paris, 1874.
Schmidt, Julian. *Geschichte der Deutschen Literatur seit Lessings Tod*. Leipzig, 1866.
Scholem, Gerhard. "Lyrik der Kabbala?" *Der Jude*. Berlin, 1921.
Simmel, Georg. *Goethe*. Leipzig, 1913.
Solger, Karl Wilhelm Ferdinand. "Über die Wahlverwandtschaften" (1809), in *Nachgelassene Schriften und Briefwechsel*. Leipzig, 1826.
Stael-Holstein, Madame la Baronne de. *De l'Allemagne*. Paris, 1861.
Werner, Zacharias. "Die Wahlverwandtschaften," in *Goethe und die Romantik*. Weimar, 1899.

COLLECTIONS OF LETTERS AND CONVERSATIONS
CITED BY BENJAMIN

Briefwechsel zwischen Goethe und Zelter in den Jahren 1796 bis 1832. Berlin, 1834.
Goethes Briefwechsel mit einem. Jena, 1906.
Goethes Gespräche. Leipzig, 1909.
Goethe ueber seine Dichtungen. Frankfurt am Main, 1901.

NOTES

INTRODUCTION: THE PHILOLOGY OF LIFE

1. *Poetic Force: Poetry after Kant* (Stanford: Stanford University Press, 2014).

2. In *Origin of the German Trauerspiel*, Benjamin describes the way in which nature and history become "entangled" in the emergence of the allegorical sign (*GS* 1.1: 344 and 378; *Origin of the German Trauerspiel*, trans. Howard Eiland [Cambridge, Mass.: Harvard University Press, 2019], 175 and 219). In "Toward the Image in Proust," time becomes subject to "entanglement" in the image (*GS* 2.1: 320–21; *SW* 2: 244–45).

3. See *GS* 2.1: 921; and Gershom Scholem, *Walter Benjamin—Die Geschichte einer Freundschaft* (Frankfurt am Main: Suhrkamp, 1975), 26.

4. This failure became definitive in the summer of 1925 when the philosophy faculty at the University of Frankfurt voted to request that Benjamin withdraw his habilitation thesis (subsequently published in 1928 by Rowolt Verlag as *Ursprung des deutschen Trauerspiels*). See Howard Eiland and Michael W. Jennings, *Walter Benjamin: A Critical Life* (Cambridge, Mass.: Harvard University Press, 2014), 231–34.

5. For a detailed and illuminating account of Benjamin's existence during these years, see Eiland and Jennings, *Walter Benjamin: A Critical Life*, 75–176.

6. This is the philological time that Benjamin describes in notes composed in 1918 as one in which the "uni-directionality" of history "inclines in the end toward the cyclical" (*GS* 6: 94). The understanding of philology in this chapter and throughout this book has been profoundly shaped by Peter Fenves's rich study *The Messianic Reduction: Walter Benjamin and the Shape of Time* (Stanford: Stanford University Press,

2011). On this definition of a time that tends to the cyclical, see especially *The Messianic Reduction*, 240–42.

7. The passage in question is from Benjamin's "Goethe's Elective Affinities" (*GS* 1.1: 165–66; *SW* 1: 328–29). I will return to consider it in detail in chapter 3.

8. Johann Wolfgang von Goethe, *Sämtliche Werke. Briefe, Tagebücher und Gespräche*, vol. 39 (Frankfurt am Main: Suhrkamp, 1999), 48–52.

9. On Goethe's technique of juxtaposition, see Goethe, "Wiederholte Spiegelungen," *Naturwissenschaftliche Schriften*, vol. 1 (Zurich: Artemis, 1964), 821–23.

10. The occurrence in "Toward the Critique of Violence" of this word—*Fortleben* (living on, or, as the published English translation reads, "continued life")—overlaps with the following passage from "The Task of the Translator," an essay that was written at the same time, namely, in 1921: "Since the important works of world literature never find their chosen translators at the time of their origin, their translation marks their stage of continued life" (*das Stadium ihres Fortlebens*) (*GS* 4.1: 10–11; *SW* 1: 254).

11. Michel Foucault, The *History of Sexuality: An Introduction*, vol. 1, trans. Robert Hurley (New York: Vintage, 1990), 140.

12. Giorgio Agamben, *Means without End: Notes on Politics*, trans. Vincenzo Binetti and Cesare Casarino (Minneapolis: University of Minnesota Press, 2000), 4 and 8. According to Agamben, a "form-of-life" is "a life that cannot be separated from its form" and that "is never prescribed by a specific biological vocation": "No matter how customary, repeated, and socially compulsory, it always retains the character of a possibility." A form-of-life or what Agamben also characterizes as "living itself" would emancipate the human being from the sovereign power of biological life (as *bíos*) that presupposes and depends upon bare life (as *zoé*). "A political life," Agamben writes, "that is, a life directed toward the idea of happiness and cohesive with a form-of-life, is thinkable only starting from the emancipation from such a division [between *zoé* and *bíos*], with the irrevocable exodus from any sovereignty" (*Means without End*, 8). The philology of life that concerns me in Benjamin's literary criticism operates in the space and time of a division that is not biological (not based on the separability of *zoé* from *bíos*) but that is also not a matter exclusively of possibility and of an ability to go beyond the biological principle.

The coherence and objectivity of the life that is at issue in this study is determined by the ambiguous possibility of a dynamic finitude confronting philology in Benjamin's sense.

13. Jacques Derrida's critique of Agamben's approach to history and time as claiming to begin always from "a decisive and founding event" may be understood as a philological intervention in the Benjaminian sense. *Séminaire. La Bête et le Souverain*, vol. 1 (Paris: Galilée, 2008), 419–21; *The Beast and the Sovereign*, vol. 1 (Chicago: University of Chicago Press, 2009), 333.

14. Walter Benjamin, *Gesammelte Briefe*, 6 vols., vol. 2 (Frankfurt am Main: Suhrkamp, 1995–2000), 137; *Correspondence, 1910–1940* (Chicago: University of Chicago Press, 1994), 176.

15. Schestag, *Philo: xenia. Erste Folge* (Basel: Urs Engeler, 2009), 48.

16. Benjamin's underlining is clear in the manuscript of the letter of February 14, 1921, to Gershom (Gerhard) Scholem, which is reproduced as part of the cover illustration for this book. Thanks are due to Stefan Litt for sending me a photograph of the letter from the National Library of Israel, Walter Benjamin Collection, ARC 4° 1598 03 64.

17. The quotation from Goethe is from a letter to Carl Friedrich Graf von Reinhard on December 31, 1809. The key phrase reads: "that poetized asserts its right like that which has taken place" (*Das Gedichtete behauptet sein Recht wie das Geschehene*). *Goethes Briefe*, vol. 3 (Hamburg: Christian Wegner Verlag, 1965), 117.

18. With regard to the definition of philology in Benjamin's February 14, 1921, letter to Scholem see Fenves, *Messianic Reduction*, 231–44.

19. The phrase "fashionable currents" is taken from the title of a book by one of Benjamin's teachers, Heinrich Rickert. This will be discussed in chapter 1.

20. Sigrid Weigel suggests that Benjamin's "concept of life" works out a "third position" beyond the opposition between "life philosophy" and natural science. See Sigrid Weigel, "Treue, Liebe, Eros. Benjamins Lebenswissenschaft in 'Goethes Wahlverwandtschaften,'" in *Benjamins Wahlverwandtschaften. Zur Kritik einer programmatischen Interpretationen* (Frankfurt am Main: Suhrkamp, 2015), 174–95, at 194.

21. On philology as friendship with language, see Werner Hamacher, *Für—Die Philologie* (Weil am Rhein: Urs Engeler, 2009), 33–34.

22. This phrase appears in a June 2, 1868, letter from Nietzsche to his friend Paul Deussen. See James I. Porter's excellent book *Nietzsche and the Philology of the Future* (Stanford: Stanford University Press, 2002), 15. As Porter observes, Nietzsche also writes of a "philologist of the future" in his notebooks on rhythm (see Friedrich Nietzsche, *Kritische Gesamptausgabe, Werke*, vol. 2.3 [Berlin: de Gruyter, 1993], 331). My next set of remarks draws on Porter's study.

23. See Porter 127–66. To compare, see Nietzsche on "atoms of time" in *Kritische Gesamtausgabe, Werke* 2.2 (Berlin: de Gruyter, 1993), 379; Porter, 85–106; and Benjamin on "atoms of writing" (*Schriftatomen*) in *Trauerspiel, GS* 1.1: 351; *Origin of the German Trauerspiel*, 185.

24. Like many of his most important intellectual entanglements, Benjamin's relation to Nietzsche is difficult to pin down to the influence of a single set of works or even a selection of specific passages from a precursor. Thus a recent book on the influence of Nietzsche on Benjamin is forced to juxtapose interpretations of key concepts in the works of each thinker. See James McFarland, *Constellation: Friedrich Nietzsche and Walter Benjamin in the Now-Time of History* (New York: Fordham University Press, 2013). Benjamin deals directly, of course, with *The Birth of Tragedy* in *Origin of the German Trauerspiel* and with the notes on the eternal return in *The Arcades Project*, to take just two examples. But the fundamental stance toward genuine historical experience that marks his thought from the student writings to the very last theses on history bears a profound connection to Nietzsche's critique of education, history, and philology from his Basel lectures *On the Future of Our Educational Institutions* to the *Untimely Meditations*. Benjamin read these works during his student years (see Eiland and Jennings, *Walter Benjamin: A Critical Life*, 25–26 and 65). I will come back to this point below in chapter 1.

25. The citation from Nietzsche is from the fragments collected as "We Philologists" (Friedrich Nietzsche, *Kritische Studienausgabe*, vol. 8 [Berlin: de Gruyter, 1988], 62). The quotation from Benjamin appears in his essay "Literary History and Literary Science" (*GS* 3: 290; *SW* 2: 464).

26. Uwe Steiner provides a detailed history of the text in Walter Benjamin, *Der Begriff der Kunstkritik in der deutschen Romantik, Kritische Gesamptausgabe*, vol. 3 (Frankfurt am Main: Suhrkamp, 2008), 165–205.

27. See Fenves, *Messianic Reduction*, 232–34.

28. Here is Benjamin's description in his late "On Some Motifs in Baudelaire": "Since the end of the nineteenth century, philosophy has made a series of attempts to grasp 'true' experience, as opposed to the kind that manifests itself in the standardized, denatured life of the civilized masses. These efforts are usually classified under the rubric of 'the philosophy of life' (*Lebensphilosophie*)" (*GS* 1.2: 608; *SW* 4: 314).

1. "TWO POEMS BY FRIEDRICH HÖLDERLIN"

1. "The Life of Students" draws on two lectures delivered by Benjamin in May and June of 1914 as part of his activity in the so-called youth movement and in particular as president of the Berlin Independent Students' Association. The essay was composed, however, after August 1914, when Heinle committed suicide, and appeared first in *Die Neue Merkur. Monatschrift für geistiges Leben* in September 1915 and in an expanded second version in *Das Ziel. Aufruf zu tätigen Geist* in 1916 (see *GS* 2.3: 916). According to the *Gesammelte Schriften*, Benjamin's first published work was "Sleeping Beauty," published in March 1911 in *Der Anfang. Vereinigte Zeitschriften der Jugend* and signed "Ardor-Berlin" (a version of a pseudonym used by Benjamin in several of his earliest publications). The first text published by Benjamin under his own name was "Moral Lessons," which appeared in *Die Freie Schulgemeinde* in July 1913 (*GS* 2.3: 889 and 899). On the biographical and historical background of Benjamin's "The Life of Students," see Johannes Steizinger, *Revolte, Eros und Sprache. Walter Benjamins "Metaphysik der Jugend"* (Berlin: Kulturverlag Kadmos, 2013), 135–58.

2. Gershom Scholem, *Tagebücher, nebst Aufsätzen und Entwürfen bis 1923*, 2 vols., vol. 1 (Frankfurt am Main: Jüdischer Verlag, 1995–2000), 390. Fenves provides a translation of this passage from Scholem's diary. Peter Fenves, *The Messianic Reduction: Walter Benjamin and the Shape of Time* (Stanford: Stanford University Press, 2011), 256.

3. Scholem notes in the account of this conversation given in his diary the following: "Time is indeed a course, but is time directed? For it is a thoroughly metaphysical assertion that time is like a straight line; perhaps it is a cycloid or something else, which has no direction at many points" (*Tagebücher*, vol. 1, 391; Fenves, *Messianic Reduction*, 256).

4. Fenves, *Messianic Reduction*, 107.

5. From the perspective of progressive time and conventional history as adopted by the German students, according to Benjamin, their years appear as an empty and "irrational period of waiting" for adulthood that must be filled with enjoyment: "German students are to a greater or lesser degree obsessed with the idea that they have to enjoy their youth. The entirely irrational period of waiting for marriage and profession had to be given some content and it had to be a playful, pseudo-romantic one that would help pass the time" (*GS* 2.1: 85; *SW1*: 45).

6. Walter Benjamin, *Gesammelte Briefe*, 6 vols., vol. 2 (Frankfurt am Main: Suhrkamp, 1995–2000), 137; *Correspondence, 1910–1940* (Chicago: University of Chicago Press, 1994), 176.

7. See Howard Eiland and Michael W. Jennings, *Walter Benjamin: A Critical Life* (Cambridge, Mass.: Harvard University Press, 2014), 65.

8. See, for example, Edmund Husserl, "Ideen zu einer reinen Phänomenologie und phänomenologischen Philosophie. Erstes Buch: Allgemeine Einführung in die reine Phänomenologie," in *Husserliana*, vol. 3.1. (Den Hag: Martinus Nijhoff, 1950), 121; *Ideas for a Pure Phenomenology and Phenomenological Philosophy*, trans. D. Dahlstrom (Indianapolis: Hackett, 2014), 104.

9. Henri Bergson, "Introduction à la métaphysique," in *La pensée et le mouvant* (Paris: Presses Universitaires de France, 2009), 177–277, at 183; *Introduction to Metaphysics*, trans. T. E. Hulme (Indianapolis: Bobbs-Merrill, 1949), 26. This essay was originally published in the *Revue de métaphysique et de morale* in 1903. Aging is also the subject of an important passage in the first chapter of *L'évolution créatrice*, which first appeared in 1907 (Paris: Presses Universitaires de France, 2009), 17–21; *Creative Evolution*, trans. Arthur Mitchell (New York: Henry Holt, 1911), 17–21. The notes in the 2009 edition of *L'évolution créatrice* provide an overview of the sources in relation to which Bergson develops his theory of aging (see 400–2).

10. Crucial to this development is the reception of Bergson's work in German philosophy during this period. For a comprehensive overview, see Caterina Zanfi, *Bergson et la philosophie allemande. 1907–1932* (Paris: Armand Colin, 2013).

11. See Uwe Steiner, "The True Politician: Walter Benjamin's Concept of the Political," trans. Colin Sample, *New German Critique* 83 (2001): 43–88, at 54. For an incisive account of how Benjamin and Heidegger become

"entangled" in Rickert's "system," in particular with respect to the concept of "mere life," see Peter Fenves, "Entanglement—Of Benjamin with Heidegger" in *Sparks Will Fly: Benjamin and Heidegger*, ed. Andrew Benjamin and Dimitris Vardoulakis (Albany: State University of New York Press, 2015), 5–14. I am indebted to Fenves's analysis of the entire question of Benjamin's relation to Rickert's concept of *Voll-Endung* and of how it diverges from that of Heidegger. Fenves suggests that Benjamin's philosophical-political project as laid out in "Toward the Critique of Violence" is a "philosophy of life that is neither *Lebensphilosophie* nor value philosophy"—a critique of *Lebensphilosophie* that also does not respond to Rickert's call for the "completion" of "mere life" through the construction of a system of value (Fenves, "Entanglement," 14). For some comments on the relevance of *Lebensphilosophie* and Rickert to Benjamin's study of Goethe in particular, see Steiner, "Exemplarische Kritik. Anmerkungen zu Benamins Kritik der Wahlverwandtschaften," in *Benjamins Wahlverwandtschaften: Zur Kritik einer programmatischen Interpretation*, ed. Helmut Hühn, Jan Urbich, and Uwe Steiner (Frankfurt am Main: Suhrkamp, 2015), 37–67, 50–54.

12. Rickert, *Die Philosophie des Lebens. Darstellung und Kritik der philosophischen Modeströmmungen unserer Zeit* (Tübingen: Verlag von Mohr, 1920), 28–29.

13. Rickert, *Die Philosophie des Lebens*, vii.

14. Rickert, *Die Philosophie des Lebens*, xiv. The connection of Benjamin's philosophical project to Rickert's critique of "*mere* life" in *Lebensphilosophie* is somewhat obscured by Giorgio Agamben's derivation of his influential concept of "bare life" from Benjamin's use of the phrase *bloßes Leben* in his essay "Toward the Critique of Violence." Recently, a number of scholars have pointed out that Agamben neglects the importance of the neo-Kantian critique of *Lebensphilosophie* in his account of the emergence of the phrase *bloßes Leben* in Benjamin's work by relying too heavily on Foucault's concept of biopower. Carlo Salzani, for example, concisely describes Agamben's transposition of Benjamin's use of the phrase "*bloßes Leben*" out of the context of the Neokantian critique of *Lebensphilosophie* and into the terms of Foucault's concept of "biopolitics":

> [He] extracts the syntagm *bloßes Leben* from its context (the turn-of-the-century, Nietzsche-influenced *Lebensphilosophie* and its Neo-Kantian critique) and

transposes it into a different context, that of a Foucault-inspired critique of biopolitics structured, however, along the (spatial) lines of Schmitt's *nomos* and theory of sovereignty. The two notions—"mere life" in Benjamin and "bare life" in Agamben—ultimately differ to such a point that they must be considered independent from one another. (Carlo Salzani, "From Benjamin's *bloßes Leben* to Agamben's *Nuda Vita*: A Genealogy," in *Towards the Critique of Violence: Walter Benjamin and Giorgio Agamben*, ed. Brendan Moran and Carlo Salzani [London: Bloomsbury, 2015], 109–23, at 117)

15. Fenves, "Entanglement," 13.
16. Rickert, *Die Philosophie des Lebens*, 178–79.
17. Rickert, *Die Philosophie des Lebens*, 179n1.
18. As Richard Gray observes, Nietzsche's fragments gathered together under the title "Wir Philologen" "could well have been called 'Vom Nutzen und Nachteil der Philologie für das Leben.'" Richard Gray, "Skeptische Philologie: Friedrich Schlegel, Friedrich Nietzsche und eine Philologie der Zukunft," *Nietzsche-Studien* 38 (2009): 39–64, at 46.
19. References to this article are to Heinrich Rickert, "Vom System der Werte," *Logos: Internationale Zeitschrift für Philosophie der Kultur* 4 (1913): 295–327. Fenves cites the notes from Rickert's summer semester 1913 lecture course (in the Heidelberg University archives) as presenting his philosophy of "completed life" as a superior alternative to *Lebensphilosophie*. See Peter Fenves, "Completion Instead of Revelation," in *Walter Benjamin and Theology* (New York: Fordham University Press, 2016), 56–74, at 57–58. Letters from this period document that both Benjamin and Heidegger attended this course.
20. Rickert, "Vom System," 295.
21. Rickert, "Vom System," 301.
22. Rickert, "Vom System," 303.
23. Rickert, "Vom System," 299.
24. Rickert, "Vom System," 297.
25. These immanent modes of completion are themselves superseded by a third atemporal or transcendental *Voll-Endung* of "eternal goods" that combines the advantages and eliminates the disadvantages of the two lower regions of completion ("Vom System," 304–5).
26. Ricket, "Vom System," 303.
27. Rickert, "Vom System," 304.

28. See Martin Heidegger, *Zur Bestimmung der Philosophie. 1. Die Idee der Philosophie und das Weltanschauungsproblem; 2. Phänomenologie und transzendentale Wertphilosophie; Anhang: Über das Wesen der Universität und des akademischen Studiums, Gesamtausgabe*, vols. 56–57 (Frankfurt am Main: Vittorio Klostermann, 1987), 129–203, and *Phänomenologische Interpretationen zu Aristoteles. Einführung in die phänomenologische Forschung, Gesamtausgabe*, vol. 61 (Frankfurt am Main: Vittorio Klostermann, 1985), 80–83.

29. Indeed, even the word *method* recalls Hermann Cohen's *infinitesimalmethode*. The use of the term "limit-concept" (*Grenzbegriff*) may allude to Cohen's discussion of this in *Kants Theorie der Erfahrung*, 2nd ed. (Berlin: Dümmler, 1885), especially 507–8). Wilhelm Windelband also evokes this concept in his *Geschichte der neueren Philosophie in ihrem Zusammenhange mit der allgemeinen Kultur und den besonderen Wissenschaften*, vol. 2 (Leipzig: Breitkopf and Härtel, 1911) in the same section that is cited by Benjamin in his dissertation on romanticism (see 225–26; I will return to this in the next chapter). Cohen's treatment of "the task" (*die Aufgabe*) that is set forth by the Kantian "thing-in-itself"—what he calls the "limiting task" (*Begrenzungs-Aufgabe*)—also illuminates the role assigned to it in relation to life in Benjamin's essay (see Cohen, *Kants Theorie der Erfahrung*, 519–20).

30. The tension between the aesthetic critique and the philological commentary corresponds to what Fenves insightfully describes as Benjamin's explication in "Timidity" of a structure that "combines—without synthesizing—the antithetical philosophical programs undertaken by Bergson on the one hand and by the Marburg School on the other" (Fenves, *Messianic Reduction*, 31).

31. Goethe's statement can be found in his December 31, 1809, letter to Carl Friedrich von Reinhard (*Goethes Briefe*, vol. 3 [Hamburg: Christian Wegner, 1965], 117).

32. See Dilthey, *Grundlegung der Wissenschaften vom Menschen, der Gesellschaft under der Geschichte, Gesammelte Schriften*, vol. 19 (Göttingen: Vandenhoeck and Ruprecht, 1982), 103; and "Die Typen der Weltanschauung und ihre Ausbildung in den metaphysischen Systemen," in *Weltanschauung. Philosophie und Religion* (Berlin: Reichl, 1911), 3–54, at 19. Another context for Benjamin's remarks is Hegel's characterization of the

"excessive warmth" of certain modern poetry, in which the genuine force of the ancient prophets becomes "cold and abstract." Hegel cites the poems of Klopstock as exemplifying this quality (Georg Wilhelm Friedrich Hegel, *Vorlesung über die Ästhetik* 3, *Werke*, vol. 15 (Frankfurt am Main: Suhrkamp, 1986), 453–54.

33. As Fenves has pointed out, the earlier and later versions of the poem correspond in neo-Kantian terms (specifically, those developed by Cassirer) to a logic of substance, on the one hand, and function, on the other (Fenves, *Messianic Reduction*, 18–43).

34. Hölderlin used Gottlob Heyne's 1798 edition of Pindar, not Boeckh's, which did not appear until 1811. See David Constantine, "Hölderlin's Pindar: The Language of Translation," *The Modern Language Review* 73.4 (October 1978): 825–34, at 825–26.

35. See Maria G. Xanthou, "Ludolph Dissen, August Boeckh, Gottfried Hermann and Tycho Mommsen: Tracing *Asyndeton*, Steering Influence," *Bulletin of the Institute of Classical Studies* 57.2 (December 3, 2014): 1–21. Xanthou provides an instructive overview of the philological dispute over asyndeton from Boeckh through Dissen to Gottfried Hermann's critique of Dissen's edition and ultimately Tycho Mommsen's reconciliation of the arguments of both sides in the late nineteenth century. Xanthou observes that Hermann's criticism of Boeckh and Dissen led to the recognition of "the need for the definition of '*Unverbundenheit*'" (disconnectedness; my translation) (Xanthou, 21). Xanthou concludes with a comment that gestures toward the interpretation of Benjamin's philological approach under consideration in this book: "This question [of clarifying the connections in Pindar's asyndeta] seems to have almost philosophical bearings and it helped to restrain a latent '*horror coniunctionis*' in Boeckh's and Dissen's theories of *asyndeton*" (Xanthou, 21).

36. *GS* 1.1: 208; *Origin of the German Trauerspiel*, trans. Howard Eiland (Cambridge, Mass.: Harvard University Press, 2019), 2. The translation of the German *Umweg* as "undirection" is meant to indicate a connection between this methodological comment in the preface to the *Origin of the German Trauerspiel* and the philological theory developed in the years leading up to this study. Benjamin's statement that "method is undirection" (*Methode ist Umweg*) places a clever turn on Friedrich Gundolf's famous dictum, "method is lived experience" (*Methode ist Erlebnis*). In the second

edition of this work, Gundolf revises this sentence to read "method is the kind of lived experience" (*Methode ist Erlebnisart*). Friedrich Gundolf, *Shakespeare und der deutsche Geist*, 2nd ed. (Berlin: Bondi, 1914), viii. Benjamin includes the 1911 edition in his list of readings on romanticism (see Steiner's edition of *Der Begriff der Kunstkritik in der deutschen Romantik* in the Kritische Gesamtausgabe of *Werke und Nachlaß*, vol 3 (Frankfurt am Main: Suhrkamp, 2008), 155.

37. On the inside-out movement of the image in the last strophe of "Timidity," as the god is trapped or bagged by the poets, see my *Poetic Force* (Stanford: Stanford University Press, 2014), 24–25.

38. The interpretation of the significance of the word *gelegen* is informed by Samuel Weber's remarks in *Targets of Opportunity: On the Militarization of Thinking* (New York: Fordham University Press, 2005), 125–33.

39. *Verlagerung* can be translated as "dislocation" or "shifting." Significantly, it is also used in geological discourse to describe the "drifting of the continents" (*Verlagerung der Kontinenten*) or the underlying "shifting" of the earth's magnetic poles (*Polverlagerung*). Alfred Wegener used the word *Verlagerung* in the latter phrase in the 1912 article in which he proposed the theory of continental drift (see Alfred Wegener, "Die Entstehung der Kontinente," *Geologische Rundschau* 3.4 (1912): 276–92, at 277). This geological signification of *Verlagerung* is in line with Benjamin's use of the word *Geschichte* in his 1921 letter to Scholem on philology. *Verlagerung des Mythologischen* (shifting of the mythological) also plays on *die Wahrheit der Lage* (the truth of the layout).

40. Hans Jürgen Scheuer, "Verlagerung des Mythos in die Struktur. Hölderlins Bearbeitung des Orpheus-Todes in der Odenfolge Muth des Dichters—Dichtermuth—Blödigkeit," *Jahrbuch der deutschen Schillergesellschaft* 45 (2001): 250–77, at 258. Scheuer traces this "shifting of the mythological" through a detailed analysis of the drafts of the poem, the manuscripts of which are available in facsimile in volumes 4 and 5 of the Frankfurter Hölderlin-Ausgabe edited by Dietrich E. Sattler. With regard to the three mythologemes to which I allude, Scheuer considers the sources in Ovid, *Metamorphoses* 11.1–70 (on Orpheus) and 2.49–62 (on Phaeton) and in Homer, *Odyssey* 5.333–350 (on Odysseus).

41. Scheuer, "Verlagerung des Mythos in die Struktur," 258.

42. Scheuer, "Verlagerung des Mythos in die Struktur," 265–66.
43. Scheuer, "Verlagerung des Mythos in die Struktur," 265.
44. "There is a fine art of passion, but an impassioned fine art is a contradiction in terms, for the infallible effect of the beautiful is emancipation from the passions." Friedrich Schlegel, *On the Aesthetic Education of Man*, trans. Keith Tribe (New York: Penguin, 2016), 64.
45. Friedrich Hölderlin, "Half of Life":

With its yellow pears
And wild roses everywhere
The shore hangs into the lake,
O gracious swans,
And drunk with kisses
You dip your heads
In the sobering holy water.

Ah, where will I find
Flowers, come winter,
And where the sunshine
And shade of the earth?
Walls stand cold
And speechless, in the wind
The weathervanes creak.
(Friedrich Hölderlin, "Half of Life," *Hymns and Fragments*, trans. Richard Sieburth [Princeton: Princeton University Press, 1984], 47)

46. On the swan song, see Michael Jakob, "*Schwanengefahr*": *Das lyrische Ich im Zeichen des Schwanns* (Munich: Hanser, 2000). On the "speechless" walls of Hölderlin's "Half of Life," see Werner Hamacher, *Two Studies of Friedrich Hölderlin*, trans. Julia Ng and Anthony Curtis Adler (Stanford: Stanford University Press, 2020), 159–63.
47. Winfried Menninghaus, *Hälfte des Lebens: Versuch über Hölderlins Poetik* (Frankfurt am Main: Suhrkamp, 2005).
48. Menninghaus, *Hälfte des Lebens*, 75.
49. Friedrich Schlegel, *Kritische Friedrich-Schlege-Ausgabe*, vol. 11 (Paderborn: Ferdinand Schöningh, 1964), 61–62.
50. Friedrich Hölderlin, *Sämtliche Werke*, 8 vols., vol. 4 (Stuttgart: Kohlhammer, 1946–85), 197. This sentence appears in Hölderlin's master's thesis, "Geschichte der schönen Künste unter den Griechen." In his massive

two-volume 1928 biography of Hölderlin, Wilhelm Böhm comments: "Unconsciously [Hölderlin] describes himself and the secret of his own poetry." Wilhelm Böhm, *Hölderlin*, vol. 1 (Berlin: Max Niemeyer, 1928), 41.

51. On Sappho's "invention" of the Adonic in her lament for the death of Adonis, Menninghaus cites Marius Plotius Sacerdos, *Artes grammaticae* in: *Grammatici latini*, vol. 6, ed. Heinrich Keil (Leipzig: Teubner, 1874), 516.

52. Menninghaus, *Hälfte des Lebens*, 19.

53. Friedrich Hölderlin, "Zwei Briefe an Casimir Ulrich Böhlendorff," *Sämtliche Werke*, vol. 6, 425–27; *Essays and Letters on Theory*, trans. Thomas Pfau (Albany: State University of New York Press, 1988), 149–51. Benjamin also cites this letter along with the *Annotations on Oedipus* in a key passage of his essay on Goethe's *Elective Affinities* (*GS* 1.1: 181–82; *SW* 1: 340–41). I will come back to this passage in chapter 3. The 1801 letter to Böhlendorff is among those contained in Benjamin's file titled "German Letters 1" that was assembled in preparation for the series published in the *Frankfurter Zeitung* in 1931 and 1932 and then later in the volume *Deutsche Menschen* that appeared in 1936. Ultimately Benjamin decided to publish a subsequent letter from Hölderlin to Böhlendorff (from 1802). The headnote composed by Benjamin for the set of three letters that includes the earlier 1801 letter from Hölderlin to Böhlendorff alludes to the "secret Germany" that would be revealed to the Germans by the collection of letters. This headnote points to the critical intervention Benjamin sought to make in the experience of German letters during these years: "The intention of this series is, rather, to reveal the lineaments of a 'secret Germany' that people nowadays would much prefer to shroud in a heavy mist. For a secret Germany really exists. It is merely that its secretness is not simply the expression of its inwardness and depth, but—albeit in a different sense—the product of raucous and brutal forces that have prevented it from playing an effective role in public life and have condemned it to a secret one. . . . Hölderlin confronts them as never before with the figure of the genius. . . . And although Hölderlin's letters were read, they were misunderstood most in what they said to the Germans about Germany" (*GS* 4: 945; *SW* 2: 466). The "secret," in other words, lies in the extremely difficult relation to national poetic property and possession set forth by the theory of the "free use of the own" in the 1801 letter.

54. According to Menninghaus's interpretation, this double inversion of this theory involves, on the one hand, the formal power of ancient verse to turn against or to invert through poetic formalization the pathos that is natural or native to the Greeks and, on the other, the poetry of the moderns that inverts the formalization of oriental pathos in Greek poetry (*Sämtliche Werke*, vol. 6, 426; *Essays and Letters*, 149). However, because the Greeks' inversion took the form of a "denial" of their native pathos, Menninghaus argues, ancient Hellenic verse offers no direct way back to the pathos of which this poetry is the complement. For the modern poet, ancient Greek poetry is, in other words, irreducibly complementary with regard to its original pathos. As suggested by his use of the Freudian term "denial" (*Verleugnung*), Menninghaus compares the status of Greek poetry for Hölderlin to the irreducibly distorted character of the signifier in the psychoanalytic theory of repression: "If Greek art delivers the 'oriental fire' to its modern devotees only in the form of masterful denial, then there is apparently no direct access to the 'ground' out of which the Greeks have spoken. Only the exact and faithful study of the artistic achievement of denial can yield negative access to that which is denied, the traces and outlines of the 'sentiment' that is transformed into 'sobriety'" (Menninghaus, *Hälfte des Lebens*, 90). But it is not so much that the Greeks "denied" the pathos as that its innateness for them defied their attempts to master or appropriate it.

55. Here is the key passage from Hölderlin's December 4, 1801, letter to Böhlendorff:

> Hence the Greeks are less master of sacred pathos, because to them it was native, whereas they excel in their talent for presentation, beginning with Homer, because this exceptional man was sufficiently sensitive to plunder the Western Junonian sobriety for his Apollonian empire and thus to veritably appropriate what is foreign. With us it is the reverse. Hence it is so dangerous to deduce the rules of art for oneself exclusively from Greek excellence. I have labored long over this and know by now that, with the exception of what must be the highest for the Greeks and for us—namely, the living relationship and destiny (*Geschick*)—we must not share anything identical with them. (Hölderlin, "Zwei Briefe," *Sämtliche Werke*, vol. 6, 426; *Essays and Letters*, 150)

56. Hölderlin, "Anmerkungen zum Ödipus," *Sämtliche Werke*, vol. 5 (Stuttgart: Kohlhammer, 1952), 195; *Essays and Letters*, 101.

57. On Benjamin's association of speechlessness with Sappho, see Weigel, *Body- and Image-Space*, 77–79.

58. An example of Wolf's characterization of the Homeric poems as the product of a people is to be found in his remarks contrasting the Homeric texts with those attributed to Ossian. See Friedrich August Wolf, *Prolegomena to Homer, 1795*, trans. Anthony Grafton, Glenn W. Most, and James E. G. Zetzel (Princeton: Princeton University Press, 1985), 204.

59. Benjamin may be understood to approach the question of the life found in the poetized along the lines of his interpretation of divine law (*Gesetz*) in his later essay on the critique of force—lines that retrace up to a point Kant's approach to the distinction between ethical and juridical constraint. Benjamin's commentary on Hölderlin's "Timidity" and on the life that is "nothing but its own" from which it arises may allude to the poet's statement in the letter to Böhlendorff cited above concerning the "free use of its own." From this perspective, the life from which Hölderlin's poem arises for Benjamin is fundamentally ethical in Kant's sense (divine or sacred in the sense worked out in the commentary on "Timidity") in that it compels or forces itself: makes "free use of its own" (*der "freie" Gebrauch des Eigenen*) in a way, however, that resists the ownership involved in making it—life—into a means to an external end. From this perspective, the insertion of the phrase "sacredly sober" into the commentary on "Timidity" would participate in the freedom of the poem.

60. Immanuel Kant, *Gesammelte Schriften* [Akademie-Ausgabe], vol. 6 (Berlin: Reimer; later, Walter de Gruyter, 1900–present), 78–82; *Religion with the Boundaries of Mere Reason* in: *Religion and Rational Theology*, trans. Allen Wood and George di Giovanni (Cambridge: Cambridge University Press, 1996), 118–21. See Fenves, *Messianic Reduction*, 190–226. See also my *Poetic Force*, 35–36.

2. THE CONCEPT OF CRITICISM IN GERMAN ROMANTICISM

1. Samuel Weber, *Benjamin's -abilities* (Cambridge, Mass.: Harvard University Press, 2009), 21. The word "esoteric" in Weber's remarks alludes to a 1918 letter from Benjamin to Scholem.

2. This debate coalesced around Dilthey's 1883 "Einleitung in die Geisteswissenschaften" and the response by Wilhelm Windelband,

especially in "Kritische oder genetische Methode" and "Geschichte und Naturwissenschaft"—lectures delivered and published in 1883 and 1894. "Kritische oder genetische Methode," in *Präludien. Aufsätze und Reden zur Philosophie und ihrer Geschichte*, vol. 2 (Tübingen: J. C. B. Mohr, 1907), 318–44; "Geschichte und Naturwissenschaft," in *Präludien. Aufsätze und Reden zur Philosophie und ihrer Geschichte*, vol. 2 (Tübingen: J. C. B. Mohr, 1907), 355–79. See Frederick C. Beiser, *The German Historicist Tradition* (New York: Oxford University Press, 2011), 322–92; and Gerhard Oexle, "Naturwissenschaft und Geschichtswissenschaft. Momente einer Problemgeschichte," in *Naturwissenschaft, Geisteswissenschaft, Kulturwissenschaft: Einheit—Gegensatz—Komplemtarität?*, ed. Otto Gerhard Oexle (Göttingen: Wallstein, 2000), 98–155.

3. Lorraine Daston and Peter Galison chart the emergence of "scientific objectivity" in the nineteenth century, but they do not deal with this concept in the context of aesthetics or "cultural science" during this same period. Lorraine Daston and Peter Galison, *Objectivity* (New York: Zone, 2010).

4. The first topic that Benjamin considered during 1916 and 1917 for his doctoral dissertation, Kant and the problem of history, also bears the marks of the debate over the validity of history as a science from a Kantian perspective that had been taken up by Windelband and the so-called Southwest neo-Kantians; Hermann Cohen who had been the leading Marburg neo-Kantian was also an important influence on Benjamin at this time. See Howard Eiland and Michael W. Jennings, *Walter Benjamin: A Critical Life* (Cambridge, Mass.: Harvard University Press, 2014), 98–99 and 102. The work of Windelband and Rickert shaped the discussion of objectivity in the cultural sciences in this academic context. Of particular importance was the former's distinction between knowledge in the natural sciences (nomothetic) as distinct from that of the "historical sciences" or the humanities (*Geisteswissenschaften*) (idiographic). Max Weber, for example, builds specifically on Rickert's elaboration, notably in the latter's 1896 treatise *The Limits of Concept Formation in the Natural Sciences*, on the distinction between nomothetic and idiographic concepts first proposed by Wilhelm Windelband in "History and Natural Science" (Windelband, "Geschichte und Naturwissenschaft," 363–64). Although originally advanced as a methodological distinction, rather than one

concerning content or subject matter, Windelband's dyad eventually came to stand for a disciplinary difference between the nomothetic natural sciences, which seek universal laws, and the idiographic historical sciences, which focus on particular facts. On the evolution of these terms, including in Windelband's own writing, see Beiser, *The German Historicist Tradition*, 381–84. Rickert argued that ideographic concepts form on the basis of values, the general validity of which rest on the universally recognized commitments of a community. The scientific character of historical knowledge—its objectivity—is understood to derive from the generalizable values that inform the ideographic concepts and that in turn shape the selection of materials for historical study. From Rickert's perspective the problems of problem-history, we might say, are ideographic concepts. The problem that concerns Benjamin in his dissertation is the concept of criticism—more precisely, "one moment" in the problem-historical "context" (*Zusammenhang*) that is represented by the romantic concept of criticism. This means primarily literary criticism since for the romantics, Benjamin observes, literature occupies the "central position among all the arts" (*GS* 1.1: 14; *SW* 1: 118).

5. Wilhelm Windelband, *Die Geschichte der neueren Philosophie in ihrem Zusammanhange mit der allgemeinen Kultur und den besonderen Wissenschaften*, vol. 2 (Leipzig: Breitkopf and Härtel, 1911), especially 221–29.

6. Windelband, *Geschichte der neueren Philosophie*, 224. Benjamin also cites Windelband at the end of the first section on the crucial difference between Fichte's subordination of being to action (the unconscious action of the "I" limiting itself) and the romantic insistence on the limitless, "absolute" character of the "medium of reflection" (*GS* 1.1: 39; *SW* 1: 132).

7. For Rickert's gloss on *Vollendung*, which he writes as *Voll-Endung*, see his "Vom System der Werte," *Logos: Internationale Zeitschrift für Philosophie der Kultur* 4 (1913): 295–327, at 301.

8. Of course, Benjamin's main point is the difference between Kant's concept of the power of judgment and the Romantics' concept of reflection: "Reflection is not, as the power of judgment is, a subjectively reflecting process; rather, it lies enclosed in the presentational form of the work an unfolds itself in criticism, in order to reach fulfillment in the lawful continuum of forms" (*GS* 1.1: 88; *SW* 1: 165).

9. The philosophical development that Benjamin attributes to the romantics is nowhere to be found in Windelband's *Geschichte der neueren Philosophie in ihrem Zusammanhange mit der allgemeinen Kultur und den besonderen Wissenschaften*. Following German romantic philosophy therefore means leaving Windelband behind. There are indeed no authoritative "sources" for this "point of departure"—except, that is, the writings of the German romantics themselves. In this respect Benjamin's critical study of the romantics mirrors the immanent theory of romantic criticism.

10. Samuel Weber, "From Reflection to Repetition: Medium, Reflexivity and the Economy of the Self," in *Thinking Media Aesthetics. Media Studies, Film Studies and the Arts* (Berlin: Peter Lang, 2013), 51–65, at 57.

11. Samuel Weber, "From Reflection to Repetition," 57.

12. Thus in the pages devoted to a discussion of Friedrich Schlegel's interpretation of Fichte Ender's focus remains entirely within the context of the self-positing "I." See Carl Enders, *Friedrich Schlegel. Die Quellen seines Wesens und Werdens* (Leipzig: H. Haessel, 1913), 301–3.

13. As Benjamin observes with regard to romantic aesthetic theory, "The value of a work depends solely on whether it makes its immanent criticism possible or not. If this is possible—if there is present in the work a reflection that can unfold itself, absolutize itself, and resolve itself in the medium of art—then it is a work of art. The mere criticizability (*Die bloße Kritisierbarkeit*) of a work demonstrates the positive value judgment made about it" (*GS* 1.1: 78–79; *SW* 1: 159–60).

14. Benjamin, *Gesammelte Briefe*, vol. 2, 26.

15. Ernst Behler notes in his "Introduction" to the *Athenaeum-Fragments* in the critical edition of Friedrich Schlegel's works that "the key to [the doctrine of romantic poetry] lies in Schlegel's early writing on the classics" that he started to develop in the mid-1790s, especially with the completion of the famous essay "On the Study of Greek Poetry" in 1795 (*Kritische Friedrich Schlege Ausgabe*, vol. 2.1 [Paderborn: Ferdinand Schöningh, 1974], xlvi).

16. Beyond this "immanent" analysis of Schlegel, Benjamin also claims support for his thesis based on the fragments of Novalis and also on the later Windischmann lectures of 1804–06. If, as the translators of the English edition note, "much of what Benjamin surmises from the later

Windischmann texts" adduced in support of his thesis is contradicted by the Jena lectures from 1800–01 that were not available to Benjamin, the reverse is the case with the philological fragments that were also not published until after he completed his study of romanticism (see *SW* 1: 186n8).

17. This nexus continues to develop in Benjamin's thinking through the fragments on justice and property composed during the years leading up to the completion of his dissertation and of the essay "Toward the Critique of Violence" that appeared as he was turning his attention to Goethe. For the fragments on justice and property see *GS* 6: 91–93, 98–100, and 104–8. For example: "To every good, limited as it is by the spatio-temporal order, there accrues a possession-character as the expression of its transience. But possession, as something caught in the same finitude, is always unjust. No order of possession, however articulated, can therefore lead to justice. Rather, this lies in the condition of a good that cannot be a possession. This alone is the good through which goods become possessionless." "Notes toward a Work on the Category of Justice," in *Toward the Critique of Violence*, ed. Peter Fenves and Julia Ng (Stanford: Stanford University Press, 2021), 65.

18. Letter dated February 23, 1918; Benjamin, *Gesammelte Briefe*, vol. 1, 433. See Uwe Steiner, *Die Geburt der Kritik aus dem Geiste der Kunst: Untersuchungen zum Begriff der Kritik in den frühen Schriften Walter Benjamins* (Würzburg: Königshausen and Neumann, 1989), 16–17; and "Zur Entstehungs- und Publikationsgeschichte," to Walter Benjamin, *Der Begriff der Kunstkritik in der deutschen Romantik, Kritische Gesamtausgabe*, vol. 3, 180–86.

19. On the links between "the poetized" in the essay on Hölderlin and "the ideal" in the discussion of Goethe in the appendix to the dissertation, see Steiner, *Die Geburt der Kritik aus dem Geiste der Kunst*, 129–41.

20. Friedrich Schlegel, *Kritische Friedrich Schlegel Ausgabe*, vol. 16.1 (Paderborn: Ferdinand Schöningh, 1981), 52.

21. Schlegel's fragments on philology have themselves been the subject of important philological work since Benjamin completed his dissertation, in particular the compilation first edited by Joseph Körner and published in the influential journal *Logos* in 1928 under the title *"Zur Philologie"* (On Philology) and more recently in 1981 in volume 16 of the *Kritische*

Friedrich Schlegel Ausgabe. A critical facsimile edition prepared by Samuel Müller also appeared in 2015 under the title *Hefte Zur Philologie*, which includes a useful overview of the emergence of these notebooks out of Schlegel's intellectual projects of the mid-1790s. See *Hefte Zur Philologie* (Paderborn: Ferdinand Schöningh, 2015), 244–48.

22. The word "continuance" translates the German *Bestand* in the following sentence from the end of the second part of the dissertation: "[Prose] is the eternal sober continuance of the work" (*GS* 1.1: 109; *SW* 1: 178).

23. On Schlegel's initial resistance to Wolf's thesis, see Behler, "Einleitung," *Kritische Friedrich Schlegel Ausgabe*, vol. 1.1, cliii.

24. *Kritische Friedrich Schlegel Ausgabe*, vol. 1.1: 515. Johann Gottfried Eichhorn, whose *Introduction to the Old Testament* (1780–83) was a key influence on Wolf, approaches this irreducible foreignness of the Biblical text as follows:

> If a nation can only be held to be original and to possess an original literature which from the lowest step of education has raised itself up by its own strength gradually upwards, has invented its own laws and religion, and the progressive gradation of whose knowledge has never been interrupted by aids from foreign learning, arts, and inventions, in that case the Jews can pass for no original people and be held to have no original literature. (Johann Gottfried Eichhorn, *Einleitung in das Alte Testament* [Leipzig: Weidmann, 1803], 3; *Introduction to the Old Testament*, trans. George Tilly Gollop [London: Spottiswoode, 1888], 1)

Here is another example:

> None of all the books which now form the canon of the Old Testament could by possibility in its journey through time retain the external shape first bestowed upon them by its author. They have all of them not merely been compelled to complete the cycle of changes which human hands have wrought upon a Homer and the rest of the great series of classical writers—partly due to injury, partly to the advantage, of posterity, sometimes from mere chance, sometimes from necessity—but their original structure has subjected them to some further changes, quite peculiar to themselves. And if Moses were now to arise from the dead, he would with difficulty recognize himself in the company in which he is placed. (Eichorn, *Einleitung in das Alte Testament*, 181; *Introduction*, 116)

25. Schlegel, *Kritische Friedrich Schlegel Ausgabe*, vol. 1.1, 116n1.

26. Schlegel, *Kritische Friedrich Schlegel Ausgabe*, vol. 1.1, 515.

27. On Schlegel's unrealized proposals to publish his philological notebooks in either in the *Lyceum* or in the *Philosophische Journal*, see Hans Eichner, "Einleitung," *Kritische Friedrich Schlegel Ausgabe*, vol. 16.1, xx; and Martina Eicheldinger, "'Zur Philologie': Entstehung, Erstdruck, Einflüsse," *Friedrich Schlegel Handbuch: Leben—Werk—Wirkung*, ed. Johannes Endres (Stuttgart: Metzler, 2017), 162–65, at 162.

28. For explicit references to philology, see Lyceum-fragments 55, 75, and 100, and Athenaeum-fragments 82, 93, 147, 231, 255, 295, 321, 391, 403, and 404.

29. On the underappreciation of the significance of philology and of Wolf in particular on the development of Schlegel's thought, see Denis Thouard, "Der unmögliche Abschluss. Schlegel, Wolf und die Kunst der Diaskeuasten," in *Antike—Philologie—Romantik. Friedrich Schlegels altertumswissenschaftliche Manuskripte*, ed. Christian Benne and Ulrich Breuer (Padeborn: Ferdinand Schöningh, 2011), 41–62, at 45n13.

30. Schlegel, *Kritische Friedrich Schlegel Ausgabe*, vol. 16.1, 37.

31. The phrase "philosophy of philology" is employed by Schlegel to describe his project in an August 1797 letter to Niethammer. It is cited by Hans Eichner in his introduction to the philological fragments in the *Kritische Friedrich Schlegel Ausgabe*, vol. 16.1, xvi.

32. As far as I am aware, Benjamin alludes only once, in passing, to Wolf: in his encyclopedia article on Goethe (*GS* 2.2: 731; *SW* 2: 181).

33. Here is Schlegel's comparison of Wolf to Kant in the first footnote to "On Homeric Poetry":

> It is the usual fate of great scientific inventions in the beginning more in general to astonish or also, as chance would have it, to be opposed, than to be understood and used. Almost every part of the entire study of antiquity may expect directly and indirectly to receive a new light, even a new shape, from *Wolf's discoveries* in Homeric poetry. Still however the Prolegomena, this masterpiece of ingenuity that is greater than that of Lessing, is often just as much misunderstood (perhaps for similar reasons) as Kant's *Critique of Pure Reason*, since they first came to the attention of the public. (*Kritische Friedrich Schlegel Ausgabe*, vol 1.1, 116n1)

34. Denis Thouard has recently demonstrated the impact of Wolf's work on the central concepts of romantic critical theory including "the idea of the infinitude of the work," "the inseparability of criticism and work," and

"the developmental historicity of texts" (Thouard, "Der unmögliche Abschluss," 43).

35. Denis Thouard makes a convincing case that the impact of Schlegel's reading of Wolf, as expressed in the 1797 philological fragments and the 1798 *History of the Poetry of the Greeks and the Romans*, "prepares the romantic theory of the Athenaeum" (Thouard, "Der unmögliche Abschluss," 58). Thouard shows how Schlegel's encounter with Wolf's philology can be understood to lead to a "response" to the problem of the "juxtaposition of antiquity and modernity" framed in the essay "On the Study of Greek Poetry" from 1795: "In this sense, the philological model allowed Schlegel to work out the principle of an infinite reflexivity between meaning and history, spirit and letter, or philosophy and philology. The intervention of criticism in the work, borrowed from the Alexandrian interpolators (*Diaskeuasten*) through the mediation of Wolf, becomes characteristic of romantic practice. The updating of the ancient authors, which then results when they are converted into a modern interpretation, is a response to the juxtaposition of ancient and modern." Thouard, "Der unmögliche Abschluss," 59–60.

36. Indeed, this appendix on early romantic aesthetic theory and Goethe was not submitted to the faculty, according to the editors of the English edition of Benjamin's works (see *SW* 1: 199n307).

37. Hölderlin, *Sämtliche Werke*, vol. 5, 285.

38. Scholem reports the "deep impression" made by Hölderlin's translations of Pindar on Benjamin as expressed to Scholem in a conversation from October 1914. Gershom Scholem, *Walter Benjamin—Die Geschichte einer Freundschaft* (Frankfurt am Main: Suhrkamp, 1975), 26.

39. Marcello Gigante, *Nomos Basileus* (New York: Arno, 1979), 92. Lukas van den Berge has offered a useful overview of the range of interpretations given to the word *nomos* from antiquity up to today and provided a context within which the limitations of the interpretations of Schmitt and Agamben can be subject to criticism on the basis of the tradition and a reading of the fragment informed by this complex tradition. Lukas van den Berge, "Law, King of All: Schmitt, Agamben, Pindar," *Law and Humanities* 13.2 (2019): 198–222. Summarizing Gigante's commentary on Pindar's Fragment 169 along with that of Hugh Lloyd-Jones, van den Berge states that *nomos* signifies "'the justice of Zeus,' the supreme and just 'law of the

universe' to which both gods and men should obey" (van den Berge, 213). The allusion to Lloyd-Jones is *The Justice of Zeus* (Berkeley and Los Angeles: University of California Press, 1983), 48–51.

40. Citing Carl Schmitt, *The Nomos of the Earth in the International Law of the Jus Publicum*, trans. Gary Ulmen (New York: Telos, 2006), 69–72, van den Berge notes: "As Schmitt explicates, *nomos* is the nominalization— the *nomen actionis*—of the Greek verb *nemo*, denoting, amongst other things, the appropriation of land: the constitutive act of spatial ordering that conceptually precedes the moral and legal order that follows from it" ("Law, King of All," 199). It is important to insist on the priority of the qualification, "among other things" over "the appropriation of land" in this sentence. The Greek verb *nemo* must be understood in this sense to signify the concept of spatial ordering or dividing that precedes all appropriations of land.

41. Benjamin's comment on the romantic theory of the novel in the passage alludes to an earlier passage on the way the novel in this theory is "neutralizing" the "rigor" of its form: given its "external license and irregularity" the novel as a genre "never oversteps its form . . . neutralizes the presentational form, which prevails only in its purity, not in its rigor" (*allein in ihrer Reinheit, nicht in ihrer Strenge in ihm waltet*) (*GS* 1.1: 98; *SW* 1: 172).

42. "It is the privilege of ancient thinkers, who sometimes pose the deepest questions of philosophy in the shape of mythical solutions, to circumscribe the problem of art, according to its entire scope, according to form and content, by means of the primal image" (*GS* 1.1: 118; *SW* 1: 184).

43. Hölderlin, *Sämtliche Werke*, vol. 5 (Stuttgart: Kohlhammer, 1970), 287.

44. Hölderlin, *Sämtliche Werke*, vol. 5, 287.

3. "GOETHE'S ELECTIVE AFFINITIES"

1. There are no exact equivalents in English for what is translated here as "subject-matter" and "truth-of-the-matter": the German terms *Sachgehalt* and *Wahrheitsgehalt*. The key challenge is double: (1) to find fitting English words to translate consistently the three basic linguistic elements of which this pair of terms is composed—especially difficult are *Sache* and *Gehalt*

(for *Wahrheit* "truth" is acceptable) and (2) to do this in a way that allows the English translation to follow Benjamin's separating and recombining of these elements in his essay. The challenge of translating *Sachgehalt* and *Wahrheitsgehalt* (as well as other similarly handled terms), in other words, confronts us from the start with the task of conveying the defining feature or signature of Benjamin's philological method in the Goethe essay. The problem begins with the question of how to translate *Sachgehalt* (just as for the critic the problem begins with the question of how to interpret the *Sachgehalt* of the literary work). According to the Grimm dictionary the oldest sense of the word *Sache*—the first element—is a case that comes before a judge for a decision. Grimm notes that *Sache* also signifies the source or basis of a conflict as well as "generally what someone has to represent, to accomplish, to do; one's assignment, task, duty, obligation." The word *Gehalt*, according to Grimm, means that which is contained, but also the precious metal contained in coins, the minerals contained in medicinal waters (*Gesundbrunnen*), or the ore contained in crude metals. Although not exactly equivalent, the English word "subject" includes some significations that resonate with the German word *Sache*. *The Oxford English Dictionary*, for example, lists "that about which a judgment is made" and "an object with which a person's occupation or business is concerned or on which his or her craft is exercised." But interestingly the English word "matter," especially when it is combined with the word "subject," also shares some significations with *Sache*. Under "matter," the *Oxford English Dictionary* includes "a subject of contention" and under "subject matter": "the ground, basis, or source of something" and "the matter in dispute." Thus, both parts of the phrase "subject-matter" connect specifically to the Gehalt or "matter" of the *Sachgehalt*, forming a kind of semantic bridge between *Sache* and *Gehalt*. This connection or bridge is indicated through the insertion of a hyphen between the two parts of the phrase. The translation of *Wahrheitsgehalt* with "truth-of-the-matter" draws on the colloquial sense in which this phrase is used to reveal what is not known, or not widely known, about a matter. This translation of *Sachgehalt* and *Wahrheitsgehalt* as "subject-matter" and "truth-of-the-matter" was suggested to me by Peter Fenves as an alternative to the translation in particular of the former as "material content," which introduces a term that is both highly significant in Benjamin's work (especially the later work) and misleading in this context.

2. The distinction between the appearance and the meaning of the essay thus corresponds to the difference between "the way of meaning" *(die Art des Meinens)* and "what is meant" *(das Gemeinte)* in "The Task of the Translator," an essay that Benjamin completed while he was working on his study of Goethe *(GS* 4.1: 13–14; *SW* 1: 257). See Paul de Man, *The Resistance to Theory* (Minneapolis: University of Minnesota Press, 1986), 86–92.

3. De Man excludes the complementarity of the relation between "the way of meaning" and "what is meant," but he does not rule out that these "may be mutually exclusive in a certain way" *(Resistance to Theory*, 88).

4. Johann Wolfgang von Goethe, *Werke, Kommentare und Register*, 14 vols. [Hamburger Ausgabe] (München: C. H. Beck, 1981). Unless otherwise indicated, all citations of Goethe are from this edition with volume number followed by page number in parenthesis. This conversation is dated February 9, 1829.

5. In a letter dated October 1, 1809, Goethe wrote to Johann Friedrich Cotta of the soon to appear *Elective Affinities*: "There is much laid into it that, I hope, will incite the reader to repeated observation" *(es ist manches hineingelegt, das, wie ich hoffe, den Leser wiederholte Betrachtung auffordern wird) (Goethes Briefe*, vol. 3 [Hamburg: Christian Wegner Verlag, 1965], 110). The composition of *Elective Affinities* was completed in late July 1809 with printing beginning in August of that year and publication in February 1810. For a summary, see *Goethes Werke* [Hamburger Ausgabe], vol. 6, 689–91.

6. Benjamin began work on Goethe's *Elective Affinities* in summer 1919 and completed the composition in summer 1922. The essay appeared in two installments in Hugo von Hoffmannsthal's journal *Neue Deutsche Beiträge* (the first two parts in April 1924 and the third part in January 1925). See *GS* 1.3: 811–22.

7. John T. Hamilton describes Goethe's early efforts to make "a name for himself by cultivating a Pindaric personality." Hamilton, "Florilegia: Influence and Cross-Pollination between Celan and Hölderlin, Pindar and Horace," *MLN* 135.3 (April 2020): 600–19, at 613. See also Hamilton's discussion of Pindar in Goethe's early "Wanderers Sturmlied," in *Soliciting Darkness: Pindar, Obscurity, and the Classical Tradition* (Cambridge, Mass.: Harvard University Press, 2004), 237–65.

8. On the link of Benjamin's approach to *Sachgehalt* to Husserl's phenomenological exposition of the *Sache*, see Fenves, "Kant in Benjamins

Wahlverwandtschaften-Essay," in *Benjamins Wahlverwandtschaften. Zur Kritik einer programmatischen Interpretation*, ed. Helmut Hühn, Jan Urbich, and Uwe Steiner (Frankfurt am Main: Suhrkamp, 2015), 221–37, at 226–28.

9. Under the entry for *Siegel* in Grimm we find both "single impression of the certificate in wax . . . as a sign of the authenticity and validity of a document" and "the instrument itself with which the impression is made." The Oxford English Dictionary defines "seal" as "a device (e.g., a heraldic or emblematic design, a letter, word, or sentence) impressed on a piece of wax or other plastic material adhering or attached by cords or parchment slips to a document as evidence of authenticity or attestation" and also "an engraved stamp of metal or other hard material used to make an impression upon wax, etc., affixed as a 'seal.'"

10. The reference in Kant is *Kritik der reinen Vernunft, Kants Gesammelte Schriften* [Akademie Ausgabe], vol. 4 (Berlin: Georg Riemer, 1911), A 141–42/B 181; *Critique of Pure Reason*, trans. and ed. Paul Guyer and Allen W. Wood (New York: Cambridge University Press, 1998), 274. See Fenves, "Kant in Benjamin's *Wahlverwandtschaften*-Essay," 223–28.

11. Rudolf A. Makkreel, *Imagination and Interpretation in Kant: The Hermeneutical Import of the Critique of Judgment* (Chicago: University of Chicago Press, 1995), 31–32. Also relevant to this point is Makkreel's discussion of what he calls "the reading of nature" in Kant (33–39).

12. The experience of the word *Sachgehalt* that Benjamin tried to prepare for the reader of his essay may be considered an example of what Werner Hamacher, echoing Friedrich Schlegel, calls a "philological affect" (*Für—Die Philologie* [Weil am Rhein: Urs Engeler, 2009], 33–37).

13. The tripartite structure of thesis, antithesis, and synthesis is made explicit in the original "fair copy" of the manuscript in the form of subtitles to each of the three parts and is provided in the outline that exists in the Benjamin archive and that is published in the apparatus of the German edition (see *GS* 1.3: 835–37). On Benjamin's instructions, the subtitles were excluded from the original publication in the *Neue Deutsche Beiträge* (see *Gesammelte Briefe*, vol. 6, 331). In an April 4, 1938, letter to Adorno, Benjamin describes the "dialectical rigor" of the tripartite structure of the Goethe essay as a possible model for "schematizing" the Baudelaire book and by extension the work on the Paris arcades (*Briefe*, vol. 6, 765). See *GS* 1.3: 822–23.

14. The Latin phrase is from Horace's *Ars Poetica*: *"Publica materies priuati iuris erit"* (public material will be private property) (l. 131). The English translation is offered by Rita Copeland in her discussion of the difference between *publica materies* (owned by everyone) and *proprie communia* (owned by no one) (l. 128). See Rita Copeland, *Rhetoric, Hermeneutics, and Translation in the Middle Ages: Academic Traditions and Vernacular Texts* (Cambridge: Cambridge University Press, 1995), 169–72.

15. To a certain extent, the absence of typographical marking identifying "elective affinities" as the title of the novel is a matter of the convention adopted by the press (of course this does not negate the effect it has of not distinguishing between the title and the phrase). For example, Friedrich Gundolf's book on Goethe, published just a few years earlier, employs a similar typographical practice (see Friedrich Gundolf, *Goethe* [Berlin: Georg Bondi, 1916], 557). The English translator of Benjamin's essay on Goethe, Stanley Corngold, notes that "elective affinities" is not definitively marked in the text as the title of a novel in a note that appears more than halfway through the essay—in note 27 to *SW* 1: 330, which corresponds to *SW* 1: 359 in the "Notes" section. In the original publication in the *Neue Deutsche Beiträge* after appearing with no distinguishing typological or diacritical marking in the title of the essay (on page 83), the word *Wahlverwandtschaften* occurs for the first time on page 88, also unmarked, and it remains so. Kant's *Metaphysics of Morals*, however, is cited as a title in quotation marks three pages earlier (on page 85) as "Metaphysik der Sitten."

16. To compare, see Ernst Cassirer's *Das Problem Jean Jacques Rousseau* (Darmstadt: Wissenschaftliche Buchgesellschaft, 1970), which was first published in the *Archiv für Geschichte der Philosophie* 41.1–2 (1932): 177–213 and 479–513. In the first paragraph of his study, Cassirer describes the "problem" of Rousseau as a matter than cannot be "reduced to a mere historical fact.... It is, rather, a movement of thought that renews itself, a movement of such strength and passion that it seems hardly possible in its presence to take refuge in the quiet of 'objective' historical contemplation." *The Question of Jean Jacques Rousseau*, trans. Peter Gay (Bloomington and London: Indiana University Press, 1963), 35.

17. Friedrich Wilhelm Riemer, Goethe's editor and literary secretary, published this conversation in 1841 in his two-volume *Mitteilungen über Goethe* (*Notes on Goethe*). Bettine von Arnim's *Briefwechsel mit einem*

Kind (*Correspondence with a Child*) is presented as an epistolary exchange consisting of letters attributed to the author and to Goethe (it was published in 1835, three years after Goethe's death). In the introduction to the edition used by Benjamin (*Goethes Briefwechsel mit einem Kinde* [Jena: Eugen Diederichs, 1906], v), Jonas Fränkel notes: "Doubtless [von Arnim] later lovingly wove into the image of her youth much that was perhaps only experienced as an impression and that only with time gradually grew in her consciousness." In the commentary to the modern edition (Bettine von Arnim, *Werke und Briefe*, vol. 2 [Frankfurt am Main: Deutscher Klassiker Verlag, 1992], 887), Walter Schmitz and Sibylle von Steinsdorff observe that it is "not possible to determine the extent of fictionalization" in the book.

18. Johann Wolfgang von Goethe, *Werke* [Hamburger Ausgabe], vol. 6 (Hamburg: C. H. Beck, 1981), 270; *Elective Affinities*, trans. R. J. Hollingdale (New York: Penguin, 1971), 50. Hereafter cited parenthetically as *HA*; *EA*.

19. Goethe, *Werke*, vol. 6, 270; *Elective Affinities*, 50.

20. Adler cites Jane Mercet's 1806 "Conversations on Chemistry" as a contemporary English example. See Jeremy Adler, *"Eine fast magische Anziehungskraft". Goethes Wahlverwandtschaften und die Chemie seiner Zeit* (München: C. H. Beck, 1987), 84–85.

21. On the contemporary understanding of "elective affinity" see Adler, 99–100. According to Grimm, "insofar as a choice is ascribed to the body, the word [elective affinity] is taken from human conditions and as such aroused the attention of Goethe" (*"Wahlverwandtschft,"* Grimms Wörterbuch, vol. 13 [1922]).

22. Adler, *"Eine fast magische Anziehungskraft,"* 116. In keeping with the Rousseauist theory of the origins of language, in other words, the "affinities" are irreducibly metaphorical and it is precisely this theory that Eduard refuses to endorse—electing instead to mythify the "affinities" by seeing them as rooted in a nature that binds human and earthly elements alike. On the irreducibly metaphorical character of the "affinities" in the novel, see J. Hillis Miller, *Ariadne's Thread: Story Lines* (New Haven: Yale University Press, 1992), especially 170–73. See also Kir Kuiken, "On the Delineation of Choice and Decision in Benjamin's Goethe's Elective Affinities," *Canadian Review of Comparative Literature* 31.3 (2004): 286–308, especially 292–94.

23. Peter Fenves, "Introduction," in Walter Benjamin, *Toward the Critique of Violence: A Critical Edition*, trans. Peter Fenves and Julia Ng (Stanford: Stanford University Press, 2021), 1–37, at 31–34.

24. Here are the main points in the outline of the topical headnotes Benjamin prepared for the book publication of his Goethe essay that did not appear. They are provided by the German editor in the notes to the essay (*GS* 1.3: 835–37).

> On the Elective Affinities
> Outline
> Part One: The Mythic as Thesis
>   I. Criticism and Commentary
>   II. The Meaning of the Mythic World in the Elective Affinities
>   III. The Meaning of the Mythic World for Goethe
> Part Two: Redemption as Antithesis
>   I. Criticism and Biography
>   II. Gundolf's "Goethe"
>   III. The Novella
> Part Three: Hope as Synthesis
>   I. Criticism and Philosophy
>   II. Beauty as Semblance
>   III. Semblance as Reconciliation

25. Hermann Cohen, *Ästhetik des reinen Gefühls*, vol. 2 (Berlin: Cassirer, 1912), 123 and 125.

26. Benjamin goes on to suggest that the naming of Eduard is "arbitrary" (*wilkürlich*) "chosen for its sound" and is thus "analogous to the displacement of the tombstones" (*GS* 1.1: 135; *SW* 1: 305). In this sense "Eduard" may be understood to belong to a purely differential order of markers with an arbitrary relation to what they are supposed to indicate.

27. In this sense, like the conversation about the "affinities," the name Eduard had become something of a stereotype of the Englishman fashionable in eighteenth-century France. In *La Nouvelle Héloïse* it is inflected, as one critic points out, by Rousseau's "attitude toward England and the manner in which his conception of English character was formed." George R. Havons, "The Sources of Rousseau's Edouard Bomston," *Modern Philology* 8.1 (July 1919): 125–39, at 125. This included, according to a note in the Pléiade edition of the novel, the image of "the '*philosophe*' . . . an

idealized Diderot." Jean-Jacques Rousseau, *Œuvres completes*, vol. 2 (Paris: Gallimard, 1964), 1412 (note by Bernard Guyon). In a comment that illuminates Goethe's Eduard, Havons argues that Edouard Bomston was in part based on the "deep impression" made on Rousseau by Prévost's *Cléveland*, which "furnished Rousseau . . . with the general conception of a man who believes himself a philosopher, but who in reality is guided by his *âme sensible* rather than by his reason" (Havons, 131).

28. The development of a line of scholarship focused on the names in Goethe's novel can be traced to Heinz Schlaffer's 1972 essay, "Namen und Buchstaben in Goethes 'Wahlverwandtschaften,'" which was first published in *Jahrbuch der Jean-Paul-Gesellschaft* 7 (1972): 84–102. Schlaffer's essay begins with an allusion to Benjamin's comment on the "poverty of naming" in Goethe's novel.

29. Norbert Oellers, "Warum eigentlich Eduard? Zur Namen-Wahl in Goethes *Wahlverwandtschaften*," in *Geneo huius loci: Dank an Leiva Petersen* (Wien/Köln/Graz: H. Böhlan, 1982), 215–34, at 220 and 223. The source cited by Oellers is Hans Bahlow, *Unsere Vornamen im Wandel der Jahrhunderte* (Limburg/Lahn: Starke Verlag, 1965), 24n24 and 81. Oellers's article belongs to an important strain of commentary on names in Goethe's novel that has focused on this question starting with an essay by Schlaffer cited above.

30. Goethe's journals attest to his reading of Schlegel's study during a summer trip to Karlsbad in 1808. See the entries for May 13 and 23 and June 22 and 23: *Goethes Werke* [Weimarer Ausgabe], vol. 3.3 (Munich: Deutscher Taschenbuch Verlag, 1987), 335, 338–39, and 350–51. Gabrielle Belsier, *Goethes Rätselparodie der Romantik. Eine neue Lesart der "Wahlverwandtschaften"* (Tübingen: Niemeyer Verlag, 1997), 65–66 and 77–80, provides a detailed account of Goethe's preoccupation with Schlegel and his study.

31. Belsier, *Goethes Rätselparodie der Romantik*, especially 77–80. The word *Verwandtschaft* (affinity) appears repeatedly in the opening paragraphs of Schlegel's study (six times in four short paragraphs) and reappears in the title of the second chapter, *"Von der Verwandtschaft der Wurzeln"* (On the Affinity of the Roots).

32. *Kritische Friedrich Schlegel Ausgabe*, vol. 8, 157. See Belsier, *Goethes Rätselparodie der Romantik*, 81–82.

33. Belsier, *Goethes Rätselparodie der Romantik*, 87.

34. *Kritische Friedrich Schlegel Ausgabe*, vol. 1, 76. Belsier interprets the baron's unorthodox grafting, which is at odds implicitly with Schlegel's approach to Indo-European roots and explicitly with his use of the metaphor of grafting in his early essay "On the Study of Greek Poetry," as a matter of parody (Belsier, *Goethes Rätselparodie der Romantik*, 75–76). This interpretation, however, assimilates Goethe's technique in the novel to the romantic theory of parody as a mode of irony (Belsier, *Goethes Rätselparodie der Romantik*, 13–14). From this perspective, Goethe's engagement with romantic theory during the composition of *Elective Affinities* (from 1808 to 1809)—documented, if not specified in detail, in his own diaries and in other contemporary accounts—is taken in this admirable study as evidence of his application in the novel of the romantic concept of parody to the later work of Friedrich Schlegel: a romantic parody of romanticism (very romantic indeed!). Benjamin's thesis, on the other hand, would refuse the assimilation of Goethe's aesthetic theory and practice to the romantic formalism elucidated in his dissertation. In this context, the question of the "subject-matter" remains critical.

35. The mythic "O" around which the character names turn may also be understood to contain an allusion to Catholic cult of the Virgin Mary and the liturgical ceremony of the "Expectant Virgin." In this sense the "O" would refer to refer to romanticism from Goethe's perspective. I will come back to this possibility below in a discussion of the connection between Goethe's *Elective Affinities* and Heinrich von Kleist's novella, "The Marquise of O."

36. Goethe, *Werke*, vol. 6, 269 and 276; *Elective Affinities*, 49 and 56.

37. The key passages in the essays by Derrida in which the figure of grafting occurs are the following from 1968–72 (thanks are due to Geoffrey Bennington for his assistance with tracing the emergence of this figure in Derrida's work): "La pharmacie de Platon," in *La dissémination* (Paris: Seuil, 1972), 69–198, at 174n67 (originally published in *Tel Quel* 32–33 [1968]); "La dissémination," in *La dissémination*, 319–408, at 395 (originally published in *Critique* 261–262 [1969]); "La double Séance," in *La dissémination*, 199–318, at 230–31n15 (originally published in *Tel Quel* 41–42 [1970]); and "Signature Événement Contexte," in *Marges de la philosophie* (Paris: Minuit, 1972), 365–92, at 376–81 (originally presented

as a lecture delivered in Montreal at the Congrès international des Sociétés de philosophie de langue française in August 1971).

38. Derrida, "La pharmacie de Platon," *La dissémination*, 174n67
39. Goethe, *Werke*, vol. 6, 269; *Elective Affinities*, 49–50.
40. Goethe, *Werke*, vol. 6, 270; *Elective Affinities*, 50.
41. Derrida, "Signature Event Context," *Margins of Philosophy*, trans. Alan Bass (Chicago: University of Chicago Press, 1982), 307–30, at 317–18.
42. The phrase *"l'homme et l'œuvre"* is from Marcel Proust's famous attack on the method of Charles Augustin Sainte-Beuve. See "Contre Sainte-Beuve," in *Contre Sainte-Beuve: précédé de Pastiches et mélanges et suivi de Essais et articles* (Paris: Gallimard, 1971), 221. Proust's critical essays on Sainte-Beuve, which were written from 1895 to 1900 but which were not published in 1954, informed the connection between literature and life that is the subject of Benjamin's 1929 essay on his great novel. Benjamin's "Toward the Image of Proust" is deeply linked to his study of Goethe.
43. The key phrase from this conversation with Eckermann on September 17, 1823, is as follows: "The world is so large and rich and life is so multi-faceted that occasions for poems will never be lacking (*es Anlässen zu Gedichte nie fehlen wird*). But these must all be occasional poems (*Gelegenheitsgedichte*), that is, reality must provide the cause and the material (*Stoff*).... All my poems are occasional poems, they are called forth by reality and are grounded and rooted in it" (Goethe, *Sämtliche Werke. Briefe, Tagebücher und Gespräche*, vol. 39, 50). There are similar allusions to "occasional poems" in *Poetry and Truth*, in particular in Books 7 and 10 of the second part. See Goethe, *Werke* [Hamburger Ausgabe], vol. 9 (München: Beck, 1981), 265 and 397.
44. For a useful if conventional survey of the explicit connections in Goethe's work to the genre of occasional poetry that does not consider the possibility suggested by Benjamin, see Ernst M. Oppenheimer, *Goethe's Poetry for Occasions* (Toronto: University of Toronto Press, 1974).
45. Among the first to promote the role of "occasional poetry" that Goethe assigns to his work was Hegel in his *Lectures on Aesthetics* from the 1820s, first published in 1835. Hegel writes of this poetry as tending to have a *"dependency* on the external occasion" (*"Abhängigkeit" von der äußeren Gelegenheit*) that is to be countered by the genuine poet who

must take it as "an inducement exclusively to use the occasion above all to express himself, his mood, joy, sadness, or attitude." Georg Wilhelm Friedrich Hegel, *Vorlesungen über die Ästhetik*, vol. 3, *Werke*, vol. 15 (Frankfurt am Main: Suhrkamp, 1986), 425.

46. The allusion to the romantics' turn to religion, religious vocation, and "conversion" is undoubtedly pointing to Friedrich Schlegel's famous conversion to Catholicism of which Goethe learned from Karl Friedrich Reinhard in June 1808 as *Elective Affinities* was being completed. See Belsier, *Goethes Rätselparodie der Romantik*, 77–80.

47. The word "allowed" cited in this sentence alludes to the end of Benjamin's "Two Poems by Friedrich Hölderlin." It points to the allowing or yielding described by Benjamin as the "sobriety" that is "allowed, that is called for" (*die Nüchternheit erlaubt, geboten, ist*) in the poem (*GS* 2.1: 125; *SW* 1: 35). In this sense, allowing is a manifestation of what Hölderlin calls "free use" in his letter to Böhlendorff analyzed above. The verb translated as "called for" (*geboten*) also makes an implicit connection between the sobriety and the opportunity granted to the poet in the sense that in German one says "when the opportunity presents itself" (*wenn sich die Gelegenheit bietet*).

48. On "dialectic," which in Benjamin's writing is, as several commentators have noticed, far from simply identical with the conventional Hegelian understanding of this term as "reconciliation" or "synthesis," see Samuel Weber, "Genealogy of Modernity: History, Myth and Allegory in Benjamin's Origin of the German Mourning Play," *MLN* 106.3 (April 1991): 467–68; and my *Writing in Parts: Imitation and Exchange in Nineteenth-Century Literature* (Stanford: Stanford University Press, 1995), 4 and 124–37. Paul de Man makes a similar observation about Benjamin's use of the term "messianic" in an exchange with Dominick LaCapra that appears after de Man's essay, "Conclusions: Walter Benjamin's "The Task of the Translator," in *The Resistance to Theory*, 103.

49. The word "synthesis" appears in the heading for this third part of the Goethe essay in the schematic outline Benjamin prepared for the project. This term has to be read in the light of the declaration in his programmatic essay on the "coming philosophy" from 1918 that "other than synthesis, another relation between thesis and antithesis is possible"— one of "a certain non-synthesis" (*GS* 2.1: 166; *SW* 1: 106).

50. The entry *"Geschwister"* in Grimm's dictionary makes this progressively more inclusive definition clear from (1) "sister" to (2) "sisters with the inclusion of brothers" to (3) "that which is alike" *(von gleichartigem)*.
51. Goethe, *Werke*, vol. 6, 270; *Elective Affinities*, 50.
52. On Benjamin's turn to the *Trauerspiel* project after the completion of the Goethe essay in the early months of 1923, see Howard Eiland and Michael W. Jennings, *Walter Benjamin: A Critical Life* (Cambridge, Mass.: Harvard University Press, 2014), 183–84.
53. J. L. Frisch, for example, in his 1741 *Teutsch-lateinisches Wörterbuch*, gives *valor* as the Latin equivalent of *Gehalt*. The Grimm dictionary registers the emergence, in the late eighteenth century, of the application of the term to aesthetics. Under the following general signification of *Gehalt* Grimm states: "Content of coins . . . what they contain of pure silver, gold, true value." Grimm notes the extension of this meaning of *Gehalt* to aesthetics with Schiller, and in particular with the 1781 preface to *The Robbers* and the phrase *"ein gewisser Gehalt von Geisteskraft"* (a certain amount of spiritual power) necessary, according to Schiller, for the adequate reception of the play *(Die Räuber, Schillers Werke*, vol. 3 (Weimar: Hermann Böhlhaus Nachfolger, 1953), 7; an English translation of the passage can be found in Schiller, *Works*, vol. 2 (Boston: Household, 1884), 136. A useful historical survey of the word *Gehalt* can be found in the *Historisches Wörterbuch der Philosophie*, vol. 3, ed. Joachim Ritter (Basel: Schwabe and Co. Verlag, 1974), 139–45.
54. Lukács identifies what he calls the "priority of content *(Gehalt)*" in Hegel's understanding of the "dialectical interaction of form and content" *(dialektische Wechselwirkung [zwischen] Gehalt and Form)*." Georg Lukács, "Hegels Ästhetik," in Georg Wilhelm Friedrich Hegel, *Ästhetik*, vol. 2, ed. Friedrich Bassenge (Berlin: Verlag das Europäische Buch, 1985), 620.
55. Lukács, "Hegels Ästhetik," 599.
56. On what might be called the substance-based ontology of Hegel's epistemology—that dialectical "sublation" *(Aufhebung)* extends the substance metaphor to the realm of "rationality" or *Geist* and ultimately requires Hegel to deny the existence of the "irrational" in nature—see Emile Meyerson, *L'explication dans les sciences* (Paris: Payot, 1921). While Hegel rejects and mocks the scientific tendency to "explain change by denying it, by affirming the identity of things through time,"

as Meyerson notes (656), the empirical facts of nature are viewed by him as including a measure of "scoria" that must be subject to "purification" by experimental science so that what exists in them—what in them is identical with reason (*Geist*)—can be separated by philosophy from what does not exist—what is not identical with reason (399–400 and 481). Thus, what Meyerson calls Hegel's "play on words" (144n2 and 399) in the term *aufheben* (to conserve and to abolish) in fact describes a process whereby the substance of *Geist* is separated from the scoria of what is not-*Geist*. Meyerson's general argument here is that Hegel "only allows within his 'science' for a unique irrational, the *Andersein*, while declaring it by the way rational, while our science [one that does not postulate the identity of reason and nature] recognizes a whole series of them" (400).

57. The critical vocabulary of potentiality is the subject of the important study by Samuel Weber, *Benjamin's -abilities*, cited at the beginning of chapter 2.

58. Benjamin cites Julian Schmidt, *Geschichte der deutschen Literatur seit Lessing's Tod* (5th thoroughly revised and expanded edition), vol. 2 (Leipzig: Grunow, 1866), 590. Digitized copies of the 1866 edition of Schmidt's book can be found online on the HathiTrust Digital Library. The reference to the passage in question is https://babel.hathitrust.org/cgi/pt?id=umn.31951002011275b&view=1up&seq=586.

59. A couple of paragraphs earlier, Benjamin introduces this motif by characterizing Ottilie as "reserved" (*verschlossen*) (*GS* 1.1: 175; *SW* 1: 336).

60. Schmidt, *Geschichte der deutschen Literatur seit Lessing's Tod*, vol. 2, 523.

61. As it happens, *Die Grenzboten* published its final issue in 1922—the year in which Benjamin completed his essay on Goethe. A farewell notice appeared in December 1922: see "Ein Abschiedswort," *Die Grenzboten* 81.45 (1922): 481. The entire run of the journal has been digitized and is available online at https://brema.suub.uni-bremen.de/grenzboten.

62. As noted above, Benjamin cites the 1866 edition of *Geschichte der deutschen Literatur seit Lessing's Tod*, vol. 2, 590, and the passage he cited alludes to page 523. In the later edition of 1890, the passage cited would have followed the first paragraph ending on vol. 4, 387, and the passage cited would have been included in the discussion of "The Marquise von O" in vol. 4, 360.

63. Similarly, the paragraph immediately preceding this one in Benjamin's essay redeems the key question Schmidt poses about the novel in spite of his "home-baked common sense" (*hausbacknen Verstand*): that of the "silencing of conscience" (*Verstummen des Gewissens*) in Ottilie (*GS* 1.1: 177; *SW* 1: 337). This passage in the 1866–67 edition of Schmidt's book also disappears from the version published in 1890 (Schmidt, *Geschichte*, vol. 2 [1866–67 ed.], 590).

64. Thus, although it is inaccurate to say that the "relations" in question exist between Goethe's novel and Kleist's novella, certainly such "relations" are at issue in the latter, specifically, with respect to the profoundly enigmatic Marquise of O. In this sense Benjamin's critical redemption of the comment on the heroines of Goethe and Kleist has interesting implications for an interpretation of the novella that Schmidt considered—at least as of 1866—closest to Goethe's novel. "The Marquise of O" appeared in the journal *Phöbus* in 1808, one year before the publication of the original two-volume edition of Goethe's novel. Moreover, the central theme of Kleist's novella, which draws on the Catholic cult of the "Expectant Virgin," had been the subject of Kleist's comedy *Amphitryon*, which was performed in 1807 and which received a decidedly negative reception by Goethe who saw in its use of Catholic imagery a sign of romanticism (see Katharina Mommsen, *Kleists Kampf mit Goethe* [Heidelberg: Lothar Stiehm, 1974], 24–25). The association of Ottilie with the Virgin Mary and the onomastic O-motif in Goethe's novel can be read as a critique of Kleist's novella and, more generally, of romanticism. On the "O" in the title of Kleist's novella and its links to the Catholic cult of the Virgin Mary, see Steven R. Huff's illuminating article, "Kleist and Expectant Virgins: The Meaning of the 'O' in 'Die Marquise von O,'" *Journal of English and German Philology*, vol. 81.3 (July 1982): 367–75. Yet the critical question remains, as in Goethe's novel, the impenetrable heroine who stands at the center of the novella's enigma concerning the nature of "relation" in the sense of *Verwandtschaft*.

65. Benjamin cites the relevant passage in Plato's *Phaedrus* (251A and 254B) from Julius Walter, *Die Geschichte der Ästhetik im Altertum ihrer begrifflichen Entwicklung nach dargestellt* (Leipzig: O. R. Reisland, 1893). Walter's discussion of "bodily beauty" (*Körperschönheit*) in Plato illuminates the divergent inflection in Benjamin's interpretation of the kind of

beauty that appears with Ottilie's "living body" (*lebendiger Leib*) (*GS* 1.1: 197; *SW* 1: 353) (Walter, *Geschichte der Ästhetik im Altertum*, 281–309).

66. Walter, for example, describes the ambiguity of the appearance of beauty as such as "the connecting link between two worlds" (*das Bindeglied zweier Welten*) (Walter, *Geschichte der Ästhetik im Altertum*, 309).

67. This veil appears near the end of Act 3 in *Faust Part Two*. The poet Euphorion, the son of Helena and Faust, has died a death like that of Icarus by soaring too close to the sun. Helena embraces Faust and leaves her veil in his arms as she vanishes. At this point Mephistopheles, in the guise of Phorkyas, urges Faust to "hold firmly" on to the veil and provides an explanation of its meaning:

> Hold fast to what from all this that remains to you.
> Do not let the garment go. Already, demons
> Pull at its corners, and wish to drag it down
> Into the underworld. Hold firmly!
> No more is the goddess, that you have lost,
> But it is divine. Serve yourself from the lofty,
> Inestimable gift, and soar on high:
> It will carry you quickly above everything common
> To the ether, as long as you can last.
> We will meet again, far away from here.
> (*Halte fest, was dir von allem übrigblieb.*
> *Das Kleid, laß es nicht los. Da zupfen schon*
> *Dämonen an den Zipfeln, möchte gern*
> *Zur Unterwelt es reißen. Halte fest!*
> *Die Göttin ist's nicht mehr, die du verlorst,*
> *Doch göttlich ist's. Bediene dich der hohen,*
> *Unschätzbaren Gunst und hebe dich empor:*
> *Es trägt dich über alles Gemeine rasch*
> *Am Äther hin, so lange du dauern kannst.*
> *Wir sehn uns wieder, weit, gar weit von hier.*)
> (Goethe, *Faust Part Two*, trans. David Luke [New York: Oxford University Press, 1994], ll. 9945–54)

Helena's veil appears as something to be held (the repetition of the imperative "hold firmly" [*halte fest*] plays on Faust's name) and as something to be appropriated ("serve yourself" [*bediene dich*], Faust is urged).

But this is from the perspective of Mephistopheles, in the form of Phorkyas who is the antithesis of Helena. Yet two veils appear in this dramatic scene: there is Helena's veil and also the clouds into which her veil is drawn along with Faust: "Helena's garments dissolve into the clouds, envelop Faust, lift him into the air, and withdraw with him," according to the stage direction (after l. 9954). As Faust holds on to the veil of Helena—or, more precisely, as he is exhorted to hold on to it—he is enveloped or veiled by the clouds.

68. In the second installment of the first edition of "Goethes Wahlverwandtschaften" published in the *Neue Deutsche Beiträge* in 1925, page 164 contains 33 lines with the dash in question appearing in the middle of line 17—the middle line. The dash appears at the very end of page 197 in the *Gesammelte Schriften*.

69. This retrospective aspect of the conclusion was largely hidden from its first readers. At that time Benjamin's critical studies were barely in circulation and the essay on Hölderlin had not been published at all (this did not happen until 1955). The print run of Benjamin's dissertation was very limited, and a substantial portion of those copies were destroyed in a fire at the Francke publishing house in October of 1923. Steiner, *Der Begriff der Kunstkritik in der deutschen Romantik, Kritische Gesamtausgabe*, vol. 3 (Frankfurt am Main: Suhrkamp, 2008), 188–90. The allusions in this passage to Benjamin's own youth and in particular to the suicide of his friend the poet Fritz Heinle in 1914 would have been legible only to a small circle of friends.

70. Youth's "readiness for death" (*Todesbereitschaft*) is to be contrasted, according to Benjamin, with a "readiness to die" (*Bereitschaft zum Sterben*) that is the characteristic of age (*GS* 1.1: 198; *SW* 1: 353). The traditional dictum that "philosophizing is learning to die" (*Philosophieren heißt sterben lernen*) suggests that this contrast between youth and age extends to the relation between literature and philosophy.

71. "*Zugestehen*" and "*Zugeständnis*," *Grimms Wörterbuch*.

72. On the significance of the name Ottilie, Benjamin writes: "In the name 'Ottilie' [Goethe] alludes to the saint who was the patron of those suffering from eye disease and to whom a convent on the Odilienberg in the Black Forest was dedicated. Goethe calls her a 'consolation for the eyes' of the men who see her; indeed, in her name one may catch a hint of the mild light which is the blessing of sick eyes and in itself the hearth of all semblance (*Heimat alles Scheines*)" (*GS* 1.1: 186; *SW* 1: 344).

73. As noted in chapter 1, in the December 4, 1801, letter Hölderlin writes: "With the exception of what must be the highest for the Greeks and for us—namely, the living relationship and destiny (*Geschick*)—we must not share anything identical with them." Hölderlin, "Zwei Briefe," *Sämtliche Werke*, vol. 6 (Stuttgart: Kohlhammer, 1969), 426; *Essays and Letters on Theory*, trans. Thomas Pfau (Albany: State University of New York Press, 1988), 150. The complex signification of *Geschick* is also crucial to a passage from Hölderlin's "Remarks on Antigone" that has multiple connections to Benjamin's reflection on Ottilie in this paragraph. The key sentence from Hölderlin is "It is the main tendency in the mode of representation of our time to designate something, to possess a skill, since the lack of destiny, the *dysmoron*, is our deficiency" (*die Haupttendenz in den Vorstellungsarten unserer Zeit ist, etwas treffen zu können, Geschick zu haben, da das Schicksallose . . . unsere Schwäche ist*). "Anmerkungen zur Antigonä," *Sämtliche Werke*, vol. 5 (Stuttgart: Kohlhammer, 1970), 270; "Remarks on Antigone," *Essays and Letters on Theory*, trans. Thomas Pfau (Albany: State University of New York Press, 1988), 113–14.

74. Benjamin's earlier reference to Bettine von Arnim's collection is to a letter purportedly sent from Goethe to Bettine on February 5, 1810—just after the publication of *Elective Affinities* (*GS* 1.1: 145; *SW* 1: 313; see above in this chapter page 20 and note 37). This correspondence "with a child" is a key to Benjamin's interpretation of the novel.

75. We do not know, however, whether Goethe ever read the letter. Indeed, based on evidence presented in the modern critical edition published in 1992, the possibility that it might have been written after Goethe's death cannot be excluded. The modern critical edition of von Arnim's text prepared by Walter Schmitz and Sibylle von Steinsdorff contains a comprehensive comparison of the *Correspondence with a Child* with the original handwritten letters in the archive of the von Arnim family that was purchased in its entirety at auction in 1929 by David Heinemann and that was donated to the Pierpont Morgan Library after his death. Schmitz and von Steinsdorff record no original manuscript in the archive that corresponds to the May 22, 1809, letter in question, which appears on pages 271–73 of their edition and which would appear on page 1129 in the apparatus if it were included. Benjamin did not have this information available to him when he completed his essay on Goethe. Nevertheless his

assumption that Goethe read the letter is true to the interpretation of it as a source for the novel.

76. The reference in Bettine's letter to Valhalla is to the "hall of slain warriors" in Norse mythology but also perhaps to the memorial conceived by Crown Prince Ludwig I of Bavaria in 1807 to which Goethe's bust was added in 1808.

77. The passage from chapter 3 of *Elective Affinities*, Part Two is Goethe, *Werke*, vol. 6, 375; *Elective Affinities*, 171.

78. The second phrase from Gundolf in the above sentence is not cited by Benjamin. It appears just before the excerpts quoted by Benjamin. I include it because it makes explicit the priority of "lived experience" (*Erlebnis*) in Gundolf's approach. Here is the entire passage:

> The historical explanation of [the work's] uniqueness has to pause on the character of Ottilie: this character derives from a unique lived experience of Goethe (*stammt aus einem einmaligen Erlebnis Goethes*), from a moment that was essentially creative of the entire work, through which the available formative elements of its entire being and condition came together to form a work of art and its inner possibilities became a represented reality. The figure of Ottilie is neither the main content (*der Hauptgehalt*) nor the real problem of *Elective Affinities*, but without the moment when Goethe saw what appears in the work as Ottilie, very likely the content (*der Gehalt*) would not have been poeticized nor the problem formulated in this way. (Gundolf, *Goethe*, 569)

79. Benjamin cites the second edition of *Goethes Gespräche*, vol. 2, prepared by Woldemar Freiherrn von Biedermann (Leipzig: F. W. v. Biedermann, 1909), 353. It is interesting and telling that in the modern edition that is "expanded and edited" by Wolfgang Herwig in 1969 immediately following the allusion to Ottilie is inserted in brackets "Minna Herzlieb" (*Goethes Gespräche*, vol. 2 [Zurich and Stuttgart: Artemis, 1969], 1109). This specification of the meaning of what "Ottilie" names contradicts Benjamin's point.

80. Goethe, *Werke*, vol. 6, 456; *Elective Affinities*, 261.

81. Although it might not have appeared so to Goethe, it is fitting that Sulpiz Boisserée is the source on which Benjamin draws to demonstrate the relevance of the romantic concept of the work to Goethe's remarks. Boisserée, along with his brother Melchior, were disciples of Friedrich Schlegel in Paris at the beginning of the century as he was writing his

study of Indo-European etymology. This connection of Boisserée to Schlegel and to romanticism made Goethe suspicious initially of the younger art historian to whom he had originally refused an audience in Weimar around the time the *Elective Affinities* appeared. See E. H. Gombrich, *Gastspiele. Aufsätze eines Kunsthistorikers zur deutschen Sprache und Germanistik* (Vienna: Böhlau, 1992), 69–87; and Hartmut Fröschle, *Goethes Verhältnis zur Romantik* (Würzburg: Königshausen and Neumann, 2002), 128–29.

82. Benjamin's allusion is to Hölderlin, "Anmerkungen zum Ödipus," *Sämtliche Werke*, vol. 5, 196; *Essays and Letters*, 102.

83. Bertolt Brecht, "Stefan Georges Stellung im deutschen Geistesleben," *Literarische Welt* 4.28 (July 13, 1928): 3–4.

84. See Eiland and Jennings, *Walter Benjamin: A Critical Life*, 147–48.

85. The 1928 article in the *Literarische Welt* is republished in *GS* 2.2: 622–24 (there is no translation in the *Selected Writings*). The 1933 article, which originally appeared in the *Frankfurter Zeitung*, is republished in *GS* 3: 392–99; *SW* 2: 706–11.

CODA: THE AFTERLIFE OF PHILOLOGY

1. The editors of Benjamin's *Gesammelte Schriften* date the note on "the dialectical" image as having been composed during the period from "the end of 1938 to the beginning of 1939" (*GS* 1.3: 1225).

2. Here are the last five lines of Hugo von Hofmannsthal's *Death and the Fool* (*Der Tor und der Tod*):

How wonderful are these beings,
Who nevertheless interpret what is not interpretable,
Who read what was never written
Masterfully binding confusion
And finding yet ways in eternal darkness.
(*Wie wundervoll sind diese Wesen,*
Die, was nicht deutbar, dennoch deuten,
Was nie geschrieben wurde, lesen
Verworrenes beherrschend binden
Und Wege noch im Ewig-Dunkeln finden.)
(Hugo von Hofmannsthal, *Der Tor und der Tod*
[Leipzig: Insel-Verlag, n.d.], 32).

3. Here is the key passage on fools and folly in Kafka from Benjamin's "Letter to Gershom Scholem on Kafka" (June 12, 1938):

> This is why, in Kafka, there is no longer any talk of wisdom (*Weisheit*). Only the products of its decomposition are left. There are two. First is rumor about true things. . . . The other product of this diathesis is folly (*die Torheit*), which, though it has entirely squandered the content that belongs to wisdom (*der Gehalt, der der Weisheit zueigen ist*), preserves the unruffled complaisance (*Gefällige und Gelassene wahrt*) that rumor utterly lacks. Folly is the essence of Kafka's favorites (*Die Torheit ist das Wesen der Kafkaschen Lieblinge*)—from Don Quixote through the assistants to the animals. . . . Of this much, Kafka was sure: first, that to help, one must be a fool (*daß einer, um zu helfen, ein Tor sein muß*); and second, that only a fool's help is real help (*eines Toren Hilfe allein ist wirklich eine*). . . . So, as Kafka says, there is an infinite amount of hope—only not for us. (Walter Benjamin, *Gesammelte Briefe*, vol. 6 [1938–1940] [Frankfurt am Main: Suhrkamp, 2000], 113; "Letter to Gershom Scholem," *Selected Writings*, vol. 3, trans. Edmund Jephcott [Cambridge, Mass.: Harvard University Press, 2002], 322–29, at 326–27.)

4. Hofmannsthal, *Der Tor und der Tod*, 20.

5. Allusions to the "book of life" can be found, for example, in the following Bible passages: Psalms 69:27–28, Philippians 4:3, and Revelation 20:12. For a summary of the biblical scholarship on this topic, see Stefan Fischer, "Buch des Lebens," in *Das wissenschaftliche Bibellexikon im Internet* (posted 2014): https://www.bibelwissenschaft.de/stichwort/15741/. Some interesting comments can also be found in Herman L. Strack and Paul Billerbeck, *Kommentar zum Neuen Testament aus Talmud und Midrasch*, vol. 2 (München: Beck, 1922), 169–70.

6. In a highly interesting commentary in *The City of God* on "the book of life" in Revelation 20:12, Augustine insists on the distinction between "the book of life" and other "books" that appear in this passage. The former have written in them things done and not done—"deeds"—whereas the latter contains "the book of life of each man." This latter "book of life," Augustine concludes, has a "divine power" of remembering: "And this *divine power* (*uis diuina*) is called a book, because in it we shall as it were read all that it causes us to remember (*Quae nimirum uis diuina libri nomen accepit. In ea quippe quodam modo legitur, quidquid ea faciente recolitur*)." *City of God*, vol. 2, trans. Marcus Dodds (Edinburgh: T & T Clark, 1871), 374.

7. For what the editors of the *Gesammelte Schriften* describe as "the lengthy and convoluted publication history" of Benjamin's Goethe essay, from which it was rescued by Hofmannsthal, see *GS* 1.3: 812–21.

8. Letter to Karl Jakob Ludwig Iken on September 27, 1827. *Goethes Briefe* [Hamburger Ausgabe], vol. 4 (Hamburg: Christian Wegner, 1967), 250.

9. On Goethe and Wolf, see Manfred Riedel, "Zwischen Dichtung und Philologie. Goethe und Friedrich August Wolf," *Deutsche Vierteljahrsschrift für Literaturwissenschaft und Geistesgeschichte* 71 (1997): 92–109. On Wolf's debts to biblical scholarship, in particular to Johann Gottfried Eichhorn, see Anthony Grafton, "Introduction" to Friedrich August Wolf, *Prolegomena to Homer, 1795,* trans. Anthony Grafton, Glenn W. Most, and James E. G. Zetzel (Princeton: Princeton University Press, 1985), 18–26.

10. I am aware of only one passing allusion by Benjamin to Wolf: in his encyclopedia article on Goethe (*GS* 2.2: 731; *SW* 2: 181).

11. As Benjamin indicates in his note, this same citation appears in convolute 15a,1 in the manuscript of *The Arcades Project* (GS 5.1: 603–4; *The Arcades Project,* trans. Howard Eiland and Kevin McLaughlin [Cambridge, Mass.: Harvard University Press, 1999], 482). In the manuscript on Paris, however, the citation from Monglond is taken down in French, as is the standard practice in that text. Thus, the English translation is directly from the French.

12. The sentence in Monglond's French text likens the process by which these images come to light to the activity of working or sculpting stone. He writes: "Only the future possesses developers active enough to work these negatives to perfection" (*Seul l'avenir possède des révélateurs assez actifs pour fouiller parfaitement de tels clichés*). André Monglond, *Le préromantisme français 1 Le héros préromantique* (Grenoble: Arthaud, 1930), xii. Among the significations of the verb *fouiller* Littré includes: "term in sculpture or architecture; to carve and hollow out ornamentation in order to give it more relief; for example, to work marble." An especially apt example of this meaning of the word—one of which Benjamin was certainly aware—is provided by a passage from Marcel Proust's *Within a Budding Grove* in which the plain and dreary Romanesque church in Balbec is contrasted to those that display "the fantasy of the later gothic builders who worked their stone as if it had been lace" (*la fantaisie des architectes gothiques qui fouillent la pierre comme de la dentelle*). Marcel Proust, *À l'ombre des jeunes filles en fleurs, À la recherche du temps perdu,*

vol. 1 (Paris: Gallimard, 1987), 456; *Within a Budding Grove*, trans. C. K. Scott Montcrieff (London: Chatto and Windus, 1924), 50. In the German translation of this text, which Benjamin completed with Franz Hessel in 1926 and published in 1927, the phrase in Proust's sentence is translated as *"Phantaisie der gotischen Architekten, die den Stein meistern wie Spitze." Im Schatten der jungen Mädchen* (*Gesammelte Schriften. Übersetzungen*, supplement 2), trans. Walter Benjamin and Franz Hessel (Frankfurt am Main: Suhrkamp, 1987), 40.

13. The adaptation of the comparison of the temporal receptivity of literary texts to photography is the explicit focus of Benjamin's comments.

14. Theodor W. Adorno, letter dated November 10, 1938, *Briefwechsel, 1928–1940* (Frankfurt am Main: Suhrkamp, 1994), 364–65; *SW* 4: 100.

15. The allusion is to Benjamin's April 4, 1938, letter to Gretel and Theodor Adorno (*Gesammelte Briefe*, vol. 6, 62).

16. Adorno's criticisms of "Paris of the Second Empire in Baudelaire" are contained in a letter from November 10, 1938. It is included in the apparatus to "Paris of the Second Empire in Baudelaire" in Benjamin's *Gesammelte Schriften* (*GS* 1.3: 1093–1100); an English translation is contained in the *Selected Writings*, vol. 4 (*SW* 4: 99–105). Benjamin's response came in a letter dated December 9, 1938 (*Gesammelte Briefe*, vol. 6, 181–93; *SW* 4: 105–15).

17. The quotations from Benjamin's December 9, 1938, letter that follow in this paragraph are from *Gesammelte Briefe*, vol. 6, 184–88; *SW* 4: 107–10.

18. For a description of the development of the tripartite plan for the Baudelaire book, see the editor's note (*GS* 1.3: 1064–65) and Benjamin's September 28, 1938, letter to Horkheimer (Benjamin, *Gesammelte Briefe*, vol. 6, 162–63). For a detailed account of the evolution of the Baudelaire project out of the Arcades Project, see Giorgio Agamben, "Introduction," trans. Martin Rueff, in *Walter Benjamin, Baudelaire* (Paris: La Fabrique, 2013): 7–20, see especially 7–11.

19. Benjamin, *Gesammelte Briefe*, vol. 6, 184; *SW* 4: 107. The passage in Adorno's letter from which Benjamin cites can be found in Benjamin, *GS* 1.3: 1096; *SW* 4: 102.

20. For an example of the translation of the ancient Greek *thaumazein* from Plato's Theatetis 155d into German as *Staunen*, see Gustav Adolf Seeck, *Platons Theaitetos: ein kritischer Kommentar* (München: Beck, 2010), 46.

21. Benjamin, *Gesammelte Briefe*, vol. 6, 184; *SW* 4: 107.

22. In a recent study, *The Benjamin Files* (London: Verso, 2020), Fredric Jameson provides a reading of the exchange between Benjamin and Adorno. Jameson's tendency to adopt Adorno's perspective (see, for example, *The Benjamin Files*, 170) does not prevent him from seeing that Benjamin's "wide-eyed presentation of facticity" is not simply an undialectical error. Yet Jameson misses the significance of philology in Benjamin's response to Adorno, describing it as an appeal to "classical philology" and downgrading the "genuine philological attitude" in favor of the supposedly more "crucial" monad (*The Benjamin Files*, 225–26). As I have suggested, philology as defined by Benjamin is fundamentally different from the historical methodology of Auerbach and Spitzer that Jameson has in mind when he writes of "the practice . . . of restoring the background of an entire world and way of life, with its implements and its laws, its concrete constituents" (*The Benjamin Files*, 225).

23. Benjamin, *Gesammelte Briefe*, vol. 6, 185; *SW* 4: 108.

24. As Benjamin writes: "Through its form the work of art is a lively center of reflection" (*ein lebendiges Zentrum der Reflexion*) (*GS* 1.1: 73; *SW* 1: 156). The allusion to the monad in Leibniz refers to Benjamin's discussion in the preface to his study of the Baroque *Trauerspiel* (*GS* 1.1: 227–28; *Origin of the German Trauerspiel*, 26–27). In an illuminating commentary on the passage from Benjamin's December 9, 1938, letter under consideration, Giorgio Agamben explicates the ambiguity of the monad in Leibniz: "The reference to the Leibnizian concept of the monad must be taken here literally. On the one hand, the fact that the monad has no window 'through which something could enter or exit' implies that its transformations 'come from its internal principle. On the other hand, since the nature of monads is 'representative,' each one of them represents also, with the entirety of the universe, 'the body that was attributed to it in particular.'" Agamben, "Introduction," 17–18. In the former case Agamben refers to *Monadology* paragraphs 7 and 11; in the latter to paragraph 62.

25. Benjamin, *Gesammelte Briefe*, vol. 6, 185; *SW* 4: 108.

26. Criticism of Adorno's supervision of Benjamin's legacy can be found already in Helmut Heissenbüttel's 1967 essay published in *Merkur*, and "Hannah Arendt amplified Heissenbüttel's charge that Adorno's editorial practices essentially continued the censorship of Benjamin's writing

undertaken by the Institute for Social Research in New York in the late 1930s." Eiland and Jennings, *Walter Benjamin: A Critical Life* (Cambridge, Mass.: Harvard University Press, 2014), 678.

27. Theodor W. Adorno, "Parataxis" in *Noten zur Literatur* (Frankfurt am Main: Suhrkamp, 1974) 447–91, at 447–48, and 252; "Parataxis" in *Notes to Literature*, vol. 2, trans. S. W. Nicholson (New York: Columbia University Press, 1992): 109–49, at 109 and 114.

28. Adorno, "Parataxis," 453–54, 115.

29. As noted in the preface, Benjamin's early essay on Hölderlin was first published in the two-volume *Schriften* edited by Adorno in the mid-1950s.

30. Adorno notes a few pages earlier that "the poetized" was a term that "first Benjamin and later Heidegger" used to characterize that which is composed poetically (Adorno, "Parataxis," 450;111–12). However, as we have seen, in applying this word to Hölderlin's poetry Benjamin was drawing on Goethe's remark on *Elective Affinities* in an 1809 letter to Reinhard (Goethe, *Briefe*, vol. 3, 117).

31. Adorno, "Parataxis," 471, 130–31.

32. Adorno, "Parataxis," 478, 137.

33. Adorno, "Parataxis," 478, 137.

34. I have offered an explication of this interpenetration of space and time that Benjamin finds in Hölderlin's poem in my *Poetic Force: Poetry after Kant* (Stanford: Stanford University Press, 2014), 24–25.

35. On this point, see my *Poetic Force*, 51–54.

36. Adorno, "Parataxis," 489, 147.

37. The translation of "Brot und Wein" is from Christopher Middleton. Friedrich Hölderlin, *Selected Poems and Letters* (Chicago: University of Chicago Press, 1972).

38. Adorno, "Parataxis," 488, 146.

39. Adorno, "Parataxis," 489, 147,

40. See Adorno, "Parataxis," 489, 147; and Benjamin *GS* 2.1: 116; *SW* 1: 28.

41. Adorno's allusion to "presence" (*Dabeisein*) seems to reintroduce the self-consistency and security on the level of aconceptual synthetic mediation that Hölderlin's paratactic poetry disrupts on the level of language. In this sense, *Dabeisein* in the relevant section of Hegel's *Encyclopedia* is precisely what the movement enacted in the first stanza of "Timidity" shatters. Hegel stresses the unified subjectivity and selfhood as such in the indispensable quality of *Dabeisein* that anchors reflection in experience. This is in direct

contrast to the self-shattering action of what Benjamin calls "spatiotemporal interpenetration." Indeed, Hölderlin's famous fragment, "Urteil und Sein," takes aim at precisely this understanding of the unified nature of the judging subject. Here is the relevant passage from Hegel's *Encyclopedia* on *Dabeisein*: "The principle of *experience* contains the infinitely important determination that human beings must themselves be *involved* when taking up a given content and holding it to be true, more precisely that they must find such content to be united and in unison with *the certainty of themselves*. They must be involved in it, whether through their external senses only or with their deeper spirit and the essential consciousness of their respective self [my emphasis]. Georg Wilhelm Friedrich Hegel, *Enzyklopädie der philosophischen Wissenschaften im Grundrisse 1, Werke*, vol. 8 (Frankfurt am Main: Suhrkamp, 1986), 49–50; *Encyclopedia of the Philosophical Sciences in Basic Outline, Part 1: Science of Logic*, trans. Klaus Brinkmann and Daniel O. Dahlstrom (Cambridge: Cambridge University Press, 2010), 35.

42. In addition to Tiedemann and his team, special recognition is due to the careful scholarship and translations of the editors of the *Selected Writings* from Harvard University Press, led by Howard Eiland and Michael W. Jennings (and supported by Lindsay Waters), as well as the work of Giorgio Agamben on the reconstruction of the plan for the unfinished Baudelaire book.

43. Paul de Man, "Return to Philology," in *The Resistance to Theory* (Minneapolis: University of Minnesota Press, 1986 (originally published in 1982 in the *Times Literary Supplement*). Examples of important recent critical work on philology relevant to a reconsideration of this topic in Benjamin's writings include Werner Hamacher, *Für—Die Philologie* (Basel: Urs Engeler, 2009) and *95 Thesen zur Philologie* (Basel: Urs Engeler, 2009); Schestag, *Philo: xenia. Erste Folge*—discussed in detail in the preface; John Hamilton, *Philology of the Flesh* (Chicago: University of Chicago Press, 2018); and Jacques Lezra, *On the Nature of Things: Translation as Necrophilology* (New York: Fordham University Press, 2018). The recent collection edited by Gerhard Richter and Ann Smock, *Give the Word: Responses to Werner Hamacher's 95 Theses on Philology* (Lincoln: University of Nebraska Press, 2019), contains many valuable essays on the significance of philology in Hamacher's work and in literary study more generally.

BIBLIOGRAPHY

Adler, Jeremy. *"Eine fast magische Anziehungskraft." Goethes Wahlverwandtschaften und die Chemie seiner Zeit.* München: C. H. Beck, 1987.
Adorno, Theodor W. *Noten zur Literatur.* Frankfurt am Main: Suhrkamp, 1974.
——. "Parataxis." In *Notes to Literature*, vol. 2, trans. S. W. Nicholson, 109–49. New York: Columbia University Press, 1992.
Adorno, Theodor W., and Walter Benjamin. *Briefwechsel, 1928–1940.* Frankfurt am Main: Suhrkamp, 1994.
Agamben, Giorgio. "Introduction," trans. Martin Rueff. In *Walter Benjamin, Baudelaire*, 7–20. Paris: La Fabrique, 2013.
——. *Means without End: Notes on Politics*, trans. Vincenzo Binetti and Cesare Casarino. Minneapolis: University of Minnesota Press, 2000.
Arnim, Bettine von. *Goethes Briefwechsel mit einem Kinde.* Jena: Eugen Diederichs, 1906.
——. *Werke und Briefe*, vol. 2. Frankfurt am Main: Deutscher Klassiker Verlag, 1992.
Augustine. *City of God*, vol. 2, trans. Marcus Dodds. Edinburgh: T & T Clark, 1871.
Beiser, Frederick C. *The German Historicist Tradition.* New York: Oxford University Press, 2011.
Belsier, Gabrielle. *Goethes Rätselparodie der Romantik. Eine neue Lesart der "Wahlverwandtschaften."* Tübingen: Niemeyer Verlag, 1997.
Benjamin, Walter. *Correspondence, 1910–1940.* Chicago: University of Chicago Press, 1994.
——. *Der Begriff der Kunstkritik in der deutschen Romantik, Kritische Gesamtausgabe*, vol. 3. Frankfurt am Main: Suhrkamp, 2008.

———. *Gesammelte Briefe*, 6 vols. Frankfurt am Main: Suhrkamp, 1995–2000.
———. *Gesammelte Schriften*, 7 vols. Frankfurt am Main: Suhrkamp, 1972–91.
———. *Origin of the German Trauerspiel*, trans. Howard Eiland. Cambridge, Mass.: Harvard University Press, 2019.
———. *Selected Writings*, 4 vols., ed. Michael W. Jennings et al. Cambridge, Mass.: Harvard University Press, 1996–2003.
———. *Toward the Critique of Violence*, ed. Peter Fenves and Julia Ng. Stanford: Stanford University Press, 2021.
Berge, Lukas van den. "Law, King of All: Schmitt, Agamben, Pindar." *Law and Humanities* 13.2 (2019): 198–222.
Bergson, Henri. *Creative Evolution*, trans. Arthur Mitchell. New York: Henry Holt, 1911.
———. *L'évolution créatrice*. Paris: Presses Universitaires de France, 2009.
———. *Introduction to Metaphysics*, trans. T. E. Hulme. Indianapolis: Bobbs-Merrill, 1949.
———. *La pensée et le mouvant*. Paris: Presses Universitaires de France, 2009.
Bialas, Wolfgang, and Anson Rabinbach. "Introduction: The Humanities in Nazi Germany." In *Nazi Germany and the Humanities: How German Academics Embraced Nazism*, 2nd ed., viii–lii. London: Oneworld, 2014.
Böhm, Wilhelm. *Hölderlin*, vol. 1. Berlin: Max Niemeyer, 1928.
Brecht, Bertolt. "Stefan Georges Stellung im deutschen Geistesleben." *Literarische Welt* 4.28 (July 13, 1928): 3–4.
Cassirer, Ernst. *Das Problem Jean Jacques Rousseau*. Darmstadt: Wissenschaftliche Buchgesellschaft, 1970.
———. *The Question of Jean Jacques Rousseau*, trans. Peter Gay. Bloomington and London: Indiana University Press, 1963.
Cohen, Hermann. *Ästhetik des reinen Gefühls*, vol. 2. Berlin: Cassirer, 1912.
———. *Kants Theorie der Erfahrung*, 2nd ed. Berlin: Dümmler, 1885.
Constantine, David. "Hölderlin's Pindar: The Language of Translation." *Modern Language Review* 73.4 (October 1978): 825–34.
Copeland, Rita. *Rhetoric, Hermeneutics, and Translation in the Middle Ages: Academic Traditions and Vernacular Texts*. Cambridge: Cambridge University Press, 1995.
Daston, Lorraine, and Peter Galison. *Objectivity*. New York: Zone, 2010.

Derrida, Jacques. *The Beast and the Sovereign*, vol. 1, trans. Geoffrey Bennington. Chicago: University of Chicago Press, 2009.
———. *La Dissemination*. Paris: Seuil, 1972.
———. *Marges de la philosophie*. Paris: Minuit, 1972.
———*Séminaire. La Bête et le Souverain*, vol. 1. Paris: Galilée, 2008.
———. "Signature Event Context." In *Margins of Philosophy*, trans. Alan Bass, 307–30. Chicago: University of Chicago Press, 1982.
Dilthey, Wilhelm. "Die Typen der Weltanschauung und ihre Ausbildung in den metaphysischen Systemen." In *Weltanschauung. Philosophie und Religion*, 3–54. Berlin: Reichl, 1911.
———. *Einleitung in die Geisteswissenschaften. Versuch einer Grundlegung für das Studium der Gesellschaft und der Geschichte*, vol. 1. Leipzig and Berlin: B. G. Teubner, 1922.
———. "Geschichte und Naturwissenschaft." In *Präludien. Aufsätze und Reden zur Philosophie und ihrer Geschichte*, vol. 2, 3rd ed., 355–79. Tübingen: J. C. B. Mohr, 1907.
———. *Grundlegung der Wissenschaften vom Menschen, der Gesellschaft under der Geschichte. Gesammelte Schriften*, vol. 19. Göttingen: Vandenhoeck and Ruprecht, 1982.
———. "Kritische oder genetische Methode." In *Präludien. Aufsätze und Reden zur Philosophie und ihrer Geschichte*, vol. 2, 3rd ed., 318–44. Tübingen: J. C. B. Mohr, 1907.
Eichhorn, Johann Gottfried. *Einleitung in das Alte Testament*. Leipzig: Weidmann, 1803.
———. *Introduction to the Old Testament*, trans. George Tilly Gollop. London: Spottiswoode, 1888.
Eiland, Howard, and Michael W. Jennings. *Walter Benjamin: A Critical Life*. Cambridge, Mass.: Harvard University Press, 2014.
Enders, Carl. *Friedrich Schlegel. Die Quellen seines Wesens und Werdens*. Leipzig: H. Haessel, 1913.
Endres, Johannes, ed. *Friedrich Schlegel Handbuch: Leben—Werk—Wirkung*. Stuttgart: Metzler, 2017.
Fenves, Peter. "Completion Instead of Revelation." In *Walter Benjamin and Theology*, 56–74. New York: Fordham University Press, 2016.
———. "Entanglement—Of Benjamin with Heidegger." In *Sparks Will Fly: Benjamin and Heidegger*, ed. Andrew Benjamin and Dimitris Vardoulakis, 3–26. Albany: State University of New York Press, 2015.

———. *The Messianic Reduction: Walter Benjamin and the Shape of Time.* Stanford: Stanford University Press, 2011.

Fischer, Stefan. "Buch des Lebens." In *Das wissenschaftliche Bibellexikon im Internet* (2014), https://www.bibelwissenschaft.de/stichwort/15741/.

Foucault, Michel. *The History of Sexuality: An Introduction*, vol. 1, trans. Robert Hurley. New York: Vintage, 1990.

Fröschle, Hartmut. *Goethes Verhältnis zur Romantik.* Würzburg: Königshausen and Neumann, 2002.

Gigante, Marcello. *Nomos Basileus.* New York: Arno, 1979.

Goethe, Johann Wolfgang von. *Elective Affinities*, trans. R. J. Hollingdale. New York: Penguin, 1971.

———. *Faust Part Two*, trans. David Luke. New York: Oxford University Press, 1994.

———. *Goethes Briefe*, vol. 3. Hamburg: Christian Wegner Verlag, 1965.

———. *Goethes Gespräche*, vol. 2. Leipzig: F. W. v. Biedermann, 1909.

———. *Goethes Gespräche*, vol. 2. Zurich and Stuttgart: Artemis, 1969.

———. *Goethes Werke* [Weimarer Ausgabe], vol. 3.3. Munich: Deutscher Taschenbuch Verlag, 1987.

———. *Naturwissenschaftliche Schriften*, vol. 1. Zurich: Artemis, 1964.

———. *Sämtliche Werke. Briefe, Tagebücher und Gespräche*, vol. 39. Frankfurt am Main: Suhrkamp, 1999.

———. *Werke, Kommentare und Register*, 14 vols. [Hamburger Ausgabe]. München: C. H. Beck, 1981.

Gombrich, E. H. *Gastspiele. Aufsätze eines Kunsthistorikers zur deutschen Sprache und Germanistik.* Vienna: Böhlau, 1992,

Gray, Richard. "Skeptische Philologie: Friedrich Schlegel, Friedrich Nietzsche und eine Philologie der Zukunft." *Nietzsche-Studien* 38 (2009): 39–64.

Grüttner, Michael. "Die nationalsozialistische Wissenschaftspolitik und die Geisteswissenschaften." In *Literaturwissenschaft und Nationalsozialismus*, 13–41. Tübingen: Max Niemeyer Verlag, 2003.

Gundolf, Friedrich. *Goethe.* Berlin: Georg Bondi, 1916.

———. *Shakespeare und der deutsche Geist.* Berlin: Bondi, 1911 (2nd ed. 1914).

Hamacher, Werner. *Für—Die Philologie.* Weil am Rhein: Urs Engeler, 2009.

———. *95 Thesen zur Philologie.* Basel: Urs Engeler, 2009.

———. *Two Studies of Friedrich Hölderlin*, trans. Julia Ng and Anthony Curtis Adler. Stanford: Stanford University Press, 2020.

Hamilton, John. "Florilegia: Influence and Cross-Pollination between Celan and Hölderlin, Pindar and Horace." *Modern Language Notes* 135.3 (April 2020): 600–19.

———. *Philology of the Flesh*. Chicago: University of Chicago Press, 2018.

———. *Soliciting Darkness: Pindar, Obscurity, and the Classical Tradition*. Cambridge, Mass.: Harvard University Press, 2004.

Havons, George R. "The Sources of Rousseau's Edouard Bomston." *Modern Philology* 8.1 (July 1919): 125–39.

Hegel, Georg Wilhelm Friedrich. *Encyclopedia of the Philosophical Sciences in Basic Outline, Part 1: Science of Logic*, trans. Klaus Brinkmann and Daniel O. Dahlstrom. Cambridge: Cambridge University Press, 2010.

———. *Enzyklopädie der philosophischen Wissenschaften im Grundrisse 1*, Werke, vol. 8. Frankfurt am Main: Suhrkamp, 1986.

———. *Vorlesung über die Ästhetik 3*, Werke, vol. 15. Frankfurt am Main: Suhrkamp, 1986.

Heidegger, Martin. *Basic Problems of Phenomenology: Winter Semester 1919/1920*, trans. Scott M. Campbell. London: Bloomsbury, 2013.

———. *Grundprobleme der Phänomenologie (1919/20)*, Gesamtausgabe, vol. 58. Frankfurt am Main: Vittorio Klostermann, 1993.

———. *Phänomenologische Interpretationen zu Aristoteles. Einführung in die phänomenologische Forschung*, Gesamtausgabe, vol. 61. Frankfurt am Main: Vittorio Klostermann, 1985.

———. *Zur Bestimmung der Philosophie. 1. Die Idee der Philosophie und das Weltanschauungsproblem; 2. Phänomenologie und transzendentale Wertphilosophie; Anhang: Über das Wesen der Universität und des akademischen Studiums*, Gesamtausgabe, vols. 56–57. Frankfurt am Main: Vittorio Klostermann, 1987.

Hofmannsthal, Hugo von. *Der Tor und der Tod*. Leipzig: Insel-Verlag, n.d.

Hölderlin, Friedrich. *Essays and Letters on Theory*, trans. Thomas Pfau. Albany: State University of New York Press, 1988.

———. *Hymns and Fragments*, trans. Richard Sieburth. Princeton: Princeton University Press, 1984.

———. *Sämtliche Werke*, 8 vols. Stuttgart: Kohlhammer, 1946–85.

———. *Selected Poems and Letters*, trans. Christopher Middleton. Chicago: University of Chicago Press, 1972.
Huff, Steven R. "Kleist and Expectant Virgins: The Meaning of the 'O' in 'Die Marquise von O . . .'" *Journal of English and German Philology* 81.3 (July 1982): 367–75.
Hühn, Helmut, Jan Urbich, and Uwe Steiner, ed. *Benjamins Wahlverwandtschaften. Zur Kritik einer programmatischen Interpretation.* Frankfurt am Main: Suhrkamp, 2015.
Husserl, Edmund. *Ideas for a Pure Phenomenology and Phenomenological Philosophy*, trans. D. Dahlstrom. Indianapolis: Hackett, 2014.
———. "Ideen zu einer reinen Phänomenologie und phänomenologischen Philosophie. Erstes Buch: Allgemeine Einführung in die reine Phänomenologie." *Husserliana*, vol. 3.1. Den Hag: Martinus Nijhoff, 1950.
Jakob, Michael. *"Schwanengefahr": Das lyrische Ich im Zeichen des Schwanns.* Munich: Hanser, 2000.
Jameson, Fredric. *The Benjamin Files.* London: Verso, 2020.
Kant, Immanuel. *Critique of Pure Reason*, trans. and ed. Paul Guyer and Allen W. Wood. New York: Cambridge University Press, 1998.
———. *Gesammelte Schriften*, 29 vols. to date [Akademie-Ausgabe]. Berlin: Reimer; Walter de Gruyter, 1900–present.
———. *Religion with the Boundaries of Mere Reason*, trans. George di Giovanni. In *Religion and Rational Theology*, 39–216. Cambridge: Cambridge University Press, 1996.
Kuiken, Kir. "On the Delineation of Choice and Decision in Benjamin's Goethe's Elective Affinities." *Canadian Review of Comparative Literature* 31.3 (2004): 286–308.
Lezra, Jacques. *On the Nature of Things: Translation as Necrophilology.* New York: Fordham University Press, 2018.
Lloyd-Jones, Hugh. *The Justice of Zeus.* Berkeley and Los Angeles: University of California Press, 1983.
Lukács, Georg. "Hegels Ästhetik." In Georg Wilhelm Friedrich Hegel, *Ästhetik*, vol. 2, ed. Friedrich Bassenge. Berlin: Verlag das Europäische Buch, 1985.
Makkreel, Rudolf A. *Imagination and Interpretation in Kant: The Hermeneutical Import of the Critique of Judgment.* Chicago: University of Chicago Press, 1995.
Man, Paul de. *The Resistance to Theory.* Minneapolis: University of Minnesota Press, 1986.

McFarland, James. *Constellation: Friedrich Nietzsche and Walter Benjamin in the Now-Time of History*. New York: Fordham University Press, 2013.
McLaughlin, Kevin. *Poetic Force: Poetry after Kant*. Stanford: Stanford University Press, 2014.
———. *Writing in Parts: Imitation and Exchange in Nineteenth-Century Literature*. Stanford: Stanford University Press, 1995.
Menninghaus, Winfried. *Hälfte des Lebens: Versuch über Hölderlins Poetik*. Frankfurt am Main: Suhrkamp, 2005.
Meyerson, Emile. *L'explication dans les sciences*. Paris: Payot, 1921.
Miller, J. Hillis. *Ariadne's Thread: Story Lines*. New Haven: Yale University Press, 1992.
Mommsen, Katharina. *Kleists Kampf mit Goethe*. Heidelberg: Lothar Stiehm, 1974.
Monglond, André. *Le préromantisme français. 1. Le héros préromantique*. Grenoble: Arthaud, 1930.
Newman, Jane O. *Benjamin's Library: Modernity, Nation, and the Baroque*. Ithaca, N.Y.: Cornell University Press, 2011.
Nietzsche, Friedrich. *Human, All Too Human: A Book for Free Spirits*, trans. R. J. Hollingdale. Cambridge: Cambridge University Press, 1996.
———. *Kritische Gesamtausgabe, Werke*, vol. 2.2. Berlin: de Gruyter, 1993.
———. *Kritische Gesamptausgabe*, vol. 2.3. Berlin: de Gruyter, 1993.
———. *Kritische Studienausgabe*, vol. 8. Berlin: de Gruyter, 1988.
Oellers, Norbert. "Warum eigentlich Eduard? Zur Namen-Wahl in Goethes *Wahlverwandtschaften*." In *Geneo huius loci: Dank an Leiva Petersen*, 215–34. Wien/Köln/Graz: H. Böhlan, 1982.
Oexle, Otto Gerhard. "Max Weber—Geschichte als Problemgeschichte." In *Das Problem der Problemgeschichte, 1880–1932*, ed. Otto Gerhard Oexle. 9–37. Göttingen: Wallstein Verlag, 2001.
———. "Naturwissenschaft und Geschichtswissenschaft. Momente iner Problemgeschichte." In *Naturwissenschaft, Geisteswissenschaft, Kulturwissenschaft: Einheit—Gegensatz—Komplemtarität?*, ed. Otto Gerhard Oexle. *Göttinger Gespräche zur Geschichtswissenschaft* 6, 98–155. Göttingen: Wallstein Verlag, 2000.
Oppenheimer, Ernst M. *Goethe's Poetry for Occasions*. Toronto: University of Toronto Press, 1974.
Porter, James I. *Nietzsche and the Philology of the Future*. Stanford: Stanford University Press, 2002.

Proust, Marcel. À l'ombre des jeunes filles en fleurs, À la recherche du temps perdu, vol. 1. Paris: Gallimard, 1987.

——. Contre Sainte-Beuve: précédé de Pastiches et mélanges et suivi de Essais et articles. Paris: Gallimard, 1971.

——. Within a Budding Grove, trans. C. K. Scott Montcrieff. London: Chatto and Windus, 1924.

Richter, Gerhard, and Ann Smock. Give the Word: Responses to Werner Hamacher's 95 Theses on Philology. Lincoln: University of Nebraska Press, 2019.

Rickert, Heinrich. Die Philosophie des Lebens. Darstellung und Kritik der philosophischen Modeströmmungen unserer Zeit. Tübingen: Verlag von Mohr, 1920.

——. "Vom System der Werte." Logos: Internationale Zeitschrift für Philosophie der Kultur 4 (1913): 295–327.

Riedel, Manfred. "Zwischen Dichtung und Philologie. Goethe und Friedrich August Wolf." Deutsche Vierteljahrsschrift für Literaturwissenschaft und Geistesgeschichte 71 (1997): 92–109.

Rousseau, Jean-Jacques. Œuvres completes, vol. 2. Paris: Gallimard, 1964.

Salzani, Carlo. "From Benjamin's bloßes Leben to Agamben's Nuda Vita: A Genealogy." In Towards the Critique of Violence: Walter Benjamin and Giorgio Agamben, ed. Brendan Moran and Carlo Salzani, 109–23. London: Bloomsbury, 2015.

Schestag, Thomas. Philo: xenia. Erste Folge. Basel: Urs Engeler, 2009.

Scheuer, Hans Jürgen. "Verlagerung des Mythos in die Struktur. Hölderlins Bearbeitung des Orpheus-Todes in der Odenfolge Muth des Dichters—Dichtermuth—Blödigkeit." Jahrbuch der deutschen Schillergesellschaft 45 (2001): 250–77.

Schlaffer, Heinz. "Namen und Buchstaben in Goethes 'Wahlverwandtschaften.'" Jahrbuch der Jean-Paul-Gesellschaft 7 (1972): 84–102.

Schlegel, Friedrich. Hefte Zur Philologie. Paderborn: Ferdinand Schöningh, 2015.

——. Kritische Friedrich Schlegel Ausgabe. Paderborn: Ferdinand Schöningh, 1958–present.

——. On the Aesthetic Education of Man, trans. Keith Tribe. New York: Penguin, 2016.

Schmidt, Julian. Geschichte der deutschen Literatur seit Lessing's Tod, vol. 2, 5th ed. Leipzig: Grunow, 1866.

Schmitt, Carl. *The Nomos of the Earth in the International Law of the Jus Publicum*, trans. Gary Ulmen. New York: Telos, 2006.
Scholem, Gershom. *Tagebücher, nebst Aufsätzen und Entwürfen bis 1923*, 2 vols. Frankfurt am Main: Jüdischer Verlag, 1995–2000.
——. *Walter Benjamin—Die Geschichte einer Freundschaft*. Frankfurt am Main: Suhrkamp, 1975.
Seeck, Gustav Adolf. *Platons Theaitetos: ein kritischer Kommentar*. München: Beck, 2010.
Steiner, Uwe. *Die Geburt der Kritik aus dem Geiste der Kunst: Untersuchungen zum Begriff der Kritik in den frühen Schriften Walter Benjamins*. Würzburg: Königshausen and Neumann, 1989.
——. "Exemplarische Kritik. Anmerkungen zu Benamins Kritik der Wahlverwandtschaften." In *Benjamins Wahlverwandtschaften: Zur Kritik einer programmatischen Interpretation*, ed. Helmut Hühn, Jan Urbich, and Uwe Steiner, 37–67. Frankfurt am Main: Suhrkamp, 2015.
——. "The True Politician: Walter Benjamin's Concept of the Political," trans. Colin Sample. *New German Critique* 83 (2001): 43–88.
Steizinger, Johannes. *Revolte, Eros und Sprache. Walter Benjamins "Metaphysik der Jugend."* Berlin: Kulturverlag Kadmos, 2013.
Strack, Herman L., and Paul Billerbeck. *Kommentar zum Neuen Testament aus Talmud und Midrasch*, vol. 2. München: Beck, 1922.
Thouard, Denis. "Der unmögliche Abschluss. Schlegel, Wolf und die Kunst der Diaskeuasten." In *Antike—Philologie—Romantik. Friedrich Schlegels altertumswissenschaftliche Manuskripte*, ed. Christian Benne and Ulrich Breuer, 41–62. Padeborn: Ferdinand Schöningh, 2011.
Walter, Julius. *Die Geschichte der Ästethik im Altertum ihrer begrifflichen Entwicklung nach dargestellt*. Leipzig: O. R. Reisland, 1893.
Weber, Samuel. *Benjamin's—abilities*. Cambridge, Mass.: Harvard University Press, 2009.
——. "From Reflection to Repetition: Medium, Reflexivity and the Economy of the Self." In *Thinking Media Aesthetics. Media Studies, Film Studies and the Arts*, 51–65. Berlin: Peter Lang, 2013.
——. "Genealogy of Modernity: History, Myth and Allegory in Benjamin's *Origin of the German Mourning Play*." *Modern Language Notes* 106.3 (April 1991): 467–68.
——. *Targets of Opportunity: On the Militarization of Thinking*. New York: Fordham University Press, 2005.

Wegener, Alfred. "Die Entstehung der Kontinente." *Geologische Rundschau* 3.4 (1912): 276–92.

Weigel, Sigrid. "Treue, Liebe, Eros. Benjamins Lebenswissenschaft in 'Goethes Wahlverwandtschaften.'" In *Benjamins Wahlverwandtschaften. Zur Kritik einer programmatischen Interpretationen*, 174–95. Frankfurt am Main: Suhrkamp, 2015.

Wellek, René. "The Early Literary Criticism of Walter Benjamin." *Rice University Studies* 57.4 (1971): 123–34.

Windelband, Wilhelm. *Geschichte der neueren Philosophie in ihrem Zusammenhange mit der allgemeinen Kultur und den besonderen Wissenschaften*, vol. 2. Leipzig: Breitkopf and Härtel, 1911.

———."Geschichte und Naturwissenschaft." In *Präludien. Aufsätze und Reden zur Philosophie und ihrer Geschichte*, vol. 2, 355–79. Tübingen: J. C. B. Mohr, 1907.

———. "Kritische oder genetische Methode." In *Präludien. Aufsätze und Reden zur Philosophie und ihrer Geschichte*, vol. 2, 318–44. Tübingen: J. C. B. Mohr, 1907.

Wolf, Friedrich August. *Prolegomena ad Homerum, sivie, De operum Homericorum Prisca et genuine forma variique mutationibus et probablili ratione emendandi*, vol. 1. Halle: Wolf, 1794–95.

———. *Prolegomena to Homer, 1795*, trans. Anthony Grafton, Glenn W. Most, and James E. G. Zetzel. Princeton: Princeton University Press, 1985.

Xanthou, Maria G. "Ludolph Dissen, August Boeckh, Gottfried Hermann and Tycho Mommsen: Tracing *Asyndeton*, Steering Influence." *Bulletin of the Institute of Classical Studies* 57.2 (December 3, 2014): 1–21.

Zanfi, Caterina. *Bergson et la philosophie allemande. 1907–1932*. Paris: Armand Colin, 2013.

INDEX

Adorno, Gretel, 11, 174
Adorno, Theodor: criticism of Benjamin's legacy, 119; lack of dialectical rigor in Benjamin's work, 14, 92, 115, 120; methodological disagreements with Benjamin, 104, 114, 115–121, 175n22; on Hölderlin, 120–124; preservation of Benjamin's writings, 119–126
Aesthetic of Pure Feeling (Cohen), 82
Agamben, Giorgio, 5, 65, 125, 132n12, 133n13, 137n14, 152n39
aging and youth, 18, 21, 101–105, 136n9, 168n70
Ardor-Berlin. *See* Benjamin, Walter
Arendt, Hannah, 14, 125
Arnim Bettine von, 79, 87, 103–104
Athenaeum-fragments (Schlegel), 59, 60, 61, 63

bare life (*zoé*). *See* philology of life: bare life
Baudelaire, Benjamin's study of: classification of Baudelaire, 22; connection between wonder and philosophy, 117–119, 175n22; entanglement with other works, 125; extension of reflection on "life," 13, 14, 114–115; Goethe's essay as model for study, 115; image-object, 118, 175n24; "lack of theoretical transparency," 116–118; shift in perspective, 118; tripartite plan, 116, 156n13. *See also*

Adorno, Theodor: methodological disagreements with Benjamin
Belsier, Gabrielle, 83
Benjamin, Walter: Ardor-Berlin pseudonym, 135n1; biographical note on George, 106–107; impact of World War I on, 2, 3, 107; methodological disagreements with Adorno, 104, 114, 115–121, 175n22; 1916 conversation with Scholem, 15; 1921 letter to Scholem, 6–7, 10, 15, 16, 26–27, 61–62, 71, 109; Rickert's seminar on Bergson's concept of time, 19; speeches to Berlin Independent Students' Association, 17, 135n1; student years, 15, 16, 24, 135n1; studies in Berlin, 2; studies in Bern, 2, 42–43; studies in Freiburg, 2, 17, 22; studies in Munich, 2; *See also* Baudelaire, Benjamin's study of; *Concept of Criticism in German Romanticism, The*; *Gesammelte Schriften*; "Goethe's Elective Affinities"; "Life of Students, The"; "Metaphysics of Youth, The"; "On Language as Such and on the Language of Man"; "On Some Motifs in Baudelaire"; *Origin of the German Trauerspiel*; "Paris of the Second Empire in Baudelaire"; philology of life; *Schriften*; "Sleeping Beauty"; "Toward the Critique of Violence"; "Two Poems by Friedrich Hölderlin"

189

Bergson, Henri, 17, 18, 19, 21, 114, 139n30
Bersier, Gabrielle, 83
Bible, philological studies of, 111–112, 172n6
"biopolitics," 5, 125, 137n14
biopower, sovereignty of, 5, 137n14
bios. See philology of life: qualified/made life
Boeckh, August, 30
Böhlendorff, Casimir Ulrich, 37, 41, 56–57, 62, 145n59
Boisserée, Sulpiz, 105–106, 170n81
"book of life," 5, 6, 110, 172n6
Brecht, Bertolt, 106
Buber, Martin, 106

Callicles, 65
Cassirer, Ernst, 25
Cohen, Hermann, 25, 82, 139n29
Concept of Criticism in German Romanticism, The (Benjamin): achievement of romantics, 53–54; analogy of critical "presentation," 70–71; as "medium of reflection," 13, 49–55, 63, 81; concepts of reflection and criticism, 44–49, 117; connection of the real, 50, 51–52; dissertation submitted, 2, 42–43, 58; divergence from critical practice in dissertation, 53–54, 55–67; entanglement with other works, 1–2, 3, 11, 12, 13, 106, 112–113, 125; esoteric dimension, 43–44, 145n1; free use doctrine, 62–63, 77, 163n47; Hölderlin's influence, 58–59, 102–103; I formation, 44–45, 48–49, 51, 53, 61, 147n6; image-object, 52, 54–55, 117, 118, 175n24; inauthentic naming, 82–83, 159n26; non-I formation, 44–45, 48; objectivity in cultural and human sciences, 46; "problem-historical investigation," 44, 146n4; relation between pure form and pure content, 63–66; rigor of form, 42, 64–66, 153n41; "second-level reflection," 48; self-limitation, 42–43, 44, 49, 51, 52, 55, 63, 65, 139n29, 147n6; subject-object formation, 51–53, 118;

"The Sources," 46–48; "the thinking of thinking," 51–52
continental drift, theory of, 141n39
Corngold, Stanley, 70
Critique of Pure Reason (Kant), 19, 65
Critique of the Power of Judgment (Kant), 20, 55
cultural sciences, 22, 146n4

Das Erlebnis und die Dichtung (Dilthey), 13, 114
"das" Geschichte. See history: layering
"death." *See* philology of life: death
Death and the Fool (Hofmannsthal), 109
de Man, Paul, 125–126
Demetz, Peter, 14, 43, 125
Derrida, Jacques, 85–87, 126
"die" Geschichte. See history
Die Grenzboten, 97
Dilthey, Wilhelm, 13, 19, 28, 114
Dissent, Ludolf, 30

"earthly life." *See* philology of life: "earthly life"
Eckermann, Johann Peter, 71, 89, 90
Elective Affinities (Goethe): beauty and modern aesthetic theory, 13, 97–104; character of the work of art, 93–95, 104; conflict between sensuality and morality, 78–83; "elective affinities" meaning and writing, 85; fear of death, 102, 124; figure of Ottilie, 13, 97–105, 124, 168n72; *Gehalt*, 73–75; Goethe's description to Eckermann, 71, 89, 90; Goethe's relationship to Ottilie, 105–106; "immanent structure," 3, 78, 79, 88, 90, 98, 104, 105; "mirroring" juxtaposition, 3–4, 111, 115, 124; missed opportunity, 3–4, 88, 90–91, 163n47; mythic economy of guilt and atonement, 81, 103; on marriage, 73–77; parody as mode of irony, 84, 161n34; role of language, 77–86; role of natural science, 93; *Sachgehalt*, 73–75; secretive stranger, 93, 96–97; "the poetized," 7, 26, 133n17; tripartite structure,

INDEX 191

4, 76, 115, 156n13; "truth-of-the-matter," 3, 68–73, 80–81, 87, 90, 91–93, 95, 153n1; use of the term *Siegel*, 74–77, 156n9; youth and age, 101–106, 168n70. *See also* Goethe, Johann Wolfgang von; "Goethe's Elective Affinities"
Enders, Carl, 54
Explanation in the Sciences (Meyerson), 94–95

Faust Part Two (Goethe), 100, 167n67
Fenves, Peter, 16, 20, 74, 81, 139n30
Fichte, Johann Gottlieb, 44–45, 46, 47–49, 51, 53, 60–61, 63
Foucault, Michel, 5, 125, 137n14
Fragment 169 (Pindar), 65
Frankfurt School, 92
free use doctrine, 57, 62–63, 77, 143, 145, 163n47
French Revolution, 17, 41
Freytag, Gustav, 97

Gair, Ulrich, 34
George, Stefan, 87, 106–107
German romantic theory of modern art: as "medium of reflection," 13 (*see also Concept of Criticism in German Romanticism, The*); fundamental concept, 54–55, 57; objective theory of, 53–54; relation between pure form and pure content, 63–66, 72, 164n54; rigor of form, 42, 64–66, 153n41. *See also Concept of Criticism in German Romanticism, The*; romantics
Germany. *See* "secret Germany"
Gesammelte Schriften (Benjamin), 119
Geschichte der neueren Philosophie in ihrem Zusammenhange mit der allgemeinen Kultur und den besonderen Wissenschaften (Windelband), 45
Gigante, Marcello, 65
Goethe, Johann Wolfgang von: concept of pure content, 63–66, 72, 87, 164n54; conversation with Boisserée, 105–106; conversation with Riemer, 78–79; fable of renunciation, 78–79, 88; method of "mirroring" juxtaposition, 3–4, 111, 115; "occasional poems," 3–4, 89, 162n45; philosophy of life, 19, 24, 67, 87; "the poetized" (*see Elective Affinities*); position on Greek poetry, 58–59, 63–64. *See also Faust Part Two; Elective Affinities;* "Goethe's Elective Affinities"; *Wilhelm Meister's Apprentice Years*
"Goethe's Elective Affinities" (Benjamin): allusion to Hölderlin's "Remarks on Oedipus," 105–106; ambiguity of *Schein* and *Leben*, 70; analysis of subject-matter, 68–70, 72–73, 87, 91–93, 153n1, 153n1; Benjamin's critical vocabulary, 96; Benjamin's sources, 77–78, 103–104, 170n81; comparison of commentator and critic, 70–71, 119; completion of, 2; connection between Ottilie and Kleist's heroines, 97–98; connection between poeticized and history, 276–277; criticism of Gundolf, 87–88, 104–105, 106; decline of myth, 76; "elective affinities" translated, 77–86, 157n15; entanglement with other works, 1–2, 3, 11, 12–13, 106, 112–113, 125; fear of life, 102; fundamental law of literature, 68; impenetrable stranger, 98–100, 166n64; inauthentic naming of Eduard, 82–85, 87, 159n26; logic of deexpiation, 81; manipulation of linguistic matter, 73–75; "The Marquise of O" as relation to, 97–98; meaning of "occasional poems," 2–3, 89, 162n45; "poverty of naming," 82–84, 87; redeeming life of missed opportunities, 3–4, 88, 90–91, 163n47; relation between life and work of author, 87–90, 104; "rigorous dialectic," 76, 81, 115, 156n13; scientific theory of virtuality, 96, 164n56; "the poetized" as "mythic material layer," 7, 26–27; true subject-matter of marriage, 74–77; "truth-of-the-matter," 3, 68–73, 80–81, 87, 90, 91–93, 95, 153n1. *See also Elective Affinities;* Goethe, Johann Wolfgang von

Greek antiquity, 36–39, 41, 59–65, 72, 91, 144n54. See *Concept of Criticism in German Romanticism, The Groundwork for the Metaphysics of Morals* (Kant), 65
Gundolf, Friedrich, 87–88, 104–105, 106, 140n36

"Half of Life" (Hölderlin), 36–37, 39, 56–57
Hegel, Georg Wilhelm Friedrich, 92, 95 104, 139n32
Heidegger, Martin, 7, 22, 24, 120–121
Heinle, Friedrich, 2, 107, 135n1
Hellingrath, Norbert von, 2, 30, 36
Herodotus, 65
history: as science, 146n4; Benjamin's definition of philology as history, 61–62, 112–113; death as true—, 109–110; *"die" Geschichte*, 6–10; entangled with nature, 131n2; layering (*"das" Geschichte*), 6–10, 12, 26–27, 62; life as historical experience, 2; linkage to philological method, 6–7, 111–112, 118; mathematical expression of, 15–16; philological—, 15, 111–112, 124; "pragmatic—," 15; term redefined, 12; "uni-directionality" of time, 131n6, 133n13; wonder and historical experience, 117–119, 124, 175n22
History of German Literature Since Lessing's Death (Schmidt), 96, 97
History of the Poetry of the Greeks and the Romans (Schlegel), 60
Hodde, Lucien de la, 114
Hofmannsthal, Hugo von, 4, 109, 110, 113
Hölderlin, Friedrich: Adorno's lecture on, 120–123; Benjamin's allusion to—in "Remarks on Oedipus," 105–106; free use doctrine, 57, 62–64, 77, 143, 145, 163n47; influence on Benjamin's dissertation, 58–59, 102–103; letter to Böhlendorff, 37, 41, 56–57, 62, 145n59; poetized of Greek poetry, 38, 51, 53, 65–67, 72, 111; seriality of Hölderlin's poetry, 120–122, 124, 176n41. See also "Half of Life"; "Letter to Böhlendorff"; "Poet's Courage, The"; Remarks on Oedipus; sobering condition; "Timidity"; "Two Poems by Friedrich Hölderlin"
Homer, 34, 37, 38, 59–62, 111, 145n58
Horace, 34, 37
Horkheimer, Max, 114
Husserl, Edmund, 19, 74, 87

Iliad (Homer), 61, 62
Illuminations (Arendt, ed.), 14, 125
"Infinite, The" (Pindar), 67
"Introduction to Metaphysics" (Bergson), 18

Journal for Social Research, 114

Kafka, Franz, 109
Kant, Immanuel: autonomy in art, 54–55; compared to Wolf, 62, 151n33; concept of power of judgment and concept of reflection, 147n8; critical philosophy, 72–73; definition of marriage, 74–75; distinction between ethical and juridical constraint, 41, 145n59; philosophy and life, 19, 20. See also *Critique of Pure Reason*; *Critique of the Power of Judgment*; *Groundwork for the Metaphysics of Morals*; *Metaphysics of Morals*; *Religion within the Boundaries of Mere Reason*; "Toward Eternal Peace"
Kierkegaard, Søren, 117
Kleist, Heinrich von, 97–98
Klopstock, Friedrich Gottlieb, 139n32

language, 9, 86–87, 111, 126. See also terminology
Larbaud, Valéry-Nicolas, 22
layering. See history: layering
Lebensphilologie, translation of, 5, 10, 21, 22, 114, 136n11, 137n14, 138n19

INDEX

Le préromantisme français (Monglond), 113
Letter to Böhlendorff" (Hölderlin), 103
life. *See* philology of life
"Life of Students, The" (Benjamin): conception of youth and student, 17–18; context of German university of the day, 17–18; divergence from critical practice, 53–54; effect of George on, 107; idea of French Revolution in, 17, 41; metaphysical structure of student life, 17; objective and subjective genitive, 20; perspectives on history, 15; terminologies of mathematics, 16, 136n5; transformation in Benjamin's writings of philosophy of life, 18–22, 101, 104; use of term "life," 17–18; "waiting period," 18, 136n5
Literarische Welt, 106
Lukács, Georg, 95
Lyceum-fragments (Schlegel), 59

Magic Flute (Mozart), 72
Makkreel, Rudolf, 74–75
Marburg school of neo-Kantian philosophy, 25, 139n30
Marivaux, Pierre de, 113
"Marquise of O, The" (Kleist), 97–98
Marx, Karl, 114, 115
Matière et mémoire (Bergson), 114
"medium of reflection," 13, 49–55, 62–63, 72, 81, 87, 112, 118, 147n6
Menninghaus, Winfried, 36, 39
"*mere* life." *See* philology of life: "*mere* life"
Metaphysics of Morals (Kant), 41, 72, 74
"Metaphysics of Youth, The" (Benjamin), 39
Meyerson, Émile, 94–95
Minor, J., 62
Mittler, Ernst Siegfried, 73
Mona Lisa, 100
Monglond, André, 113
Mozart, 72
mythology, comparisons to, 30, 36–37, 40

natural science, 93, 94, 133n20, 146n4
nature entangled with history, 131n2
Ng, Julia, 81
Niethammer, Friedrich Philipp Immanuel, 60
Nietzsche, 10, 17, 18–19, 21–22, 134n24
Novalis, 45, 46, 47, 57

object. *See* philology of life: life as object
Odyssey (Homer), 61, 62
Oellers, Norbert, 83
"On Homeric Poetry" (Schlegel), 60
"On Language as Such and on the Language of Man" (Benjamin), 86–87
"On Some Motifs in Baudelaire" (Benjamin), 114. *See also* Baudelaire, Benjamin's study of
"On the Concept of History" (Benjamin), 9, 110
On the Language and Wisdom of the Indians (Schlegel), 83
"On the Study of Greek Poetry" (Schlegel), 59, 60, 84
Origin of the German Trauerspiel (Benjamin), 94–95, 131n2
Ovid, 34, 37

"Paris of the Second Empire in Baudelaire" (Benjamin), 114–116
pathos, 37, 119, 144n54
Phaedrus (Plato), 85
philological method: Benjamin's definition as history, 61–62, 110–113; Benjamin's focus on language, 24, 29–30, 140n36; cyclical time, 12; described, 9; distinction between aesthetic and philological commentaries, 24–26, 31, 139n30; emergence from dynamic field of force, 1, 2; "enigmatic" time, 9–10; layering of (*schihten*), 7–10; linkage to history, 6–7, 110; movement from connections and disconnections, 31, 140n36; spirit of classicism and, 62. *See also* philology of life

philology of life: afterlife of, 33, 119; as historical experience, 2, 110; bare life (*zoé*), 5, 9, 10, 20–22, 33, 125, 132n12, 137n14; "being alive," 33; Benjamin's attribution of—to Goethe, 4; Benjamin's definition of, 6–8, 15, 86–87, 114, 118, 132n12; Benjamin's interweaving and interpolation of textual elements, 4, 13–14; completed life, 24, 138nn19, 25; concept of, 24, 122–123; connection between experience and language, 4, 162n42; "death," 4, 109–110; "earthly life," 4; "elective affinities" as true content of, 87, 164n54; factual recollection, 114; feeling of life, 22; "form-of-life," 5, 132n12; language-character of, 86–87; life as object, 20; life as subject, 20; linkage between life and philology, 4–5, 13, 27–28; "lived experience," 13, 88, 104–105, 114–115, 169n73; "living beings," 33; "living on," 4; "*mere* life," 19, 20, 24, 28–29, 136n11, 137n14; modes of completion (*Voll-Endung*), 23, 138n25; mythical layers, 7, 26–27, 29, 33–34, 36–37; Nietzsche's understanding of, 18, 19–22; opposition between "life philosophy" and natural science, 133n20; parts of, 4; qualified/made life (*bíos*), 5, 9, 10, 20, 33, 132n12; Schestag's definition of, 6–9; term redefined, 12–13, 135n28; "true experience," 115; true meaning, 20; true "memory," 114; use of phrase, 4–5; value-philosophy as progressive completion of, 23. *See also* "book of life"; philological method
philology of the future, 10
Philosophische Journal, 60
philosophy. *See* value philosophy
The Philosophy of Life (Rickert), 19–20
photography and time, 113–114
Pindar, 30–31, 36, 39, 41, 51, 65, 67, 72, 90
Plato, 22, 85, 98, 117
poetry: art connected to life, 27–28; as prose, 55, 59, 62–63; "life in," 122; prosaic test, 35, 62; relation to poetized, 26–27, 38, 40
"Poet's Courage, The" (Hölderlin): Adorno's interpretation, 123–124; duality of man and god, 32–33; philological comparability to "Timidity," 29–31, 122; sobering condition, 40. *See also* "Two Poems by Friedrich Hölderlin"
Prolegomena to Homer (Wolf), 59–60, 62

qualified/made life (*bíos*). *See* philology of life: qualified/made life

reflection: "canonical" form of, 51–53, 118; "center of reflection," 54–55; objective—, 55; "reflective judgment," 48; reflective thinking, 48–49, 147n8; romantic philosophy of, 49, 118; "second-level reflection," 48; self-limitation in, 49; "third-level reflection," 50–51, 118. *See also Concept of Criticism in German Romanticism, The*
Reflections (Demetz, ed), 14, 125
Reinhard, Carl Friedrich von, 26, 133n17
Religion within the Boundaries of Mere Reason (Kant), 41
"Remarks on Oedipus" (Hölderlin), 105–106
Rickert, Heinrich, 17, 19–25, 44, 45, 136n11, 137n14
Riemer, Friedrich Wilhelm, 78–79
romantics: critical theory as philosophical problem, 48, 146n4; link between— theory and neo-Kantian philosophy, 46; objective theory of art, 53–54, 57, 111; turn toward religion, 92, 163n46, 166n64; value of work of art, 55, 58, 148n13. *See also Concept of Criticism in German Romanticism, The*; German romantic theory of modern art; reflection
Rousseau, Jean-Jacques, 22, 82, 113

Sappho, 36–37, 39, 41
Satire (Horace), 35
Schestag, Thomas, 6–9, 10

Scheuer, Hans Jürgen, 33, 35
schihten. *See* philological method: layering of
Schiller, Friedrich von, 35, 95
Schlegel, Friedrich: concept of form, 63–64, 66, 72; concept of philology, 60–62; conversion to Catholicism, 163n46; "criticizability" of the work, 46, 47, 57–58, 111; Goethe's allusion to—in *Elective Affinities*, 83; historical character of literary work, 61, 63; objective aesthetic theory, 62; poetized in Greek poetry, 38, 40; public sentiment in Pindar's poems, 36; theory of reflection, 49–50, 52–54; theory of the prosaic, 62; Wolf's impact on, 60, 62, 111, 151n33, 152n35. *See also Athenaeum-fragments*; *On the Language and Wisdom of the Indians*; "On the Study of Greek Poetry"
Schmidt, Julian, 96–99
Schmitt, Carl, 65, 152n39
Scholem, Gershom: mathematical expression of history, 15–16, 135n3; 1916 conversation with Benjamin, 15; 1921 letter from Benjamin, 6–7, 10, 15, 16, 26–27, 61–62, 71, 109
Schriften (Benjamin), 14, 119, 125
"secret Germany," 37, 143n53
"Signature Event Context" (Derrida), 86
Simmel, Georg, 19
"Sleeping Beauty" (Benjamin), 135n1
sobering condition: Hölderlin's "sobriety" of ancient Greek art, 3–4, 13, 13, 36–41, 56–59, 62–67, 77, 90, 103, 144n54, 145n59, 163n47; in construction of philological object, 110; silence marked out by Benjamin, 39–40
Southwestern school of Neo-Kantianism, 25
space. *See* time: spatiotemporal interpenetration
Star of the Covenant (George), 107
stress, concept of, 10
Sturm und Drang movement, 19, 54, 55, 62
subject. *See* philology of life: life as subject

terminology, 9, 16. *See also* philology of life: Benjamin's definition of
Theatetis (Plato), 117
thinking, dimension of, 48
Tiedemann, Rolf, 14, 119, 125
time: Bergson's theory of, 18; chronological, 9; concept of, 8, 9, 133n13; cyclical—, 12; direction of, 15, 135n3; "enigmatic"—, 9–10, 15–16, 136n5; "entanglement" in the image, 131n2; historical—, 15, 113–114, 131n6; philological—, 9; spatiotemporal interpenetration, 30, 122, 124, 132n12, 176n41; true—, 17
"Timidity" (Hölderlin): Adorno's interpretation, 123–124; affirmation of poetic power, 90–91; changed "concept of life," 122; death of the poet, 36–37, 122; distinction between forces, 33, 58–59; "foot" as mortality and animality, 33–34; force of form over matter, 35; "hands" inseparable from "foot," 33–35, 103; layering of myths, 34, 36–37, 141n40; philological comparability to "The Poet's Courage," 29–31; sobering condition, 3–4, 37–40, 57, 90, 103; "transformation" at hands of poets, 28–29, 31, 32–33; use of the word *gelegen*, 3–4. *See also* "Two Poems by Friedrich Hölderlin"
"Toward Eternal Peace" (Kant), 75
"Toward the Critique of Violence" (Benjamin), 1, 20, 27, 65, 76, 80, 81, 136n11
"Toward the Image of Proust" (Benjamin), 162n42
"true historian," 6, 109. *See also* "On the Concept of History"
"truth content," 14, 121–122, 164n54
"Two Poems by Friedrich Hölderlin" (Benjamin): comparison of commentator and critic, 70–71; distinction between aesthetic and philological commentaries, 24–26, 31, 35, 139n30, 142n44; entanglement with other works, 1–2, 3, 11–12, 13, 106, 112–113, 125; impact of George on, 107; impact of World War I on, 2;

"Two Poems by Friedrich Hölderlin"
(Benjamin) (*continued*)
life as preexisting space and time, 124, 176n41; life by the poem, 25–30, 32, 124; "limit-concept," 25, 139n29; linguistic and syntactic connections, 30–31, 121; mythical layer, 36–37, 103; philological comparability of the poems, 29–30, 122–124; poem and life, 25–29; sign of the cross immortalized, 32; "the poetized," 25, 27, 120–121, 176n30. *See also* "Poet's Courage, The"; "Timidity"; "Two Poems by Friedrich Hölderlin"

"value-philosophy," 22–24
Voll-Endung. See philology of life: modes of completion

Weber, Max, 44
Weber, Samuel, 43, 53
Wegener, Alfred, 141n39
Wilhelm Meister's Apprentice Years (Goethe), 97
Winckelmann, Johann Joachim, 59, 60, 62
Windelband, Wilhelm, 44–45, 139n29
Wissenschaftslehre (Fichte), 44
Wolf, Friedrich August: compared to Kant, 62, 151n33; impact on Schlegel, 60, 62, 63, 152n35; influence on Boeckh, 30; texts of Greek antiquity, 13, 37, 38, 40, 59, 60–62, 111–112, 145n58
wonder, connection to philosophy, 117–119, 175n22
World War I, 2, 3

youth and aging. *See* aging and youth

zoé. *See* philology of life: bare life

Kevin McLaughlin was Dean of Faculty at Brown University from 2011–22. He is George Hazard Crooker University Professor of English, Comparative Literature, and German Studies at Brown. He is the author of *Poetic Force: Poetry after Kant* (Stanford University Press, 2014), *Paperwork: Literature and Mass Mediacy in the Age of Paper* (University of Pennsylvania Press, 2005), and *Writing in Parts: Imitation and Exchange in Nineteenth-Century Literature* (Stanford University Press, 1995), and the co-translator with Howard Eiland of Walter Benjamin's *Arcades Project* (Harvard University Press, 1999).

IDIOM INVENTING WRITING THEORY
Jacques Lezra and Paul North, series editors

Werner Hamacher, *Minima Philologica*. Translated by Catharine Diehl and Jason Groves

Michal Ben-Naftali, *Chronicle of Separation: On Deconstruction's Disillusioned Love*. Translated by Mirjam Hadar. Foreword by Avital Ronell

Daniel Hoffman-Schwartz, Barbara Natalie Nagel, and Lauren Shizuko Stone, eds., *Flirtations: Rhetoric and Aesthetics This Side of Seduction*

Jean-Luc Nancy, *Intoxication*. Translated by Philip Armstrong

Márton Dornbach, *Receptive Spirit: German Idealism and the Dynamics of Cultural Transmission*

Sean Alexander Gurd, *Dissonance: Auditory Aesthetics in Ancient Greece*

Anthony Curtis Adler, *Celebricities: Media Culture and the Phenomenology of Gadget Commodity Life*

Nathan Brown, *The Limits of Fabrication: Materials Science, Materialist Poetics*

Jay Bernstein, Adi Ophir, and Ann Laura Stoler, eds., *Political Concepts: A Critical Lexicon*

Willy Thayer, *Technologies of Critique*. Translated by John Kraniauskas

Julie Beth Napolin, *The Fact of Resonance: Modernist Acoustics and Narrative Form*

Ann Laura Stoler, Stathis Gourgouris, and Jacques Lezra, eds., *Thinking with Balibar: A Lexicon of Conceptual Practice*

Nathan Brown, *Rationalist Empiricism: A Theory of Speculative Critique*

Gerhard Richter, *Thinking with Adorno: The Uncoercive Gaze*

Kevin McLaughlin, *The Philology of Life: Walter Benjamin's Critical Program*

Alenka Zupančič, *Let Them Rot: Antigone's Parallax*

Adi M. Ophir, *In the Beginning Was the State: Divine Violence in the Hebrew Bible*

www.ingramcontent.com/pod-product-compliance
Lightning Source LLC
Chambersburg PA
CBHW020409080526
44584CB00014B/1244